Indo-European Mythology and Religion

Essays

by

Alexander Jacob

Indo-European Mythology and Religion. Essays.
Alexander Jacob

© Manticore Press, Melbourne, Australia, 2019.

All rights reserved, no section of this book may be utilized without permission, except brief quotations, including electronic reproductions without the permission of the copyright holders and publisher. Published in Australia.

Thema Classification:
QRS(Ancient Religions and Mythologies), QRD (Hinduism), 1QBA (Ancient World), DB (Ancient Texts), NHC (Ancient History), QRAX (History of Religion).

978-0-6484996-1-9

MANTICORE PRESS
WWW.MANTICORE.PRESS

CONTENTS

Preface — 5

I. The Origins of the Indo-European Religions — 7

II. Pralaya — 25
Cosmic Floods, the Sun and the First Man

III. Sāmkhya-Yoga, Shramana, Brāhmana, Tantra — 67
The religious traditions of the ancient Indians

IV. Vedic and Tantric Rituals — 139
A comparison

V. Reviving Adam — 177
The sacrificial rituals of the Indo-Āryans and the early Christians

VI. Dionysus and Muruga — 211
Notes on the Dionysiac Religion

VII. On the Germanic gods Wotan and Thor — 249

I. THE ORIGINS OF THE INDO-EUROPEAN RELIGIONS

THE RECENT COMPARATIVE linguistic and mythological studies of scholars such as Giovanni Semerano[1] and M.L. West[2] have made it clear that the origins of Indo-European religion are to be found in and around the ancient Near East and that the erstwhile tendency to distinguish, on the basis of the linguistic difference between agglutinative and inflected languages, the Egyptian civilisation from the Sumerian and both from the so-called 'Indo-European' cultures of the Indo-Iranians and the Hittites and Greeks has ignored the possibility that they may have all been derived from a common source.[3] The similarities between the

---

[1] See Giovanni Semerano, *Le Origini della Cultura Europea: Rivelazioni della linguistica storica*, Firenze: Leo Olschki, 1984-94. The etymological dictionary provided in this work gives Akkadian and Sumerian origins for many of the ancient Greek, Latin and German words.

[2] See M.L. West, *The East Face of Helicon*, Oxford: Clarendon Press, 1997.

[3] Indeed, it will be necessary henceforth to rename the current linguistic term "Proto-Indo-European" as "Proto-Āryan", since "Proto-Indo-European" better denotes the original proto-Dravidian/Hurrian language to which Semitic, modern Dravidian and Āryan are related

cosmological religions of the three most ancient historic civilisations of Sumer, Egypt, and the Indus Valley indeed give credence to this possibility. The references in the Sumerian epic of *Enmerkar and the Lord of Aratta*, 141-6, to a time when all the peoples of the region "in unison/ To Enlil[4] in one tongue [gave praise]," as well as in *Genesis* 11:1 to the sons of Noah [Shem, the Semite; Japheth, the Āryan, and Ham the Hamite] speaking the same tongue originally reinforce this theory. The common solar cosmological and philosophical orientation of the religions of Sumer, Egypt, and India also suggests that these three civilisations may indeed be derived from a common source. Prof. Petr Charvat has also recently noted the emergence of the first "universal religion of Mesopotamia" already in the Chalcolithic cultures of Tel el Halaf in northern Mesopotamia and Ubaid in southern Mesopotamia dating back to the 6th millennium B.C.[5]

***

As regards the original home of the people who developed the cosmological insights shared by the most ancient religions of the region, the major evidence we have is that of the so-called "Flood" story. The Flood story is a cosmological account of the birth of the universe and its light after the destruction of the cosmos at the end of a cosmic age. The "boat" which survives the flood bears the seeds of universal life and comes to rest atop a

---

than the earliest form of the Japhetic/Āryan language. Proto-Indo-European must include Semitic elements as well since Semitic is one of the oldest branches of it.

[4] Enlil, the Sumerian god of Wind, is the same as [Skt.] Vāyu, [Avestan] Wāta, [Germanic] Wotan, who represent the life-breath of the supreme deity in his macroanthropomorphic form.

[5] P. Charvat, *Mesopotamia Before History*, London: Routledge, 2002, p.236.

mountain, which is indeed the location in which the light of the universe arises – as the Egyptian evidence makes clear. The story of the deluge, however, is transferred to a terrestrial setting in the popular flood stories of Sumer, India, and Israel. The "ark", or boat, which sails over the flood, lands on a terrestrial mountain and this mountain is considered to be the originating point of the race itself since the survivor is described as a primeval king or sage.

In the Indian account of the Flood in the *Bhāgavata Purāna*, the survivor of the Flood is Manu (Man), who is called Satyavrata, King of Drāvida, and his boat comes to rest upon an unnamed "northern" mountain (VIII, 24). In the Babylonian history of Berossos, the boat of Xisouthros, the survivor of the Flood, lands in Armenia. According to Nikolaos of Damascus, a contemporary of Augustus, the Armenian mountain on which the boat landed is the Baris mountain, which may be the same as Mt. Ararat (north of Lake Van) mentioned in the biblical Flood story of *Genesis* 8:3. According to Berossus, the Babylonians moved to different parts of Babylonia from Armenia. In the Ethiopian version of the Greek Pseudo-Callisthenes, the Brāhmans are called the sons of Adam's son, Seth, and Noah was considered a transmitter of the wisdom of Seth. Since Adam is, as we shall see, indeed the Cosmic Man and not a human, we may assume that the Brāhmans referred to here are associated with the preservation of the Divine Consciousness of Brahman which arises from the Cosmic Egg and is later conveyed to humanity by Manu/ Noah.

Since the earliest centres of high culture are those of the Canaanites, Hatti, Elamites, Sumerians, and Egyptians, it is possible that the region around Mt. Ararat was the central region from whence the proto-Dravidians travelled to Palestine, Anatolia, Egypt, Mesopotamia and the shores of the Black Sea.⁶ It is probable also that one of the earliest regions to be settled by the Noachidian peoples from neighbouring Armenia was Anatolia. This is suggested by the great antiquity of the Neolithic archaeological finds at Çatal Hüyük in (ca. 7th millennium B.C.). The civilisation of Syro-Palestine may be even as old as that of Anatolia since settlements in Jordan are traceable from the late 7th millennium B.C. and in Byblos from the 6th. Following the archaeological finds from Anatolia and Syro-Palestine are those from Susa in Elam, in southwestern Iran. Speiser, along with Frankfort, conjectured that the source of this culture may have been in Armenia itself since the farthest northern site to yield pottery of the Susa I type is Mt. Ararat. As for the biblical account of the earliest Elamites, it considers Elam as a son of Shem. This suggests that a major constituent of the proto-Dravidian population in Elam must have been proto-Semites, probably proto-Akkadian Semites.

Of the early Ubaid culture of southern Mesopotamia, Eridu, which dates from the sixth millennium B.C., shows marked Elamite affinities. It is important to note that, according to Speiser, the original name of Ku'ara (near Eridu) in the first dynasty of Uruk—HA.A^{ki}—may be of Subarian, or Hurrian origin. The very term "subari" or, more precisely, "suwari", is related to Suvalliyat (Suvariya)/Sūrya, which is also the Hititte/Indic name of the sun-god. Hurri then would be the Iranian pronunciation of the same name, as the Iranian name of the sun-god, "Hvare", suggests. The original Noachidian or proto-Dravidian race is thus most probably identifiable with the proto-Hurrians who inhabited the Anatolian-Halafian settlements associated with the Subarians/Suwarians/Hurrians from the seventh millennium B.C. These earliest Hurrians

---

⁶ The northern shores of the Black Sea, in present-day Ukraine, may be identified as the homeland of the Japhetic Āryans.

spoke an agglutinative language that possessed Dravidian characteristics and F. Bork and G.W. Brown have revealed the intimate linguistic relationship between Hurrian (along with its Mitanni dialect), Elamite, and Dravidian. The Semitic, Japhetic and Hamitic peoples mentioned in the Bible are all closely related to this group whose very name points to a characteristic religious worship of the sun.

The earliest sites of northern Mesopotamian culture are to be found in Tel el Halaf, dating back to around 5000 B.C. The powerful influence of the Halafian culture is attested in the imitations of its pottery in southern Armenia as well as in northeastern Syria. The Tel el Halaf pottery is marked by bucranium designs which associate it with the seventh-millennium shrines of Çatal Hüyük in eastern Anatolia, which may have been established by the earliest proto-Dravidians or Hurrians. Charvat has revealed that the fundamental social and religious forms of later Mesopotamian culture, including that of Uruk in Sumer, are evident already in embryonic form in the early Chalcolithic sites of northern Mesopotamia. Crematory practices associated with fire-rituals are noticed here and Tell Arpachiyah (TT6) also gives the first evidence of the use of the white-red-black colour triad which persists from Chalcolithic times to Uruk[7] and is representative of the three original castes of the Indo-Europeans, priests, warriors, and the people (i.e. agriculturists and artisans).

***

[7] P. Charvat, *Mesopotamia Before History*, p.92. In Greek antiquity, black may have denoted prime matter, red matter and white spirit (*ibid.*, p.93). This corresponds to the three basic energies in Indian philosophy, Tāmas, Rajas, Sattva.The association of the three Indian castes, brahman, kshatriya and shūdra, with these colours is due to the predominance of the sattvic, rājasic, and tāmasic elements, respectively, in them.

The imperfect state of archaeological researches in the regions under investigation prohibits any definite identification of the original people which created the spiritual culture of these earliest civilisations of mankind. However, since all these civilisations are situated in the south and, according to Gordon Childe, the predominant element in the earliest graves in the region from Elam to the Danube is the 'Mediterranean',[8] we may presume that these early cultures were founded by the genius of that broad group. The dolichocephalic Mediterranean people may thus have constituted the earliest strata of the populations of Asia, Egypt, and Europe. They may be identified as the "proto-Dravidian" or "proto-Hurrian" or even proto-Indo-Europeans.

Of the three historic linguistic branches associated with the sons of Noah, Shem, Japhet, and Ham,[9] the earliest literary evidence is mostly of the Semitic proto-Akkadian. Many of the words of the earliest Uruk tablets that were designated as "proto-Euphratean" by B. Landsberger are most probably of proto-Akkadian origin, as G. Rubio has recently pointed out. Langdon, however, noted that most of the Semitic names were concentrated in the north, and this suggests the "entrance of the Semites into the northern area at Kish and Maer at a very early period". The Semitic Akkadian culture of northern Mesopotamia must have been related also to that of Elam, which is described in *Genesis* 10:20 as a "son" of Shem. It is not surprising that the earliest Akkadians were closely associated with Hurrian tribes as well, with whom they seem to have shared a common historical tradition. We have here an

---

[8] See G. Childe, *The Dawn of European Civilization*, London: K. Paul, Trench, Trubner and Co., 1961, p.109. The German evidence for this type dates from the late chalcolithic period (early 4th millenium B.C.) called Danube III.

[9] By 'sons' and 'fathers' is obviously meant later and earlier tribes of with their divergent physical and linguistic traits.

indication of the great antiquity of the Semitic Akkadian family.

***

Although the earliest attested religions are those of the Semites and the Sumerian and Egyptian Hamites, the Japhetic Āryans may indeed have been older than the Hamites, since Ham is represented in the earliest Jahvist version of the Bible as "the youngest son of Noah".[10] The Āryans are generally divided into eastern, "shatem" and western, "centum" Āryans. Regarding the western Āryan peoples, we may note that, in *Genesis* 9:2, the eldest son of Japheth [the Āryans] is called Gamer, representing the Cimmerians, who are described by Herodotus (IV,14) as having had their initial home "on the shores of the Black Sea". The Cimmerians are probably identical to the most ancient Celts, since the Welsh (who are a southern Celtic people like the Bretons) call themselves, to this day, "Cymry". Diodorus Siculus (*Bibliotheca Historica* V,32) also states that the Celts living close to the Black Sea are scattered "as far as Scythia" and the northernmost of these Celtic tribes are the wildest and most powerful having apparently "wandered across and laid waste the whole of Asia, under the then name of Cimmerians". The northern Celts are no doubt the Goidelic but the fact that the ancient name is preserved chiefly among the Bretonic Welsh may be due to the predominance of the conservative Druidic element among the latter.

The "brothers" of Gamer include Magog (the Magi or Iranians), Madai (the Medes/Mitanni/Indo-Iranians), Javan (Greeks), Tubal (uncertain), Meschech (Cappadocians, according to Josephus) and Tiras (Thracians, according to Josephus). The eastern Japhetic

---
[10] See *Interpreter Bible*, I:560.

Iranians are represented in Herodotus as worshipping the "circle of heaven" (Ahura, from Ashur/Anshar – circle of heaven) as well as the heavenly bodies. The Iranians discussed by Herodotus, however, did not build temples or worship statuary representations of their deities (I,131), and this emphasises their ancient affiliation with the Scythians, whereas the Mitanni – and the Hittite-Hurrians, however, were certainly not averse to such representations. Besides, the Iranian rituals are described by Herodotus as not involving fire, even though the later Zoroastrian religion—like the Indic—is indeed typified by its worship of fire, Atar. This suggests that the later Iranians must have come into contact in the south with the Purūrava Ailas [Elamites/Hurrians], who, as we shall see,[11] derived their worship of fire from the Gandharvas who are related to the settlers of the Bactro-Margiana Archaeological Complex in Afghanistan.[12]

The earliest historical branch of the Indo-Āryans is manifest in the 16th century B.C. in northern Mesopotamia, in the kingdom of the Mitanni. The original home of the Mitanni remains uncertain. The Mitanni themselves may be identifiable with the Medes, and, as Herodotus (VII,69) reveals, the Medes were once universally called Arians. The Medes may have been related to the proto-Iranians, since several Median words are traceable in Old Persian. The Mitanni kings have Sanskritic names distinguished by their charioteering affiliation, and this expertise is reflected also in the names (Keres-aspa, Pourus-aspa) of the Iranian branch of the Āryan family, as well as in the extraordinary prestige ascribed to the horse by the Indo-Āryans in their sacred rituals. The close relation between the Indo-Āryans and Iranians and the Scythians is confirmed by the veneration of the horse among the

---

[11] See p.96.

[12] See p.72.

Scythians reported by Herodotus (IV,61). However, the Mitanni exhibit an adherence to a Vedic (and not to the later Zoroastrian Avestan) form of religion, along with a worship of Hurrian deities, thus establishing the relative lateness of the Zoroastrian religion.

The sons of Gamer, in the biblical Table of Nations, include Ashkenaz (the Scythians, who are eastern, shatem-language speaking Japhetites), Riphath (Paphlagonians, according to Josephus) and Thokarmah (Phrygians, according to Josephus, or Armenians, according to Hippolytus of Rome).[13] The Celts and the Scythians are closely associated, as is indicated by Strabo (XI,7,2), who states that the Greek authors called all the northern populations Scythians or Celtoscythians. Also, Asclepiades of Thrace (4th c. B.C.) refers to the legendary king Boreas as a king of the Celts while in other authors he appears as a king of the Scythians, even though the Scythians are younger than the Cimmerians. The Scythians are located by Herodotus north of the Black Sea in close proximity to the Cimmerians. According to Herodotus (IV,3), the Scythians considered themselves as the "youngest of all nations". However, the wide territory of the Scythians extended through Russia to Central Asia. The Scythians are also closely associated with the Indo-Iranians with whom they shared an eastern "shatem" Āryan language and much of their religious practices. The predominance of the Iranian language in the regions inhabited by Cimmerians and Scythians, that is, from the Danube to the Dnieper, is evidenced also by the names of the Danube, Dnieper, and Dniester, which employ the Avestan term "danu" for river. Indeed, this area corresponds to that inhabited by the Slavs and we may

---

[13] That the name may denote the Armenians is made probable by the fact that their ancestor is called Tᶜorghom (see A.E. Redgate, *The Armenians*, Oxford: Blackwell Publishers, 1998, p.14).

reasonably consider the Scythians as the forebears of the latter.

Herodotus' account of the Scythians (IV,59) however suggests that they did not possess much sophistication in their religious rituals. Darius I (522-486 B.C.) himself refers to the Sakas as "unruly" and not devoted to Ahura Mazda. Herodotus' account of the religious customs of the Scythians (IV,59) indeed reveals their sharp focus on martial life, since they apparently did not set up altars or statues to any god except Ares, god of war. Eliade's researches also point to a very rudimentary practical application of the spiritual bases of the cosmological religion of the ancient Near East to quasi-shamanistic rituals. This also explains their ancient designation as "hoamavarga", or "soma-drinking", Scythians.

Indeed all the Āryan peoples may be traced back ultimately to the Hut Grave and Catacomb Grave cultures of the Ukraine (ca. 2800 B.C.) and, earlier, to the Yamnaya Culture (fourth millennium B.C.), also north of the Black Sea. But it is interesting to note that both the Indians and the Avestan Iranians seem originally to have been nomadic peoples akin to the Scythians, as is attested by the language of the Old Avesta, wherein the cosmos is viewed as an enormous tent. However, there may have been other waves of Indo-Āryans that settled in the Bactria-Margiana Archaeological Complex [situated in present-day Afghanistan and Turkmenistan] around 2200–1700 B.C. and the Gandhara region [around Peshawar] around 1700 B.C., for these seem to have followed a religion based on fire-rituals. Elaborate fire altars are evident in the ruins of the BMAC complex which correspond to the Āryan fire-sacrifices. The temples also contain rooms with "all the necessary apparatus for the preparation of drinks extracted from poppy, hemp and ephedra" that may have been used for the soma-rituals.[14]

When we investigate the crucial issue of the institution of fire-rituals among the Indo-Āryans, we should remember that neither the earliest Iranians, nor the Mitanni Indo-Āryans, nor the Scythians give any evidence of such fire-worship. In the Purāṇas, Purūravas, the early Aila [Elamite?] king, is said to have obtained sacrificial fire from the "Gandharvas", who also taught him the constitution of the three sacred fires of the Āryans. This suggests that the early Hurrians of Elam and the earliest Iranians did not worship fire and learnt it from a later wave of Āryans. However, even the Gandharvas are included among the Aila [Elamite?] dynasties in the Purāṇas, which suggests that they too were a northern and eastern branch of proto-Hurrians identifiable with the Japhetic.

***

As for the western "centum" Aryans, even though the Cimmerians or Celts, represented by Gamer, are considered the first-born of Japheth, the earliest historical evidence of a "centum" language is from Anatolia, among the Hittites. The so-called Hittites were, unlike the native Hatti, Āryans. But they, like the Cimmerian Japhetites (as well as the Semites and Hamites) do not provide archaeological evidence of any fire-rituals in their religious worship. The Hittite kingdom also shows a strong neo-Hurrian cultural influence from the fifteenth century B.C. and many of the Hittite queens bear Hurrian names, just as in the case of the Mitanni. The Hittite religion is

---

[14] See J.P. Mallory and V.H. Mair, *The Tarim Mummies: Ancient China and the Mystery of the Earliest Peoples from the West*, London: Thames and Hudson, 2008, p.262.

fully Sumero-Hurrian but has particular affinities with the Mitanni and Indo-Āryan as well.

Greeks most probably arrived in the Helladic region around 2200 B.C. from Anatolia, though it is possible that Japhetic tribes from the shores of the Black Sea moved overland to Greece as well. The pre-Greek Minoan culture of Crete, however, was instrumental in developing the Linear A script (before 1700 B.C.) which preceded the Āryan Mycenean Linear B (1300 B.C.). And just as the Cretan script is at the base of the Mycenean, so too their religion is continued unchanged by the later immigrants. It is not surprising thus that the Cretan Zeus, who is identifiable with Dionysus, is called Zagreus, which suggests an origin of the deity in the Zagros mountains of western Iran.

Farther west, one of the oldest branches of the Germanic peoples is called the Alemanni. According to Snorri Sturluson, the author of the *Prose Edda*, the Germans first derived their religion from Anatolians who moved into Europe. The first Anatolian (one of the "Aesir" [Asuras]) who migrated into Germany is said to be "Voden" or "Odin", the god of Wind [the original Germanic form, Wotan, is clearly related to the Indo-Iranian Wāta, a form of the wind-god, Vāyu]. Odin, however, is said to be a distant descendant of "Tror" or "Thor",[15] the son of a Trojan king called Mennon or Munon [=Manu?] who had married a daughter of King Priam. Thor himself is said to have first wandered to Thrace and then to other parts of the world. We will note that Thrace is also the source of the Dionysiac cult.

Odin's three sons, Vegdeg, Beldeg (Baldur) and Sigi ruled over East Germany, Westphalia, and France, respectively. Further expeditions took Odin to Denmark,

---

[15] Cf. Ch.VII.

Sweden, and Norway, whereby he succeeded in spreading the "language of Asia" all over Europe. We see therefore the centrality of Anatolia as the land whence most of the western Indo-European cultures were derived, even though the Celtic Cimmerians were largely located north of the Black Sea.

According to Tacitus, Mannus [cognate with the Indic Manu] was the ancestor of the Germanic race, and he had three sons represented by the Ingaevones (the north Germans including the Scandinavians and the ancestors of the Anglo-Saxons), Herminones (the West Germans including the Goths, Burgundians and Lombardians) and Istaevones (the Low Germans, Franks, Dutch and Belgians). The first Germanic tribe to have crossed the Rhine and ousted the indigenous Celts were the Tungri (a Belgic tribe), whose other name, Germani, was used for all the tribes.

The chief god of the Germans is said by Tacitus to be the creator god Tuisto [from Tvashtr/Tvoreshtar/Tartarus], though Ingvi, another name for Freyr, must have been the god of the Ingaevones just as Hermin, a name for Wotan, must have been the chief deity of the Herminones, while Istae remains obscure.

***

As regards the cosmological and philosophical insights that inform the ancient religions, it is likely that they were developed first through yogic meditation, as the *Brahmānda Purāna* I,i,3,8, for instance, declares. It is significant that, in the *Mahabhārata*, Shalyaparva, 44, Skanda or Muruga, the Dionysiac god of the Dravidians, is described as being endowed with yogic powers while his father Shiva is in *Mahābhārata*, Anushāsanaparva, 14, addressed as the "soul of yoga" and the object of all yogic meditation. Since it is most likely that the Noachidian people were proto-Dravidian/proto-Hurrian, it is probable that this profound yogic knowledge of the universe is characteristic of it.

The religion of the ancients was based on a spiritual vision of the formation of the cosmos.[16] After the cosmic deluge which marks the end of the first cosmic age (kalpa), the Divine Soul, Ātman, within the cosmic ocean (the Abyss) gradually recreates the cosmos assuming the form of an Ideal Macroanthropos, or Cosmic Man. The breath or life-force (Vāyu/Wotan) of the cosmic Man first unites with matter (Earth) to form a closely united complex of Heaven (the substance of the Purusha) and Earth. But the temporal aspect (Kāla, Chronos) of the rapidly moving breath or wind also separates the two elements, an event represented as a castration of the Purusha. The semen that falls from the castrated phallus impregnates the Purusha himself with a Cosmic Egg from which emerge the manifest cosmos comprised, again, of Earthly substance and Heavenly light (Brahman). This luminous Brahman is also represented anthropomorphically as a Cosmic Man.

However, this light, again represented in anthropomorphic form, continues to possess a stormy quality which is a persistence of Chronos in the manifest cosmos. This force, represented as Zeus/Seth/Ganesha, shatters the light and forces it to descend to the lower regions of Earth, where it lies moribund as, for instance, Osiris. However, the same storm-force has, in its assault on the manifest light, swallowed the divine phallus and it eventually revives the moribund light in the underworld with its potency. Separating the substance of Earth, into which the cosmic light has sunk, into the earthly regions

---

[16] For a more elaborate study of the cosmology of the ancient Indo-Europeans see A. Jacob, *Ātman*.

and heaven of our universe, it emerges through the cleft between the two into the mid-region of the stars as a universal Tree of Life, or Phallus. The seed of this newly formed universe is then emitted within our galaxy, first as the moon, and then the solar force finally emerges above the top of the Tree (Phallus) as the sun.

The process of developing life on earth is supervised by the seventh Manu of our age whom we have encountered as the King of Drāvida. This Manu is responsible for the continuance of mankind on the earth as well as for its spiritual evolution. In this task, he is assisted by seven sages, who represent the wisdom and culture of enlightened man. The brāhmans derive their ancestry from these seven sages and so we see that the Brāhmanical religion is indeed the oldest and one originally marked by yogic spiritual elevation.

Since we have identified the proto-Indo-Europeans as proto-Hurrians or proto-Dravidians, we may pause to consider what the earliest form of their religion may have been. We have noted that the Cimmerians are the most ancient of the Japhetic Aryans and we know that their priests were called Druids, so it is possible that the Druids are indeed descendants of the proto-Dravidians themselves. The phonetic similarity of "Druid" to "Drāvida" is obvious.[17] In classical texts, the name of the Druids appears mostly in a plural form, as "druidai" (Gk.) or "druidae" or "druides" (Lt.).[18] In Irish, "drai" or "druí" is the singular form of a word meaning "wise man", of which "draod" or "druid" is the plural. The association of the Druids with the Greek word for "oak", first made by Pliny (*Historia Naturalis* XVI,95), is probably a later one due to the importance of tree-worship among the ancient

---

[17] In ancient Indo-European 'v' is typically pronounced 'u'.

[18] See S. Piggott, *Prehistoric India to 1000 B.C.*, London: Cassell, 1962, p.89.

Druids, as well as amongst most of the ancient Indo-European peoples, since the sacred tree serves as a symbol of the divine phallus representing the life of the universe.

The Druids seem to have been the priests of the Cimmerian Celts, especially in Gaul and Britain. Since there is no evidence of them in other Celtic territories such as the Danube, Cisalpine and Transalpine Gaul it is possible that they are themselves of non-Celtic origin.[19] However, among the Gauls, the Druids, along with the "equites", constituted the higher "castes". Piggott believed that the Druidic tradition may go back to at least the second millennium B.C. since it has much in common with the Indo-European language and ideology, especially the Sanskritic and Hittite.[20] However, it is quite possible that the Druids were settled in Europe even earlier than the Āryans, perhaps as early as the third millennium B.C. The three-headed god attributable to the Druids in the Marne and the Côte d'Or is possibly related to the three (or four) headed god[21] of the Indus Valley of the third millennium B.C.[22] Hence it is not surprising that Clement of Alexandria believed that the Pythagorean and Greek philosophers derived their wisdom from the Gauls and other barbarians,[23] by which he no doubt meant the Druidic priestly core of these tribes. Dio Chrysostom (1st c. A.D.) considered the Druids as being similar to the Persian Magi, Egyptian priests, and Indian Brāhmans. It may be recalled that F.E. Pargiter once maintained that Brāhmanism itself may not have been originally Āryan

---

[19] The Druidic type is perhaps most evident today among the Welsh.

[20] See S. Piggott, *op.cit.*, p.74.

[21] The fourth head of the god is invisible since it is turned backwards.

[22] See, for instance, M. Jansen, *Die Indus-Zivilisation: Wiederentdeckung einer frühen Hochkultur*, Köln: DuMont, 1986.

[23] See S. Piggott, *op.cit.*, p.81.

but adopted into Indo-Āryan religion from Dravidian.²⁴ However, Pargiter did not consider the possibility that both Āryan and later Dravidian may have been derived from a proto-Dravidian/Hurrian spiritual culture.

The religion of the Druids was clearly cosmological, as is attested in the commentaries of Caesar, who attributed to them much knowledge of the stars and their motion, and of the size of the world.²⁵ Ammianus Marcellinus declared that they investigated "problems of things secret and sublime".²⁶ Diodorus Siculus, following Posidonius, maintained that they held that "the souls of men are immortal, and that after a definite number of years they have a second life when the soul passes to another body",²⁷ which is also the doctrine of the proto-Dravidians who formulated the original tenets of Indian religion.

Although the Celtic religion included sacrifices, even human, there is no evidence however of fire-worship among the Druids such as became characteristic of the Indo-Āryans and Iranians. However, the veneration of fire among the ancient Celts may be dimly detected in the relative frequency of the appellation "Áed" (fire) among the legendary and early historical high-kings of Ireland.²⁸ It is only among the proto-Aryans that the Indo-European religious rituals become centred on fire-worship, which entails an external dramatisation of cosmic events and particularly the birth of the sun within the sacred sacrificial fire, Agni.

However, with the rise of the later Hamitic cultures of Sumer and Egypt, the adoration of the cosmic forces

---

[24] See F.E. Pargiter, *Ancient Indian Historical Tradition*, London: Milford, 1922, Ch.26.

[25] *Ibid.*

[26] See S. Piggott, *op.cit.*, p.101.

[27] *Ibid.*, p.102.

[28] For instance, Áed Rúad (see the *Lebor Gabála Érenn*).

assumed anthropomorphic forms and idolatrous temple-worship became the rule, as it did in later Hinduism as well. At the same time, it should be noted that the temples of the ancient Indo-Europeans, as well as the fire-rituals of the Āryans, are both equally built on a sacred ground-plan (mandala) of the Purusha who is revived, through the various rituals performed therein, to his original cosmic solar splendour. In the Indo-Aryan sacrifices the sacrificer undergoes a ritual death and rebirth as the sun, whereas in the Hamitic temple worship, the sacred idol is adored as a living representation of the nascent and developing sun. Both these forms of worship are naturally related to the Tantric yogic exercises that employ the correspondences between macrocosm and microcosm to divinise the adept himself.[29]

The gods of the various cultures that emerged from the original homeland of the Indo-Europeans symbolise the various vital aspects of the macroanthropomorphic Purusha. Thus Enlil, Vāyu, Wotan, representing the divine breath or life-force, are chief gods among the Sumerians, Indians, and Germans; Zeus, Indra, Perun represent the storm-force, among the Germans, Greeks, Indians, and Slavs; and Atum, An, Brahman, Mithra, Helios, Sol are worshipped by the Egyptians, Sumerians, Indians, Zoroastrians, Greeks and Mithraists as the cosmic Light. While the fire-sacrifices and temple-rituals of the ancient Indo-European religions were considered necessary for the well-being of the Purusha and the proper functioning of the universe, the aim of the truly enlightened sage, however, was to transcend the cosmic incarnation altogether through yogic ascesis.

---

[29] For a more detailed examination of the rituals of the ancient Indo-Europeans see A. Jacob, *Brahman: A Study of the Solar Rituals of the Indo-Europeans*, Hildesheim: Georg Olms, 2012.

II. PRALAYA
Cosmic Floods, the Sun and the First Man

IN SURVEYING THE origins of the Indo-Europeans as well as its cosmological myths and religious rituals we may do well to start with the Indo-European accounts of the creation of the cosmos itself.

Naimittika Pralaya

The story of the Deluge which we are familiar with from the account in Genesis 6-9 is indeed a popular representation of the cosmic floods which usher in the recreation of the material universe after the collapse of the cosmos at the end of a cosmic age. The first flood that engulfs the cosmos at the end of a kalpa, or 'day' of Brahman is called Naimittika Pralaya (periodic dissolution) and the second that precedes the formation of our universe and our sun is called Chākshusha Pralaya (dissolution of the Chākshusha Manvantara).

The prehistory of the cosmos is presented in greatest detail in the Indic Purānic literature,[30] where we get a glimpse not only of the cosmic events that marked the creation but also of their psychological significance. In

---
[30] The Flood stories are to be found also in the Tamil Purānams.

the *Bhāgavata Purāṇa*[31] III,xi,18-22, a day of the supreme Lord is calculated as equalling 1000 Chaturyugas, each Chaturyuga[32] being 12,000 divine years long (that is, years as prevalent in the realm of the gods),[33] or 4,380,000,000 terrestrial years.[34] After creating and sustaining the cosmos for this extraordinarily vast period of time, comes the night in which the Lord "sleeps". This night is equally as long as the day of the Lord and is the period when the cosmos is dissolved into its original subtle constituents in the flood called Naimittika Pralaya (*BP* XII,4,3).

Each kalpa is divided into fourteen "manvantaras" or ages of Manu, a Manu being a prototype of enlightened mankind. Each Manvantara lasts for 71 odd Chaturyugas, or 310,980,000 years (*BP* III,11,24). A lifetime of Brahma lasts hundred years totalling around 155,520,000,000,000 terrestrial years. The first kalpa of the first half (parārdha) of Brahma's life was called Brahma Kalpa (*BP* III,11,33ff.), since it was marked by the perfect light of Brahma, and the last of the same half was called Padma Kalpa (the age of the lotus), since it was in this kalpa that Earth was formed in the shape of a lotus. We live in the first kalpa of the second half of Brahma's life, called Varāha Kalpa (the age of the Boar) in which the divine light is transferred to the material universe.[35]

---

[31] The following abbreviations are used in this essay: *BP=Bhāgavata Purāṇa*, *BrdP=Brahmāṇḍa Purāṇa*, *RV*=Rgveda, *SB=Shatapatha Brāhmana,* W=Warka, W.B.=Weld-Blundell Collection (Ashmolean Museum, Oxford).

[32] A chaturyuga is made up of four ages, Krita, Treta, Dvāpara and Kali, corresponding to a Golden, Silver, Bronze and Iron Age, in the course of which the divine virtue is gradually diminished. We now live in the fourth, degenerate, age (Kaliyuga) of the Varāha Kalpa.

[33] A divine day is as long as a terrestrial year.

[34] A terrestrial year is the period taken by the sun to revolve through the twelve constellations of the zodiac (*BP* III,11,13; V,22,5).

[35] Current astrophysical theories suggest that the cosmos is roughly

The Naimittika Pralaya which occurred at the end of the previous Padma Kalpa is described in some detail in the *Brahmānda Purāna*. In the *Brahmānda Purāna* III,iv,132, the cosmic cataclysm is said to have begun with a drought in which the sun burnt everything up with his "seven rays", while the "Samvartaka" fire[36] burnt the four worlds of Earth, the Mid-Region, Heaven and "Mahar" (the supracelestial realm):

> Seven rays of the sun that blazes in the sky sucking water, drink water from the great ocean. Being illuminated with that intake, seven suns are evolved. Then those rays that have become suns, burn the four worlds in the four directions. Those fires burn up the entire universe.

The Earth is thus enveloped in flames until the seven suns merge into one, and then the samvartaka fire burns up the underworld, Rasatala, as well (153). The three worlds as well as the superior, Maharloka, are thus burnt up entirely and the universe "assumes the form of a huge block of iron and shines thus" (159).

All the creatures of the universe are reduced to the state of the "mahābhūtas" (principal elements) (231). Brahman himself as the sustainer of the creation gets merged into the Mahat (the principle of manifestation),[37] which in turn

---

14 billion years old whereas, according to the *BP*, the cosmos is approximately 13,140,000,000 years old (the first day and night of the Lord plus half of the second day). The latter is likely to be more accurate since it is not based on fallible empirical observation but on spiritual intuition.

[36] The burning of the universe at the end of a cosmic age is called "kalpadaha" in *BrdP* I,i,5,122.

[37] See *BrdP* III,iv,2,115: "The manifest part evolving out of the unmanifest one is gross and it is called Mahan (Mahat)".

becomes Avyakta (the unmanifest) and the three gunas, or energies (Sattva, Rajas, Tamas) are restored to their initial perfect balance. Thereafter arise Samvartaka "clouds" which also "group themselves in seven, identifying themselves with the suns" and these clouds succeed in extinguishing the fire when they shower as torrential rains. Through these torrential rains, everything mobile and immobile is dissolved into one undifferentiated ocean of water in which the supreme deity Brahman "sleeps" during his long "night".

In the *Shiva Purāna,* the endless ocean into which the universe is dissolved at the end of the process of cosmic destruction is also called Mahādeva, that is, Shiva himself, since he is the destructive aspect of Brahman.[38] A little earlier the same ocean is called the "ocean of mundane existence" since it is the inchoate source of the life that will infuse the new universe.[39]

It is in this universal water (ambhas) called Ekarnava, Salila or Naras (*BrdP*,III,iv, 174-8) that the deity, gradually waking, begins to recreate the cosmos, first assuming the form of the macroanthropos, Purusha. Then he extracts, in the form of a Cosmic Boar, the material substance of the universe called Earth, which lies sunken, from the previous cosmos, in the Ocean. This Brahman is interestingly also called Kāla (185ff.), who is the same as Shiva, for it is the latter who, at the end of the divine "night" is the secret impetus to the recreation of the universe. Kāla/Chronos/Kumarbi, representing Time, features prominently in the Hurrian-Greek cosmogonies as well, as the producer of the Cosmic Egg and its light.[40]

---

[38] See S. Shastri, *The Flood Legend in Sanskrit Literature*, Delhi: S. Chand and Co., 1950, p.91.

[39] *Ibid.*, p.66.

[40] See p.224.

The process of the formation of the macroanthropos is described in detail in the *Brahmānda Purāna*. The initial unmanifest form of the deity in the waters is that of the supreme Soul, Ātman: "This entire dark world was pervaded by his Ātman" (I,i,3,12), with its three essential energies, Tāmas, Rajas, and Sattva, maintained in perfect balance. This unmanifest deity begins to be gradually manifested when one of the energies begins to predominate over the others. The first and highest, sattvic, form of the deity is as Vishnu, the ideal macroanthropos, while the rājasic is Brahman, who creates the material universe, and the tāmasic is Rudra, who will destroy the universe at the end of a cosmic age.

The transformation of Vishnu first into Brahman, the self-conscious, enlightened form of the supreme deity, is accomplished by virtue of intense Yogic meditation (I,i,5,6). The first act of the macroanthropos is to recover Earth through the force of his "breath" which emerges from his nostrils in the form of the wind-god Vāyu assuming the shape of a "Boar". This is followed by the intelligible creation beginning with the lower tāmasic and proceeding to the sattvic, the creation of the gods, of the "sages" who are intellectual creations of the deity, and, finally, of human life (I,i,5). Then Brahman manifests himself materially as the Light of the universe. The close union of the Light with Earth is destroyed by Time, Chronos, who is, in Hesiod's *Theogony*, 170ff, said to have castrated his father 'Heaven'. This castration results in the development of a Cosmic Egg which develops within the ideal macroanthropos, Purusha. The light of Brahman then constitutes the upper half of this egg while the lower half is constituted of the newly recovered Earth in the form of a lotus. The development of the egg is given in more scientific detail in the *Vishnu Purāna* I:

> Then (the elements) ether, air, light, water and earth, severally united with the properties of sound, and the rest existed as distinguishable according to their qualities as soothing, terrific, or stupefying; but possessing various energies, and being unconnected, they could not without combination create living beings, not having blended with each other. Having combined, therefore, with one another, they assumed, through their mutual association, the character of one mass of entire unity; and from the direction of spirit, with the acquiescence of the indiscreet principle, intellect, and the rest, to the gross elements inclusive, formed an egg, which gradually expanded like a bubble of water.[41]

It must be remembered that the earlier cosmic age (Padma Kalpa) was also marked by the creation of a universe or universes, since the Naimittika Pralaya begins with a conflagration due to the "suns". However, it is possible that there was no human life in it, since that is mentioned only in our cosmic age (Varāha Kalpa), whose seventh Manu, Manu Vaivasvata, is responsible for the transmission of the seeds of life to earth as well as for the mortality of the forms that spring from these seeds.[42] According to *BrdP* I,ii,6, the natural destruction of the earlier cosmos was followed by the intermediate period (pratisandhi) between two kalpas when the deity returned anew to his task of creation. However, this time it is clear that he proceeded farther in his material manifestation than in the previous cosmic age.

In the *Padma Purāna* I,39,48ff., Vishnu (the form of the supreme lord as macroanthropos) is said to have taken

---

[41] See W.J. Wilkins, *Hindu Mythology, Vedic and Puranic,* London: Thacker, Spink & Company, 1882, p.348.

[42] See p.40.

four forms in the process of destroying the universe. First, he appears as the sun with which he "dried up the oceans" and at the same time removes the sense of "sight" itself, the sun being traditionally associated with sight in India as well as in Egypt and Mesopotamia. At this point, he dives into the Abyss to search out Earth, the embryonic new universe which lies hidden there. Vishnu next appears as a gale (wind) which "convulsed the entire world" and at the same time destroyed "inspiration, expiration and all the forms of breath". The third form he assumes is that of fire, which reduces the universe to ashes, and finally, he assumes the nature of water as a "hundred dark whirling clouds" which "gratified the Earth with ghee-like divine water".[43] This impregnation causes "the subtle world [i.e. of the senses of sight and breath], with the sun, wind and the sky" to be enclosed in the Earth that has been recovered from the abyss. The last step of the process described here would have occurred at the time of the formation of the Cosmic Egg.

For another account of the stages which mark the new creation after the destruction of the previous cosmos, we may turn to the *Bhāgavata Purāna*. The emergence of the light of the universe—which is called Protogonos/Phanes in the Orphic theogonies[44]—occurs in the first manvantara of the Varāha Kalpa, since Protogonos' Indic counterpart, Priyavrata, is said to be the son of the very first Manu, Swāyambhuva Manu. This manvantara is also marked by the emergence of Earth and its division into seven islands (called continents in the Iranian sacred literature) which represent various galactic formations (*BP* V,1,30ff.). Like Protogonos/Mitra, it was Priyavrata who created the divisions of Earth by riding around

---

[43] See S. Shastri, *op.cit.*, p.34f.

[44] See M.L. West, *Orphic Poems*, Oxford: Clarendon Press, 1983, p.70.

Mt. Meru in his chariot.[45] Of the seven islands, the one we inhabit is the central one and called Jambudweepa (*BP* V,16,5ff.), which itself is divided into nine Varshas, of which one, Bharatvarsha, is the region which humans inhabit after the cosmic flood (*BP* V,19.9ff.).

The Varāha Kalpa, is marked by several other 'avatārs' or incarnations of the supreme Lord[46] that are assumed by the latter throughout the developing life of the cosmos in order to elevate the creation spiritually. After the Boar, the next incarnation of the Lord in our cosmic age is that of Prithu, who extracts the life-giving qualities from Earth when it has assumed the form of a Cow (in the sixth manvantara) (*BP* IV,18; *BrdP* I,ii,36,110ff.).

Chākshusha Pralaya

The sixth manvantara of the Varāha Kalpa, called the Chākshusha Manvantara or the manvantara of Chākshusha, is indeed the one at the end of which the 'deluge' occurs that is recounted in the various flood stories of antiquity as if it had occurred on earth. This flood also precedes the appearance of the seventh Manu,

---

[45] This is reflected in the Hieronyman Orphic fragment (78) also, where Protogonos wheels round the world in his chariot to bring light to it (see M.L. West, *op.cit.*, p.214).

[46] According to *BP* I,3, there are twenty-two avatārs of Vishnu, beginning with

[Krita Yuga] Chatursana (the four sons of Brahma), the boar Varāha, Nārada, Nara-Nārāyana, Kapila, Dattatreya, Yajna, Rishabha,

[Treta Yuga] the fish Matsya, the tortoise Kūrma, Dhanvantari, Mohini, Narasimha, Vāmana, Parashurāma, Vyāsa, Rāma,

[Dvāpara Yuga] Balarāma, Krishna,

[Kali Yuga] the Buddha, Kalki.

Vaivasvata whose task it is to preserve the life of the universe (*BP* I,3,15).

The flood is caused by Shiva (Enlil) when he breaks open the Cosmic Egg. Shiva begins the flood by splitting "asunder these seven worlds,[47] and breaking the [golden cosmic] egg higher than the highest". Shiva is said to be "robed in Indra's thunder-bolts"[48] as he goes about his task of devastation. In the Akkadian *Atrahasis* epic as well as in the Sumerian *Gilgamesh* (Tablet XI), it is Enlil (counterpart of Shiva) who causes the flood. For it is Enlil (or his son) who attacks the divine light An and forces it down into the underworld and into our universe. Shiva/Chronos' breaking open of this egg is indeed the start of the transfer of the life contained within it to our universe.

The solar force that is shattered by the force of Shiva/Enlil is forced into the 'underworld' where it lies in a moribund state, 'castrated' as it were by Time/Chronos. However, it is a continuation of Chronos' force, called his 'son', Zeus, that eventually revives the dormant solar force in the underworld so that it can rise into our universe as the sun. This heroic figure in the evolution of the sun is called Zeus/Ganesha/Seth in the mythologies of Greece, India, and Egypt.[49] The descent of the perfect light of Osiris-Horus the Elder/Brahman into the Abyss thus precedes its rise again as the light of our universe.

During this flood, the Lord (Vishnu in the *BP*) reposes on the serpent Anantasesha (the eternal Sesha), a form of Shiva,[50] that inhabits Pātāla, the seventh and last circle of

---

[47] That is, the seven "continents", or galactic formations of the universe.

[48] See S. Shastri, *op.cit.*, p.88.

[49] For a detailed study of the formation of the sun see A. Jacob, *Ātman: A Reconstruction of the Solar Cosmology of the Indo-Europeans*, Hildesheim: Georg Olms, 2005.

[50] As Hedammu no doubt is a form of Kumarbi in the Hurrian

the underworld (*BP* V,24,30). Since the lord of the abyss in Sumer, Egypt, as well as in the Vedas is traditionally Enki/Osiris/Varuna, the Vishnu that sleeps on the serpent Sesha must be the same as Varuna himself as the reviving solar energy. Varuna's association with Vishnu (as well as with Mitra, the "sun-god") is confirmed by the Egyptian identity of Osiris as Lord of the Abyss (abdu/Abydos) and the Underworld, who is at the same time the brother, or rather, vital aspect, of Horus the Elder, and father of the sun-god Horus the Younger. This explains Vishnu's other names, Nārāyana, Lord of the Waters, which is typical of Varuna/Enki/Osiris, and Anantaseshasāyī, the Lord who reposes on the eternal Sesha. Vishnu at this stage corresponds to Osiris in the underworld surrounded by the serpent Nehaher.[51] Vishnu/Varuna's trance-like sleep in the Purānas is indeed the same as the "death" of Osiris caused by his *alter ego* Seth.

In *BP* V,25,1, the serpent Sesha is described as being the tāmasic or Māyā-associated aspect of the supreme lord which sustains this universe by the magical effect of sympathy. In the *Vishnu Purāna*, it is stated that "Vishnu assumes the form of Rudra [Shiva/Kāla] and inclines towards destruction in order to withdraw the entire creation into himself".[52] Rudra, however, is not only the same as Time but also "the flame of Time" which "turns into the blasting breath of Sesha [the serpent]".[53] We see here an identification of Time with Māyā as agents of the illusion that sustains the incipient universe.

The serpent representing Shiva has both a benign and a malign aspect. This dual role is particularly observed in the Egyptian representations of the serpent (sometimes

---

"Kingship in Heaven" myth (see p.36).

[51] See below.

[52] See S. Shastri, *op.cit.*, p.48.

[53] *Ibid.*, p.49.

called Mehen, the "World-encircler", sometimes Nehaher, "the one with the fearful face"), which first holds together the corpse of Osiris and then accompanies the emergence of his son, the incipient sun, Horus the Younger.[54] Thus, when Osiris dies and descends into the underworld, his decaying corpse (represented as a mummy) is depicted as being held together by Nehaher.[55] In the Indic accounts of Manu and the Flood,[56] this serpent of the Abyss is the same that serves as a rope between the boat and the horn of the piscine form of the supreme deity that saves Manu during the flood.

The dual aspect of the serpent as both destructive and creative is highlighted in the last scene of the Egyptian *Book of Caverns*, which depicts a serpent within a mound of earth that helps regenerate Osiris as Horus the Younger along with another serpent encircling the solar beetle (Khepry) that is cut into pieces.[57] In the *Amduat* too, while the serpent Apop is destroyed in the seventh hour, in the eleventh and twelfth hours[58] the emergent sun itself appears within the bounds of the serpent called "World encircler".[59]

---

[54] See E. Hornung, , *The Ancient Egyptian Books of the Afterlife*, , tr. D. Lorton, Ithaca: Cornell University Press, 1999, pp.33ff; cf. R.T. Rundle Clark, *Myth and Symbol in ancient Egypt*, London: Thames and Hudson, 1959, pp.167ff.

[55] See *The Book of Caverns* (cf. R.T.Rundle Clark, *op.cit.*, p.169).

[56] See *Shatapatha Brāhmana*, I,viii,

[57] See E. Hornung, *op.cit.*, p.90.

[58] It may be noted, in passing, that the "hours" of the Egyptian books of the underworld certainly do not refer to our terrestrial hours but, rather, to divine ones. We have seen that, according to the *BP*, a divine day is as long as a terrestrial year. It is possible that the sun's yearly revolution as well as its diurnal passage may have been considered in Egypt to be repeated rehearsals of the original creation.

[59] E. Hornung, *op.cit.*, pp.33ff.

In Egypt, as Usener pointed out,[60] the solar aspect of the flood is also evident in the account of the sailing of Amun-Ra on the back of the cow, called itself the Great Flood (Mehet Ouret)—a form of Hathor/Nut[61]—holding on to her "horns". We will encounter this bovine image of the goddess of the primaeval waters and of the dawn also in the Indic sacred literature. The hymn to Amun-Ra in the Darius temple to this deity declares that the original seat of Amun-Ra was the high ground of Hermopolis Magna, where the "eight gods" of the Ogdoad were worshipped. Amun-Ra is said to have left this oasis and appeared in the moist, hidden egg along with the goddess Amente. Then he takes his place on the Great Flood. At that time, "there were no plants. They began when … the water rose to the mountain".[62]

We note that the "great flood" in Egypt is not, as in the Biblical story, the setting for the preservation of merely the Noachidian race on earth but for the emergence of the sun in our universe along with the life of the universe.

In the fragmentary Hedammu epic of the Hurrians, too, Kumarbi produces a dragon Hedammu (resembling the flood Narmada and Hathor) to destroy mankind.[63] The fact that, in the Hurrian epic of 'The Kingship in Heaven', Anu's seed (as well as his phallus) is contained in the belly of Kumarbi (Chronos/Kala/Shiva) also suggests that the creative waters of the flood caused by Shiva serve as the amniotic fluid of the incipient universe.

In the Greek Orphic theogonies, Chronos is represented as a serpent twined around the cosmic axis of

---

[60] See H. Usener, *Die Sintfluthsagen*, Bonn: Friedrich Cohen, 1899, p.260.

[61] See PT 829 d/e; cf. R.T. Rundle Clark, *op.cit.*, p.184.

[62] *Ibid.*

[63] See J. Siegelova, "Appu Märchen und Hedammu-Mythus", *Studien zu den Bogazköy-Texten*14.

Ananke, Necessity.⁶⁴ This confirms the identity of Shiva/Chronos/Kumarbi with the serpent, especially in its creative role, since, as we shall see, Shiva represents Time as well as the aspect of Egoity which informs the universe.⁶⁵

The basic quality of the serpent, however, is that of the resistant force of matter which must be overcome to allow the light of the sun to emerge in our universe. Hence the rise of the solar energy is typically preceded by a battle of a heroic god representing the storm-force of the incipient sun against a serpent of restriction. Indra in the Rgveda is described as freeing the "cows" from the "vala", a rocky enclosure in which these animals are hidden by the evil Panis.⁶⁶ The "cows" in the vala myth (X,67,1-12) in fact symbolise the radiant solar energy, since RV I,164,3 suggests that this is the secret name of the rays of the dawn. In RV X,108,5, the "cows" are described as "flying around to the ends of the sky". The Panis themselves are described in BP V,24,30 as serpentine, Asuric creations of Diti and Danu and inhabit Rasātala, the sixth of the seven subterranean regions of the material universe bordering on the last, Pātāla, in which lies the serpent Sesha.⁶⁷ "Vala", significantly, is the same term that is used in the Avesta ("vara") for the ark which bears Yima during the flood which accompanies the birth of the sun.

***

---

[64] See M.L. West, *op.cit.*

[65] See p.65.

[66] For a reference to the cows confined in the vala by the Panis see RV I, 32,11.

[67] In the Egyptian *Book of the Heavenly Cow* too the underworld is described as being populated by serpents supervised by Geb [Earth] (see E. Hornung, *op.cit.*, p.149).

The reason of the flood itself is given in the Egyptian *Book of the Heavenly Cow*, where the eye of Re, which is equated with Hathor, is said to be the instrument of the punishment of degenerate "mankind", by which we may understand a form of mankind that emerged early in the creational activities of Brahman. Re embarks on this course of punishment in conjunction with the lord of the Abyss, Nun. A part of "humanity" is destroyed by the flood, but the remainder are saved by the sun-god's decision to stop Hathor's work of devastation by causing her to become drunk on blood-red beer.[68] The sun then rises to the heavens on the back of the celestial cow.

This Egyptian account is perhaps the source of the Hebrew story, in *Genesis* 6:7, of the Flood:

> And the Lord said, I will destroy man whom I have created from the face of the earth; both man, and beast, and the creeping thing, and the fowls of the air; for it repenteth me that I have made them.

It is clear, however, that the Hebrew Flood is inaccurately located on earth and dated *after* the creation of Noah/Manu, when in fact the latter appears ages after the Flood, in the seventh manvantara.

In the Babylonian 'Epic of Erra', Marduk, the counterpart of the solar force, Ninurta/[69] Muruga, takes the place of his father Enlil in causing the flood:

---

[68] Cf. E. Hornung, *op.cit.*, p.149. The reference to beer is significant, since we note that inebriation by beer is in fact characteristic of Seth, whose name, according to a Leiden papyrus, represents the intoxicating power of beer (see H. te Velde, *Seth God of Confusion: A Study of his Role in Egyptian Mythology and Religion*, Leiden: E.J. Brill, 1967, p.3ff.). Seth is the counterpart of the Vedic Indra, who also raises the sun into the heavens infused with the force of Soma.

[69] For Marduk as one of the epithets of Ninurta, see K.

> I got angry long ago: I rose from my seat and contrived the deluge,
>
> I rose from my seat, and the government of heaven and earth dissolved.
>
> And the sky, lo! shook: the stations of the stars in the sky were altered, and I did not bring [them] back to their [former] positions.
>
> ...
>
> The offspring of the living diminished, and I did not restore them
>
> Until, like a farmer, I should take their seed in my hand.[70]

We see that Marduk too destroys some early form of life in the cosmos while preserving some part of it to be propagated in our universe.

In the relatively late Greek legend of the Flood, in which Prometheus' son, Deucalion, is represented as the survivor, who reaches safety on Mt. Parnassus, Zeus is anachronistically said to have caused the deluge because he 'would destroy the men of the Bronze Age'.[71] In Ovid's *Metamorphoses*, I, 177ff, Zeus' anger is aroused by the inferiority of humankind compared to the demi-gods:

> Now I must destroy the human race, wherever Nereus sounds, throughout the world. I swear it by the

---

Tallquist, *Akkadische Götterepitheta (Studia Orientalia* 7), Helsinki, 1938, p.422. For Ninurta as the solar force, see p.49.

[70] Tr. L. Cagni, *The Poem of Erra*, Malibu, CA: Undena Publications, 1977, p.32.

[71] See Apollodorus, *Library*, I,7,2.

infernal streams, that glide below the earth through the Stygian groves. All means should first be tried, but the incurable flesh must be excised by the knife, so that the healthy part is not infected. Mine are the demigods, the wild spirits, nymphs, fauns and satyrs, and sylvan deities of the hills. Since we have not yet thought them worth a place in heaven let us at least allow them to live in safety in the lands we have given them.

Manu of the Sun

The course of the sun's emergence in our universe coincides with that of the first Man, who is called Manu Vaivasvata, or Manu of the Sun (Vivasvant). This primal man is of interest in a study of the flood since it is he who is said to preserve the life of the universe in a boat that is at once a solar barque, as in Egypt, and an ark that carries the seeds of universal life through the flood to safety atop a mountain (from whence the sun too will arise). Manu is thus the divine ancestor of the race that is to inhabit the universe. As a personification of enlightened humanity the role of a Manu is to maintain the cosmic order at the time of the creation of the universe (*BP* VIII,14,3).

Manu Vaivasvata is also called Shraddhādeva (*BP* VIII,13,1) and is the seventh Manu of our kalpa (*BP* VIII,13, there being fourteen Manus in all in each kalpa.[72] The seventh manvantara of the Varāha Kalpa is thus called Vaivasvata (of Vivasvant, the sun) Manvantara (*BP* VII,8; VIII,7,12,18), or the Age of Manu of the Sun. Since each manvantara has a duration of around 317,000,000 years (*BP* III,11,24), life on earth must have

---

[72] The names of the first six Manus of this kalpa are Swāyambhuva,

There is also an intimate connection between Hathor and the Tree of Life, which springs up from the waters of the abyss, just as there is between Aditi and Indra in the Vedas, and Narmada is a form of Aditi as well as Pārvathi. Both Hathor and Aditi represent the basis of universal creation after the periodic destruction of the cosmos, and the Tree of Life is the form of the material universe itself which arises from the abyss through the divine seed represented by Indra/Ninurta/Marduk.

It is clear that Mārkandeya is a form of the solar force itself, and we may conclude that Manu, whom he replaces, is, as the "son" of the sun, equally one. Both Manu and Mārkandeya are thus 'superhuman' solar figures that are considered ancestors of the human race.

***

We may now consider some special aspects of the flood story of Manu that may require elucidation. In the *Shatapatha Brāhmana* Manu[80] is warned of the deluge by a fish (representing Vishnu/Prajāpati in his piscine Matsya avatār). Manu saves himself in a ship which is tied to the "horn" of the fish[81] and is borne by the latter to the heights of "the northern mountain", which, not being specified as a Himalayan one, may well be the

---

[80] The ancient Germans too considered the ancestor of the Germanic people to be 'Mannus', according to Tacitus, *Germania*, Sec.2.

[81] See *SB* I,viii,1,5. It is hard to determine what the "horn" of the fish might be (unless it were a sword-fish). On the other hand, we may recall the image of Re emerging as the sun by holding on to the horns of the Cow Mehet-Ouret. The Indic imagery may be a hybrid transformation of the Egyptian. This impression is reinforced by the fact that Manu's daughter, Ida, who in *SB* I,viii,1,11-12 is said to characterise "cattle", is, in *TS* I,7,1 and II,6,7, represented as a cow produced by Mitra-Varuna. We shall see below that Ida is the same as Narmada.

Ararat of the Armenians mentioned in *Genesis* 8:4.[82] In the *Mahābhārata,* the divine identity of the fish is revealed to be that of Prajāpati/Brahman (the name of the supreme god in his luminous, creative aspect), since the fish declares to the "seven sages"—who, unlike in the *SB* version of the story, accompany Manu in the ship —"I am Brahma, lord of progeny [Prajāpati] ... I in the form of a fish have delivered you from this peril".[83] The fish goes on to state that Manu should create all creatures including "gods, asuras, and men and all the worlds and what moves and what does not move [i.e. animal and vegetable life]."

In the *Matsya Purāna,* too, the fish that saves Manu is said to be a form of the supreme lord, Janārdana (Vishnu), while the rope that Manu ties between the fish's "horn" and the boat is the serpent, Vasuki, identifiable with the serpent of the Abyss, Sesha.[84] We note here again a similarity also between the Ship of Life and the Tree of Life since both bear the serpent at one end and both bear the seeds of universal life as well as the solar force – the latter represented by Manu himself as well as by the sun that arises atop the branches of the Tree.[85] Besides, the Ship of Life containing the seeds of life of the universe comes to rest atop a mountain, and the sun too appears atop the phallic, mountain-like, Tree of Life.

***

In the Dravidian *Cikalittala Purānam* of Arunāchalakkavirayar, we get further glimpses into the

---

[82] See p.9.

[83] *Mbh* II, 187, 2ff. (cited S. Shastri, *op.cit.*, p.9); cf. H. Usener, *op.cit.*, p.28ff.

[84] See S. Shastri, *op.cit.*, p.28.

[85] See A. Jacob, *Ātman*, Ch.XXIII.

nature of the ship of life. The divine personages who survive the flood are said to be Siva himself and his wife Uma. The boat which saves Siva and his wife are considered as being symbolic of the sacred sound "Om" itself, while the resting place of the boat is a "shrine" which stands as firm as "Dharma".[86] We may remember also that Ziusudra is blessed, at the end of the deluge, with immortality in the sacred land of "Dilmun". The original form of Dilmun may well have been "Dharman" and represented the perfect holiness that this concept signifies in Vedic religion.[87] Dilmun is also identified with the sacred "mountain" from which the light of the universe arises and which is the terrestrial source of the "me's".[88] This suggests that the phallic 'mountain' and 'tree' of life are identical.

The mountain atop which the boat comes to rest is also considered to be situated at the centre or navel of the universe. For the concept that the sanctuary is to be found atop a mountain at the navel or centre of the universe is to be found in Jewish (and later Muslim) theologians as well,[89] who no doubt derived it from Babylon. The mountain and navel clearly represent the phallic deity Shiva and his consort Pārvathi (representing

---

[86] See D. Shulman, 'The Tamil Flood Myths and the Cankam Legend', *Journal of Tamil Studies*, 14 (1978), 10.31.

[87] It is unlikely that Dilmun originally had anything to do with the little island of Bahrain which later came to be identified with it.

[88] The Sumerian 'me' corresponds to the Vedic 'rta', which are principles of the divine ordering of Nature. 'Mey' is also the Tamil word for "just" (see K. Mutturayan, "Sumer: Tamil of the First Cankam", *Journal of Tamil Studies*, 8 (1975), p.51). Cf. also Y. Rosengarten, *Sumer et le sacré*, Paris: Editions E. de Broccard, 1977, p.56. The epithet "great "mountain" of the pure me's" is applied to other sacred Mesopotamian lands, such as Aratta and Sumer, as well (*ibid.*, pp.54ff.).

[89] See A. Wensinck, "The Ideas of the Western Semites concerning the Navel of the Earth", *Verhandelingen der Koninklijke Akademie van Wetenschappen*, XVII (1916), no.1, pp.15f, 19ff, 40.

the cosmic vulva), so that they together constitute the entire emergent universe.

In the Vedic literature Indra, infused with the potency of Soma, swells into a universal Tree of Life through which the sun emerges. In order to release the sun, however, Indra has (in the vala myth, *RV* 10.67,1-12) to first free the "cows" from the "vala", a rocky enclosure in which they are hidden by the evil Panis. The "cows" symbolise the radiant solar energy, since *RV* I,164,3 suggests that this is the secret name of the rays of the dawn.[90] In *RV* X,108,5, the "cows" are described as "flying around to the ends of the sky". The Panis themselves are described in *BP* V,24,30 as serpentine, Asuric creations of Diti and Danu and inhabit Rasātala, the sixth of the seven subterranean regions of the material universe bordering on the last, called Pātāla, below which lies the serpent Sesha. The Panis are thus related to Sesha/Vrtra. "Vala", significantly, is the same term that is, as we shall see, used in the Avesta ("vara") for the ark which bears Yima during the flood which accompanies the birth of the sun.

David Shulman has pointed out that the creation stories in the Dravidian versions emphasise the importance of the shrine as the centre of the universe and seat of the renewed creation after the deluge.[91] Shiva interestingly names this shrine "the root of the universe", which is situated on a hill rather like the primordial hill from which the light of the cosmos arises in Egypt. The shrine, therefore, is the foundation of the universe itself. In the related Dravidian accounts of the deluge which engulfed the sacred city of Madurai, the latter city serves as an analogue of the shrine whence the universe emerges. In these stories, the flood is said to have been caused by

---

[90] H.P. Schmidt, *Brhaspati und Indra*, Wiesbaden: Otto Harrassowitz, 1968, p.222.

[91] See D. Shulman, *op.cit.*

Varuna [Enki] at the instigation of Indra.[92] The flood caused by Varuna, Lord of the Underworld, precedes the formation of the new sun. Shiva is the god who protects the city Madurai from the flood, no doubt that it may serve as the sacred foundation of our universe. The shrine atop the mountain is secure (as also is the sacred city of Madurai) from any destructive flood which may well up from the netherworld, Pātāla.[93]

The *Mahābhārata* also includes the crucial detail missing in *SB*, that Manu was instructed to carry on board the boat "seed of every sort". That the seed that is preserved during the cosmic deluge is indeed the divine seed which informs all life in the universe is made clear in the Dravidian accounts of the flood, which state that Shiva instructed Brahman/Prajapati to safeguard in a golden pot (a substitute for the boat) the Vedas and other scriptures along with the seed of creation.[94] After the flood, the pot comes to rest at a sacred spot and Shiva reappears to release the contents of the pot and thus initiate the terrestrial creation.[95]

---

[92] See the *Tiruvilai* of Paranjoti, 12, 18, 19 (see D. Shulman, *op.cit.*).

[93] The spire (gopurum) of the Hindu temple represents this mountain while the sanctum is dark and mysterious as the Apsu/Abyss whence the universe and its light emerge.

[94] The common Vedic notion that the Vedas precede the actual creation of the universe is copied in the Hebrew rabbinical literature which maintains that there are seven things created before the world: "the Tora, conversion, the Garden of Eden, Gehenna, the divine Throne, the Sanctuary, the name of the Messiah" (see A. Wensinck, *op. cit.*, p.17). This confirms the cohabitation of Indic and Hebrew peoples in the Near East and dates back perhaps to the contacts in the 17th c. B.C. between the Hurrian-Mitanni and the Habiru who served as their mercenaries (see B. Landsberger in J. Bottero, *op.cit.*, p.160; cf. M. Salvini, "Un royaume hourrite en Mésopotamie du Nord à l'époque de Hattušili I", in M. Lebeau (ed.), *About Subartu: Studies devoted to Upper Mesopotamia* (Subartu IV,1), Turnhout: Brepols, 1998, p.307).

[95] D. Shulman, *op.cit.*

The curious passage in *Atrahasis,* III,20, where Ea (Akkadian for Enki) speaks to the "reed wall" of Atrahasis' dwelling may also be explained by the frequent Indian references to the lake of "reeds" in which the golden seed of Siva is dropped after being infused with his fiery form, Agni.[96] In a Sumerian magical text, Urn.49, the holy reed is said to rise from the swamps of Engur (Abzu).[97] The "reed" thus is an analogue of the ship of Life itself, since both contain the seeds of the incipient universe as well as its light. Thus it is not surprising to find that the boat of Ziusudra is also made of "reed".

The fact that this 'ship of life' is the same as the one through which the sun arises into our system is made quite clear in the Egyptian *Book of the Gates.* The solar journey is undertaken in a barque which is called the "barque of the Earth",[98] since Earth is the region from which the sun is manifest. In both this book and in the *Amduat*, the solar journey through Earth is undertaken within the coils of the World Encircler, the gigantic serpent representing Time.[99]

In the Heliopolitan myth of the sun too, Seth, though the murderer of Osiris, the divine Light, helps Horus the Younger fight the serpent Apop on the barque of Re in order to ensure Re's emergence as the solar light.[100] The barque itself represents the material universe, which bears the light of the universe, Re. Seth overcomes Apop using

---

[96] See *RV* X, 51-3; *SB* 6, 3.1.31; *RV* X, 32.6.

[97] See H. Steible, *Die altsumerischen Bau- und Weihinschriften*, Wiesbaden: F. Steiner, 1982 (*FAOS* 5) I:110.

[98] See E.T. Hornung, *Ancient Egyptian Books*, p.60.

[99] *Ibid.* In the *Enigmatic Book of the Underworld*, the *ouroboros* serpents represent the birth and end of time (*ibid.*, p.78). In the Nordic Eddas, the Midgard serpent is called the "encircler of Earth" ('Voluspa', 60).

[100] See H. te Velde, *Seth, God of Confusion*, Ch.4.

his characteristic rage (nšn),[101] corresponding to the Indic 'manyu' and Iranian 'mainyu' which are associated with Shiva/Indra (*RV* X,83; *AV* IV,31,5).

In Mesopotamia, Ninurta, like Shiva's son, Skanda, represents the seed of Enlil.[102] The reference to Enki's 'makurru' boat in *Lugal e* (l.107), the sun-barque which is featured prominently as Ninurta's own, makes it clear that Ninurta is a continuation of Enki, the Lord of the Waters (Varuna/Osiris). In fact, Enki is said to have received the "lofty sun-disk" in Eridu (l.121) showing that as ruler of the underworld he is identical to the "dead" Osiris who is transformed into Horus the Younger. In the poem 'Enki and Inanna', Enki is depicted embarking on a "magur" boat, also called "the Ibex of the Abzu", which is a symbol of Enki's shrine itself. It may also be the Sumerian counterpart of the sun-barque in Egypt. Enki's voyage, in the myth, does not take him on a patently solar course but moves from region to region in "Mesopotamia" and the surrounding lands since Mesopotamia is considered a microcosm of the universe.[103]

The mountain rising from the foothills is the Mid-region of the universe, and the seed of the "primordial hill", Ninurta himself, will finally emerge atop it as the sun of our system. Indeed, in the epic, Ninurta, having accomplished his great deed, finally assumes his natural role as the sun by boarding his barque:

---

[101] See H. te Velde, *op.cit.*, p.101.

[102] So in the myth "Lugal-e" (see T. Jacobsen, *Treasures of Darkness: A History of Mesopotamian Religion*, New Haven: Yale University Press, 1976, p.131).

[103] See S.N. Kramer and J. Maier, *The Myths of Enki, the Crafty God*, Oxford: OUP 1989, p.42ff. The fact that the name of Sumer is itself probably derived from that of the primordial mountain at the centre of Earth, Meru, makes it likely that these geographical regions reflect cosmological ones.

> The Hero had crushed the Mountain; when he moved in the steppes, he appeared
>
> as the [S]un (?),
>
> ...
>
> Ninurta went joyously towards the "magur", his beloved boat,
>
> The Lord set his foot on the Makarnunta'e (boat).[104]

In the Babylonian epic, *Atrahasis*, Enki particularly advises Atrahasis to "roof [the ark] over like the Apsu/ So that the sun shall not see inside it", which indicates that the vehicle which contains the seed of all animals is, like the Abyss, completely dark.

The fact that the ship of life represents the entire universe is suggested also by the similar detail in the Ugaritic texts relating to Baal and the construction of his "palace" by his craftsman Kothar-and-Hasis. There Baal specifically objects to the inclusion of any windows in his "palace", since Mot (who represents Mortality) would enter through such an aperture. Unfortunately for Baal, Kothar-and-Hasis disobeys him and thus allows Mot to enter in, whereupon Baal is killed and thereby rendered subject to his rule. It is only after Baal's consort, Anath's destruction of Mot that Baal is resurrected (no doubt as the sun), in a manner resembling Osiris' resurrection as Horus the Younger.

If we turn to the Iranian Vendidad, we find that Yima the son of Vivanghvant (the sun)[105] is warned by Ahura

---

[104] J. Van Dijk, *Lugal ud me-lam-bi Nir-gal*, Leiden: E.J. Brill, 1983, p.137 (my translation of van Dijk's French).

[105] In Iranian mythology the twins Yama and Yima represent death

Mazda of a "snow storm" which will turn into a flood on melting.[106] In the Avesta, as in the Purānas, Yima (Manu) is mentioned in connection with the seventh incarnation of Verethraghna (Vishnu). In order to escape the cataclysm, Yima is asked to construct a "vara" [ark] which will bear the best examples of men, animals, and plants, and especially the "cows" which are on the mountains as well as in the valleys in "closed stalls".[107] Special reference is made to the fact that the "window which lets in the sunlight" be closed. That the Iranian version closely follows the Babylonian in this detail (which is perhaps found also in the original Sumerian though lost in its present fragmentary state), while at the same time leaving out the crucial reference to the Abyss, suggests that the Āryan flood stories, as well as the Mesopotamian, are based on an older proto-Dravidian/Hurrian original.

At the end of the Iranian Vendidad account of the deluge, Ahura Mazda explains that "the lights which shone in the vara" were "natural and human lights. All eternal lights shine from above, all human lights shine below in the inside (of the vara). Along with them, one sees the stars, moon, and sun shining in space". It is clear that the "human lights" are souls and that the vara, or the Ship of Life contains the light of the manifest universe, including the stars of the Mid-region.

---

and life. Yima is called the first king and the founder of civilisation and his fabulous dwelling is in Airyanem Vaego, corresponding mythologically to the Indian Yamasadanam (in the lower Heavens) and etymologically to Āryāvarta, the name applied to the Indo-Gangetic Plain settled by the later Indo-Āryans.

[106] The "snow storm" is a reference to the icy state of the incipient universe that prevents the manifestation of the solar energy.

[107] See H. Usener, *Die Sintfluthsagen*, p.208ff.

The Seven Sages

In the *Mahābhārata* version of the Flood, Manu is said to be accompanied in his boat by "seven sages", and it is worth studying their significance for an understanding of the exalted spirituality of the first enlightened humanity. Each of the Manu's in a kalpa is accompanied by seven sages (*GP* I,87) and these sages appear in order to consolidate the transition between cosmic ages with their special knowledge and powers.

The seven sages that accompanied the first Manu Svāyambhuva were called Marichi, Atri, Angira, Pulastya, Pulaha, Kratu and Vasishta.[108] In *Brahmānda Purāna* I and *Bhāgavata Purāna* VI, these sages are considered to be the "intellectual progeny" of Brahma who antedate the Ādityas, the twelve suns of the manifest universe. In the *BrdP* III,iv,2,29, the sages of the family of Angiras are said to be located in the Bhuvarloka, which is the Mid-region between Earth and Heaven. At *BrdP* III,iv,2,49ff., however, all the sages including Angiras are said to originally reside in Janarloka, the fifth world, which holds the seeds of mankind.

---

[108] In *BrdP* II,iii,1,7f. there are seven sages, whose names are given at II,iii,1,50 as Bhrgu, Angiras, Marīci, Atri, Pulastya, Pulaha, and Vasishta. In *Manusmriti* III,195ff. too there are seven, though Viraj takes the place of Pulaha. In *BrdP* II,iii,1,21, however, there are eight sages, Bhrgu, Angiras, Marīci, Pulastya, Pulaha, Kratu, Atri and Vasishta. In the *BrdP* I,i,5,70 there are nine sages, Bhrgu, Angiras, Marīci, Pulastya, Pulaha, Kratu, Daksha, Atri, and Vasishta. In *BrdP* I,ii,32,96-7 Manu is included after Kratu to make a total of ten sages. However, given the relative frequency of seven as the number of the sages in the Purānas, the *Mahābhārata*, in Sumerian literature, as well as in Indian astronomy, we may assume that this was the original number, which was later amplified by the addition of such figures as Manu himself as a sage.

The seven sages that accompany the Manu of the present seventh manvantara, Manu Vaivasvata, are, in *BrdP* I,ii,38,26-33, called Vishvāmitra [who was originally a Kshatriya and not a Brāhman], Jamadagni [who is a descendant of Bhrgu], Bharadvāja [who is a descendant of Angiras], Saradvan, Atri, Vasuman, and Vatsara.[109]

The seven sages are found also in the Sumerian accounts of the flood. In the tablet W 20030,[110] we find that each of the antediluvian kings (or, rather, gods) is accompanied by an extraordinary being called "apkallu" and, since this tablet lists only seven such kings, there are seven "apkallu" in all.[111] The apkallu are the sages who arise from the Abyss to reveal science, art, and civilisation to mankind. The names of these apkallu are u-an, u-an-du-ga, en-me-du-ga, en-me-galam-ma, en-me-bulug-ga, an-en-lil-da and u-tu-abzu,[112] and their respective appearances are in the reigns of "a-a-lu", "a-la-al-gar lugal", "am-me-gal-an-na lugal", "e[n-m]e-usumgal-an-na lugal", "dumu-zi sipa lugal", and "en-me-dur-an-ki lugal".[113] From

---

[109] In the *Baudhāyana Shrauta Sūtra*, there are eight such sages, and they are Vishvāmitra, Jamadagni, Bharadvaja, Gautama, Atri, Vasishta, Kashyapa and Agastya. Agastya is obviously a later addition as the sage who transmitted Vedic learning to the "Tamils", i.e. proto-Tamils/Sumerians.

[110] See J. van Dijk, "Die Inschriftenfunde: II. Die Tontafeln aus dem res-Heiligtum" in *XVIII. vorläufiger Bericht über die von dem Deutschen Archaeologischen Institut und der Deutschen Orient-Gesellschaft aus Mitteln der Deutschen Forschungsgemeinschaft unternommenen Ausgrabungen in Uruk-Warka (1959/1960)*, Berlin: Heinrich J. Lenzen, 1962, pp.44ff.

[111] These apkallu are complemented in the postdiluvian section of this list by the "ummannu", or the scholars who aided the several postdiluvian kings in their respective reigns.

[112] See J. van Dijk, *op.cit.*, p.44.

[113] *Ibid*. In WB 1923, 444, the names are "a-lu-lim" and "a-lal-gar" reigning in Eridu, "en-me-en-lu-an-na", "en-me-en-gal-an-na" and "dumu-zi sipa" in Bad-tibira, "sipa-zi-an-na" in Larak, and "en-me-en-

WB 1923,444 and W 20030,7, it is apparent that these kings ruled in Eridu, Bad-tibira, Larak, and Zimbir respectively, which establishes that the "apkallu" appeared during the development of the solar force in the underworld. The first of these apkallu, U-An (identifiable with Adapa),[114] is characterised in Berossus' list by a piscine form which may correspond to the Matsya incarnation of the supreme Lord, though the piscine Matsya incarnation of the supreme Lord in the Indian Purāṇas appears later, during the flood, with the seventh Manu, of the Treta Yuga.

In Egypt too it is most probable that there was a tradition of seven sages who preceded the establishment of monarchy after the "deluge". The Palermo Stone, for instance, contains the names of nine kings of Lower Egypt, while the Cairo fragment which may have formed part of the former contains a list of "kings" who clearly precede the kings of the Palermo dynastic list.[115] Of these kings seven bear the double crown of Upper and Lower Egypt.[116] Since these "kings" precede Menes (who represents Manu himself), we may reasonably conclude that these "kings" are indeed the same as the seven sages who ruled heaven and earth, which are represented in this list as Upper and Lower Egypt.

---

dur-an-na" in Zimbir. In W 20030,7 the names are given as "a-a-lu", "a-la-al-gar", "am-me-lu-an-na", "am-me-gal-an-na", "enme-usumgal-an-na", "dumu-zi sipa" and "en-me-dur-an-ki" respectively (*ibid.*, p.46).

[114] *Ibid.*, p.48.

[115] Breasted thought that the Cairo fragments must also have originally contained a set of kings of Upper Egypt who followed those of Lower Egypt (see S. Mercer, *Horus Royal God of Egypt*, Grafton, MA: Society of Oriental Research, 1942).

[116] See S. Mercer, *op.cit*, p.16. The set of seven "kings" of a united Upper and Lower Egypt is followed by the kings of Lower Egypt (in the Palermo Stone).

In the Avesta, the Amesha Spentas, the "well-doing ones", correspond to the Seven Sages, though they are deprived of their mythological form and considered as abstract mental qualities. In the *Bundahishn* I,53, after the creation of the primal astral bodies, the Mazdean creation is said to continue with the production of the Ameshaspends, the "seven fundamental Beneficent Immortals":

> of the material creations created in the spirit the first are six, He Himself as the seventh; for both spirit first and then matter are of Ohrmazd. He created forth Vohuman... then Ardwahisht, then Sahrewar, then Spendarmad, then Hordad and Amurdad [the seventh in the order of immortal beings is Ohrmazd himself].

These are derived directly from the Wind, the Lord of Duration. We may remember the wind god Vāyu in the Vedic literature who emerges from the nostrils of the macroanthropos in the form of a boar. The Amesha Spentas also correspond psychologically to the faculties of the Ideal Man, Purusha, namely intelligence, intellect, feeling, thinking, knowing and explication, along with the soul, represented by Ahura Mazda himself (*Bundahishn*, XXVIII).

In the Hebrew Bible the ante-diluvian patriarchs before Noah are the counterparts of the Seven Sages and the Sumerian apkallu and Egyptian antediluvian kings.[117] In Genesis 5, there is a reference to the descendants of Adam, starting with Seth, and continuing with Enos, Ca-i'nan, Mahal'aleel, Jared, Enoch, Methu'selah, Lamech and Noah. Since the brāhmans are, in the the Ethiopian version of

---

[117] See H. Zimmern, "Biblische und babylonische Urgeschichte", *Der Alte Orient*, II (1901), pp.26ff.

Pseudo-Callisthenes,[118] said to be the sons of Adam's son, Seth,[119] and Noah was considered a transmitter of the wisdom of Seth,[120] we may assume that the personages from Enos to Lamech are the Hebrew counterparts of the seven sages.

Since Adam is indeed the Cosmic Man and not a human, we may assume that the brāhmans referred to here are associated with the preservation of the Divine Consciousness of Brahman which arises from the Cosmic Egg and is later conveyed to humanity by the seventh Manu/Noah. As for Seth, Josephus declares that Seth

> strove after virtue and, being himself excellent, left descendants who imitated the same virtues. All of these, being virtuous, lived in happiness in the same land without civil strife, with nothing unpleasant coming upon them until after their death. And they discovered the science with regard to the heavenly bodies and their orderly arrangement.[121]

The brāhmans are also considered in the Indian tradition to be descended from the seven sages, though, in Indian astronomy, the "seven sages" are typically represented by the Pleiades. So Seth himself may be the same as the Egyptian deity Seth (Ganesha), who is the son of Horus the Elder/Brahman. Manu/Noah, however, is the first man rather than an antediluvian sage or patriarch.

---

[118] This work incorporates information culled from the anonymous *History of the Blessed Men who Lived in the Days of Jeremiah the Prophet*.

[119] See E.A.W. Budge, *The Alexander Book in Ethiopia*, London: OUP, 1933, pp.74ff.

[120] See A. Annus, *Standard Babylonian Epic of Anzu*, Helsinki: The Neo-Assyrian Text Corpus Project, 2001, p.xxix.

[121] See Josephus, *Jewish Antiquities*, I:70-1.

***

In the Vedic *Shatapatha Brāhmana*. Manu, the son of Vivasvant (*SB* I,viii,1),[122] is described as offering a sacrifice after the flood, and from this sacrifice arises, first, a "daughter" Idā [a variant of Ilā],[123] from whom is derived the human race. In the *SP*, Idā is called the "potency of Shankara [Shiva]",[124] that is, a reincarnation of his consort Pārvathi herself, and is identified with Narmada "who destroys sin and delivers (mankind) from transmigration". Narmada is, as we have seen, the power of the Flood itself which has borne aloft the incipient sun and the life of the newly formed universe.[125] Since Idā is the "potency" of Shiva, we have here a reminder that Manu must be a form of Shiva himself.

Manu's daughter Idā represents an original lunar dynasty while her brother Ikshvāku begins the solar dynasty.[126] These two primal dynasties of the Indian king-lists may be representative of the Elamite and the Kish/Akshak cultures of Mesopotamia, which began the great civilisations that marked the beginning of our Kali Yuga,

---

[122] In *KYV* VI,5,6, Vivasvant is called an Āditya (sun) whose offspring are men and the one born after the first four Ādityas. In the *SB* III,1,3,3 Vivasvant is identified with Mārtānda, the eighth Āditya, who is at first unformed but later moulded into a man who generates the creatures of Earth.

[123] Ilā and Idā are interchangeable in the *BP* (Ilā: IX,16,22) and other Purānas (Idā: *BrdP*III,60,11, *VP* 85,7) In *SP* (Vaishnava Khanda), it is a name of Narmada, the mighty river (and consort) of Shiva (see S. Shastri, *op.cit*, p.72).

[124] See S. Shastri, *op.cit.*, p.72.

[125] See above; cf. S. Shastri, *op.cit.*, p.81.

[126] It may be noted, in passing, that the Edda ('The Deluding of Gylfi') too records the first human beings as a girl called Embla and a boy called Ask.

which is dated traditionally around 3100 B.C.[127] The Sumerian, as well as the Egyptian, culture is attributed in Genesis 10:6 to the Hamitic branch of the Noachidian family, as Cush and Mizraim respectively. Ikshvāku has four sons, Nimi, Nābānadishtha, Sharyāti, and Nabhāga, who constitute solar dynasties.[128] The son of Ilā is called Purūravas and it is he who is supposed to have learned the secrets of fire-worship from the Gandharvas, or Gandhāras.[129]

If we consider Josephus' description of the lands associated with Noah, who is said to have preserved the wisdom of Seth, we find that the land of Seth is said to be located around "Seiris". In the Christian *Opus Imperfectum in Matthaeum* of Pseudo-Chrysostom, the books of Seth were supposed to have been hidden by Noah in the land of Šir, and the so-called "cave of treasures" in which they were hidden is identifiable with Mt. Ararat.[130] In Genesis 14:6, the Horites, or Hurrians, are particularly identified with Mt. Seir. But, since Manu is the same as Noah, who is the last of 'the sons of Seth' and, according to *BP* VIII,24, Manu is King of Drāvida, the brāhmans who are considered to be the "sons of Seth" may have originally constituted the priesthood of an original proto-Hurrian/proto-Dravidian population.[131] F.E. Pargiter maintained

[127] This is the calculation of the 5th c. astronomical treatise, *Sūrya Siddhānta*.

[128] See F.E. Pargiter, *op.cit.*, p.84f.

[129] See above p.16.

[130] See G.G. Stroumsa, *Another Seed: Studies in Gnostic Mythology*, Leiden:E.J. Brill, 1984, p.117.

[131] The term "Hurrian" (derived from Suwalliyat/Suwariyat/Sūrya; see above) however may not be equated with "Āryan" since both Iranian and Indian have distinct terms for the sun (sūrya, hvare) and for the community of Āryans (ārya, eira), respectively. Hurrian certainly includes a strong Dravidic element in it (see G.W. Brown, "The possibility of a connection", pp.273-305).

that Brāhmanism itself was not originally Āryan but adopted into Indo-Āryan religion from Dravidian.[132] However, Pargiter did not consider the possibility that both Āryan and later Dravidian may have been derived from a proto-Dravidian/Hurrian spiritual culture.

One of the earliest regions to be settled by the Noachidian peoples from neighbouring Armenia must have been Anatolia.[133] This is suggested by the great antiquity of the Neolithic archaeological finds at Çatal Hüyük in (ca. 7th millennium B.C.). The civilisation of Syro-Palestine may be even as old as that of Anatolia since settlements in Jordan are traceable from the late 7th millennium B.C. and in Byblos from the 6th.[134]

As regards the identity of the Noachidian family, which may be considered proto-Dravidian/Hurrian, we may remember Lahovary's pioneering research into the Mediterranean people, which he equated with the Dravidian, as being the original inhabitants of the ancient Near East 'in its largest meaning, that is including

> Anatolia, Syria, Palestine, Caucasia, Persia, Mesopotamia with its extensions towards India, as well as Arabia and the African regions facing Arabia,

---

[132] See F.E. Pargiter, *op.cit.*, Ch.26.

[133] Though the urban Neolithic achievements at Çatal Hüyük seem to be older than those in Armenia, there is evidence of similar development at the border of ancient Armenia in Jarmo (see D. Lang, *Armenia: Cradle of Civilization*, London: George Allen and Unwin, 1980., p.61).

[134] See G.W. Ahlstrom, *The History of Ancient Palestine*, Minneapolis, MN: Fortress Press, 1993; J. Cauvin, *Religions néolithiques de Syro-Palestine*, Paris: J. Maisonneuve, 1972; S.A. Cook, *The Religion of ancient Palestine in the Light of Archaeology*, London: Oxford University Press, 1930; for Jericho, see K.M. Kenyon, *Digging up Jericho*, London: E. Benn, 1957.

i.e. from the Nile valley to the high tablelands of East Africa.[135]

Lahovary goes on to remark that

It was from this world of Anterior Asia, where the foundations of civilization had been already laid, that the bearers of the neolithic and chalcolithic civilizations of the Near East spread, by successive migrations, in general of relatively small groups over a period of more than three thousand years, first towards North-East Africa, and later, during the fourth, third and second millennium, towards Europe.

The proto-Dravidians are most probably identifiable with the proto-Hurrians. The geographical region in which the earliest Hurrians are found corresponds to the earliest Anatolian-Halafian settlements associated with the Subarians/Suwarians/Hurrians from the seventh millennium B.C. These earliest Hurrians spoke a language that possessed Dravidian characteristics and F. Bork[136] and G.W. Brown[137] have revealed the intimate linguistic relationship between Hurrian (along with its Mitanni dialect),[138] Elamite, and Dravidian. Thus Elamite, which is today generally considered a Dravidian

---

[135] See N. Lahovary, tr. K.A. Nilakantan, *Dravidian Origins and the West: Newly Discovered Ties with the Ancient Culture and Languages, including Basque, of the pre-Indo-European Mediterranean world*, Bombay: Orient Longmans, 1963, p.2.

[136] See F. Bork, "Die Mitanni Sprache", *MVAG*, I and II, 1909.

[137] See G.W. Brown, "The Possibility of a Connection between Mitanni and the Dravidian languages", *JAOS*, 50 (1930), pp.273-305.

[138] For the dialectal relationship between the language of Tushratta's letter to Amenophis III and Hurrian, see Knudtzon, *Die el-Amarna Tafeln*, 2 vols., Leipzig: Hinrichs, 1915, no.24; cf. S. Smith, *Early History of Assyria*, London: Chatto and Windus, 1928, p.71.

language,[139] is also related to the Hurrian. However, Elamite and Dravidian are possibly later dialects than the northern Hurrian, since they lack the initial 's' of Hurrian personal pronominal forms.[140] The Dravidian of the Brahui-speakers in northwestern India itself retains archaic elements resembling Hurrian which are lost in the southern Dravidian languages.[141] This confirms the route taken by the Dravidians from northern Syria and Elam to South India.

Although the Hurrians are attested in historical records only from the Old Akkadian period and more particularly in the following Ur III period,[142] the fact that the Hurrians, as Wilhelm has shown,[143] are in all probability identical to the Subarians may advance their presence in Mesopotamia

---

[139] See D. McAlpin, "Linguistic Prehistory: The Dravidian Situation", in M.M. Deshpande and P.E. Hook (ed.) *Aryan and Non-Aryan in India*, Ann Arbor, MI: Center for South and Souteast Asian Studies, The University of Michigan, 1979, pp.175-190.

[140] See G.W. Brown, *op.cit.*, p.290f. For further discussions of the connection between Dravidian and Āryan, see F.C. Southworth, in *Aryan and Non-Aryan in India*, 191-234; cf. also J. Harmatta, "Proto-Iranians and Proto-Indians in Central Asia in the 2nd Millennium B.C. (Linguistic Evidence)", F.R. Allchin, "Archaeological and Language-historical Evidence for the Movement of Indo-Aryan speaking Peoples into South Asia", in *Ethnic Problems of the History of Central Asia in the EarlyPeriod (second millennium B.C.)*, Moscow, 1981, and A. Parpola, "On the Protohistory of the Indian Languages in the Light of archaeological Evidence: An Attempt at Integration", in *South Asian Archaeology*, Leiden, 1974, pp.90-100.

[141] See G.W. Brown, *op.cit.*, p.297.

[142] The calcite tablet of Tisadal, king of Urkis, composed entirely in Hurrian dates from this period (see E.A. Speiser, "The Hurrian participation in the civilizations of Mesopotamia, Syria and Palestine", *Cahiers d'Histoire Mondiale*, I,2 (1953), p.313).

[143] See G. Wilhelm, *The Hurrians*, tr. J. Barnes, Warminster: Aris and Phillips Ltd., 1989, p.1.

to a much earlier date.[144] Subartu itself may have referred later to the north-eastern lands bordering on the Tigris, and particularly Assyria,[145] but it is likely that the Elamites too formed a southern branch of the same people.[146] The gentilic "subari" is, according to Speiser, in its original form, "suwari", which suggests that it may be derived from the name of the sun-god "suvalliyat/suvariya" (Skt. sūrya/Av. hvare). It is also related to the later ethnic term "hurri", which would be the Iranian pronunciation of the same name, as the Iranian name of the sun-god, "Hvare", suggests. And the entire Hurrian ethnos may have been characterised by sun-worship.

The Hurrians, who are found widespread throughout the ancient Near East, are closely associated in the seventeenth century B.C. with the Indo-Āryan Mitanni[147] (who spoke a Hurrian dialect as well as a sacred Sanskritic

---

[144] In the Hebrew Bible, the Hurrians are referred to variously as Horites, Hivites or Jebusites (see *Interpreter's Bible*, p.665) and are not listed separately in the 'Table of Nations'.

[145] See S. Smith, *Early History of Assyria*, London: Chatto and Windus, 1928, p.70.

[146] See G.Wilhelm, *ibid.*; cf. A. Ungnad, *Subartu: Beiträge zur Kulturgeschichte und Völkerkunde Vorderasiens*, Berlin: Walter de Gruyter, 1936, p.113f.

[147] The Mitanni themselves may be identifiable with the Medes, for, as Herodotus (VII,69) reveals, the Medes were once universally called Arians, as well as perhaps with the proto-Iranians, since several Median words are traceable in Old Persian (see P.O. Skjaervo, in G.Erdosy, (ed.) *The Indo-Aryans of Ancient South Asia*, Berlin: Walter de Gruyter, 1995, p.159). That the name "Mede" may be related to the term Mitanni was suggested by J. Charpentier, "The Date of Zoroaster", *BSOS* 3 (1923-25), 747-55; B. Landsberger and T. Bauer, "Zu neueroeffentlichen Geschichtsquellen", *ZA* 37 (1927), 61-98; E. Forrer, "Stratification des lanuges et des peoples dans le Proche-Orient préhistorique", *JA* 217 (1930), pp.227-52; and F. Cornelius, "Erin-Manda", *Iraq* 25 (1963), pp.167-70.

language) as well as with the Hittites.[148] The Mitanni themselves may be identifiable with the Medes, who, as Herodotus (VII,69) reveals, were once universally called Arians,[149] as well as perhaps with the proto-Iranians, since several Median words are traceable in Old Persian.[150] However, the Mitanni represent an Indo-Āryan religious tradition rather than an Avestan or Zoroastrian since the list of Indic gods in the treaty of the Mitanni-Hurrian king Šattiwaza and the Hittite king Šuppililiumas I dating from the sixteenth century B.C.[151] includes the names Mitra-Varuna, Indra, and Nāsatyas – and Indra and Naonhaithya were considered to be demons by the Zoroastrians.

***

Epilogue

In the Indic cosmogonical accounts, our manvantara, that of Manu, of the Sun, will be followed by seven other manvantaras ruled by other Manus, called Savarni, Dakshasavarni, Brahmasavarni, Dharmasavarni, Rudrasavarni, Devasavarni, and Indrasavarni respectively

---

[148] Although the so-called Hittites were Āryans, the Hittite kingdom also gives evidence of a strong neo-Hurrian cultural influence from the fifteenth century B.C. and many of the Hittite queens bear Hurrian names, just as in the case of the Mitanni. The Āryan language of the Hittites and Mitannis may have been limited to the male members of an Āryan aristocracy.

[149] That the name "Mede" may be related to the term Mitanni was suggested by J. Charpentier, "The Date of Zoroaster"; B. Landsberger and T. Bauer, "Zu neueröffentlichen Geschichtsquellen"; E. Forrer, "Stratification des langues"; and F. Cornelius, "Erin-Manda".

[150] See P.O. Skjaervo, in G.Erdosy, *op.cit.*, p.159.

[151] See D. Yoshida, *Untersuchungen zu den Sonnengottheiten bei den Hethitern*, Heidelberg: Universitätsverlag C. Winter, 1996, p.12; cf. V. Haas, *Geschichte der hethitischen Religion*, Leiden: E.J. Brill, 1994., p.543.

(*BP* VIII,13). At the end of our kalpa there will be another Naimittika Pralaya.

In the Egyptian *Book of the Dead*, Ch.175, too, Atum declares:

> in the end I will destroy everything that I have created,
> the earth will become again part of the Primeval Ocean,
> like the Abyss of waters in their original state.
> Then I will be what will remain, just I and Osiris,
> when I will have changed myself back into the Old Serpent
> who knew no man and saw no god.[152]

The deluge that Atum threatens to overwhelm the universe with will mark the dissolution of the material universe into its original state in the Abyss Nun and the flood Hehu.[153]

However, the seeds of the universe are contained in the phallic Tree of Life and will renew themselves after every cosmic cataclysm. Thus the 'fig tree' which symbolizes the entire emergent universe at the centre of the cosmic streams is described in the *Skanda Purāna* as being unshaken by the "doomsday hurricane".[154] In the Nordic *Edda*, too, the cosmos will be renewed after Ragnarök:

> Now do I see the earth anew
> Rise all green from the waves again[155]

---

[152] See R.T. Rundle Clark, *Myth and Symbol in Ancient Egypt*, London: Thames and Hudson, 1959, p.140f.

[153] See K. Sethe, *Amun und die acht Urgötter von Hermopolis* (*Abhandlungen der preussischen Akademie der Wissenschaften*, 1929, Nr.4), p.64.

[154] See S. Shastri, *op.cit.*, p.65.

[155] "Voluspa"; cf. *The Prose Edda*, Ch.XVII. Also, R. Cook, *The Tree of*

***

At the end of the lifetime of Brahma, however, there will be a different sort of flood called a Prākrita Pralaya (*BP* XII;4,5-6) which will dissolve not just the gross form of the universe but even the subtle elements of Nature (Prakriti).

***

For the total extinction of the cosmos the destruction of the final crucial knot of Egoity (Ahamkāra) that prevents individual consciousness from realising its identity with the Divine perfect Yogic enlightenment is required. Such a liberation of the individual as well as of the cosmos would then result in what may be called an 'Ātyantika Pralaya' (*BP* XII,34) – or a dissolution without end.

Life: Symbol of the Centre, London: Thames and Hudson, 1974, p.12.

III. SĀMKHYA-YOGA, SHRAMANA, BRĀHMANA, TANTRA
The Religious Traditions of The Ancient Indians

I hail the superhuman;
I call it death-in-life and life-in-death.

- W.B. Yeats, 'Byzantium'

THE QUESTIONS REGARDING the original enlightenment of mankind, the race that was first endowed with a spiritual vision of the universe, and the beginnings of Yogic wisdom are all obscured by the mists of antiquity. If we attempt to discern the spiritual sources of the early Indo-Europeans, of the first Yogis, the Āryan fire-worshippers and the later Hamitic temple worhippers, we are forced to rely on—apart from the fragmentary archaeological and the relatively late Greek literary evidence—the mythological literature of the ancient Indians for some clues that may allow a reconstruction of the development of religious thought among the various branches of the early Indo-Europeans.

I. Sāmkhya-Yoga and Shramana

28th Chaturyuga, Treta Yuga

The extraordinary cosmological and philosophical insights that inform the religions of the ancient world could have been achieved only through divine revelation or through the exercise of such techniques of mind- and body control as developed by the various systems of Yoga. The probability that Yoga was the source of this wisdom seems to be confirmed by the *Brahmānda Purāna* (I,i,3,8), for instance, and we note that, in the *Mahābhārata*, XIII (Anushāsana Parva) 14,[156] Shiva himself is constantly addressed as the "soul of yoga" and the object of all yogic meditation. Similarly, his son, Skanda (the god Muruga of the Dravidians) is described as being endowed with yogic powers in *Mbh* IX (Shalya Parva), 44. We may recall also the extraordinary description of the different forms of primal Light that is to be found in the yoga-based *Mandalabrāhmana Upanishad*, II,[157] where the state of enlightenment itself is described in terms of an identification with the supreme Light:

> When the triputi[158] are thus dispelled, he becomes the kaivalya jyotis[159] without bhāva (existence) or abhāva (nonexistence), full and motionless, like the ocean without the tides or like the lamp without the wind.

---

[156] Cf. *MBh* VII (Drona Parva), 202, where Shiva is identified with Yoga.

[157] The most substantial information regarding the original Yogic system is perhaps that to be gleaned from the yoga-based Upanishads derived largely from the Krishna and Shukla Yajur Vedas (see K. N. Aiyar, *Thirty Minor Upanishads,* Madras: Vasanta Press, 1914).

[158] Modifications of the mind.

[159] The light of isolation [from the phenomenal world].

The aim of all enlightenment, whether it be through the fire-worship of the Āryans or the forms of worship evident in Tantra, is indeed the ultimate identification of the individual soul, ātman, with Brahman. The term "yoga" itself means "yoking" and may signify the union of the individual soul to the supreme which is brought about through several strict physiological and mental austerities.[160]

In all of these ancient religions, the understanding of the relation between the macrocosm and the microcosm also seems to be derived from a Yogic source. For instance, the Tantric Yogic notion of the Kundalini serpent and the awakening of this serpentine form to the light of Brahman lies at the basis of the Egyptian drama of Osiris in the underworld, as well as of the concept of the universal tree of life which features in the cosmologies of all the ancient Indo-European cultures.

All of the ancient Indo-European religions are, furthermore, based on a vision of the Godhead as a Supreme Soul (Ātman) that manifests itself first as an Ideal and then as a Cosmic Man, or Purusha. This Purusha is castrated by his son (Chronos/Shiva/Time), though his seminal force is restored in our universe as the sun by a son of Chronos (Zeus/Dionysus/Muruga).[161] While this Purusha cosmology informs all the early religious forms of the Indo-Europeans, we will see that Brāhmanism and the

---

[160] For the contrasting understanding of Yoga in Jainism see p.82.

[161] For a full discussion of this cosmology, based on the literary evidence of the Purānas, the Vedas, the Brāhmanas, the Avesta, the Bundahishn, the records of the religions of Egypt, Sumer, Akkad, Assyria and the Hurrians, as well as the earliest western Āryan theogonies of the Hittites, the proto-Stoic and Orphic Greeks, and the ancient Germans, see A. Jacob, *Ātman: A Reconstruction of the Solar Cosmology of the Indo-Europeans*, Hildesheim: G. Olms, 2005; cf. A. Jacob, *Brahman: A Study of the Solar Rituals of the Indo-Europeans*, Hildesheim: G. Olms, 2012, Chs.I-III.

later Tantra employ this mythology in their various rituals mostly in order to revive both the macrocosm and the microcosm spiritually. Sāmkhya-Yoga and the Shramana traditions following it, on the other hand, use it mostly as a theoretical background for ethical systems that seek to escape from cosmic manifestation and earthly incarnation altogether. In this focus on the escape from the cycle of birth, death, and rebirth they take special care to stress the importance of the precept of non-violence, which sets them in direct opposition to the sacrificial rituals of the Brāhmans.

As regards the original form of the ancient Indo-European wisdom, we note that among the Krita Yuga avatārs of Vishnu listed in the *Bhāgavata Purāna* I,3,162 Kapila (the name of the historical founder of Sāmkhya Yoga) precedes Yajna (representing Vedic sacrifice), who in turn precedes Rishabha (the name of the historic founder of Jainism). The avatārs of the Krita Yuga are of course cosmic phenomena rather than earthly, but the sequence of these names suggests that Sāmkhya-Yoga may indeed have preceded Vedic Brāhmanism, which in turn preceded Jainism. At any rate, regardless of the greater or lesser antiquity of these various traditions, when we compare the complexity of the rituals in Brāhmanism and Tantra that seek to revive the Purusha—through fire—altars, temple structures, idols and the adept's body itself – with the stark precepts of saintly conduct and asceticism

---

[162] According to *BP* I,3, there are twenty-two avatārs of Vishnu, beginning with

[Krita Yuga] Chatursana (the four sons of Brahma), the boar Varāha, Nārada, Nara-Nārāyana, Kapila, Dattatreya, Yajna, Rishabha,

[Treta Yuga] the fish Matsya, the tortoise Kūrma, Dhanvantari, Mohini, Narasimha, Vāmana, Parashurāma, Vyāsa, Rāma,

[Dvāpara Yuga] Balarāma, Krishna,

[Kali Yuga] the Buddha, Kalki.

in the Shramana traditions we may be forced to conclude that the former have indeed retained more of the original Yogic, as well as of the original Vedic, spiritual knowledge than the latter.

Sāmkhya

The theoretical basis of Yoga is Sāmkhya, which is a dualistic school of thought which distinguishes Purusha as the spiritual principle from Prakriti, or matter. Liberation (kaivalya) from matter consists of the disentanglement of the spiritual principle from the material matrix into which it has sunk. One of the most principal metaphysical doctrines propounded by this school is that of the three degrees (guna's) of spiritual refinement—or the lack of it— that characterise any manifest being: sattva (luminosity), rajas (vigorousness), and tamas (lethargy).

Sāmkhya is generally attributed to the sage Kapila. Although, as mentioned, there is an avatār of Vishnu called Kapila who appeared already in the first of the four ages, the Krita Yuga (*BP* I,3,10), in *BP* III Kapila is described as the son of Kardama and his wife Devahūti. According to *Rāmāyana*, Uttarakanda,100, Kardama was the same as Manu and king of Bāhlika (Bactria).[163] The son of Kardama is said to be Ila, the founder of the Lunar Aila dynasty.[164] The association with Bactria makes it plausible that the historic Kapila lived in the Treta Yuga beginning with Manu Vaivasvata. It was he who expounded the system of Yoga to his mother:

---

[163] Cf. S.B. Chaudhuri, *Ethnic Settlements in Ancient India: A Study on the Puranic Lists of the Peoples of Bharatvarsha*, Calcutta: General Printers and Publishers, 1955, p.110.

[164] See p.92.

The discipline of yoga of relating to the soul for the sake of complete detachment from whatever pleasure and distress, is the ultimate benefit for mankind that carries My approval.[165]

In the *Baudhāyana Sūtra* he is considered to be the son of the Vaishnava saint and Daitya[166] prince, Prahlāda. He is said to be the sage who created the four orders, or āshramas,[167] of brahmachārya, grihastya, vānaprastha and sannyāsa in such a way that he extolled the last ascetic āshrama as superior to the early ones committed to sacrificial worship. He is also credited with the propagation of the doctrine of non-violence, which, as we will see below, is the first of the five abstentions (yama's) that the Yogic system begins with. Sāmkhya is clearly the source of the Shramana sects of Jainism and Buddhism, which are both critical of the Brāhmanical sacrificial rituals and exhort asceticism as the way of liberation from the net of samsāra, or the world.

The association of Kapila with Bactria[168] is particularly interesting since there happens to be clear evidence of Indic settlement in the Bactro-Margiana Archaeological Complex (BMAC) from 2200-1700 B.C., that is, a little later than the rise of the Hamitic cultures of Egypt and Mesopotamia at the beginning of the Kali Yuga. The BMAC is not far north of Mundigak, where from 3000 B.C. we notice extensions of Elamite culture resembling

---

[165] *Srimad Bhāgavatam* (tr. Aanand Aadhar), III,25,13.

[166] That is, an Asura, or lesser god, born of Diti, the earth goddess, who is the sister of Aditi, the mother of Indra and the solar Ādityas.

[167] That the āshrama system is not originally Brāhmanical is probable, since Brāhmanism, as we shall see, focuses mostly on the first two stages and not on the latter two, which are more central to the Shramana doctrines.

[168] Bactria spreads across modern Afghanistan, Uzbekistan and Tajikistan.

that of the Indus Valley.[169] It is difficult to determine whether the Āryan settlements of BMAC represent a continuation of the early Elamite Hurrians of Mundigak or are new immigrants from the Andronovo culture associated with the Indo-Āryans (1800-900 B.C.).[170] The latter is indeed the more probable. The Andronovo culture is itself derived from the Hut Grave and Catacomb Grave culture of 2800-2000 B.C.[171] and the Sintashta culture of the southeast Urals (2300-1900 B.C.),[172] which is marked by chariot burials and may have been proto-Āryan rather than proto-Indo-Āryan. There is also clear evidence of fire-worship in the BMAC, which suggests that it was the site of Brāhmanical Āryans as well. Since there is little evidence of such fire-worship in Mundigak it is probable that the former is derived from the Andronovo rather than from the Elamite colonies – and may have included adherents of the Sāmkhya-Yoga system as well as of Brāhmanism.

Yoga

Yoga in its late, classical form (Rāja Yoga) as formulated by Patanjali (2nd c. B.C.) employs an eight-fold path that begins with five "abstentions" (yama's): non-violence,

---

[169] Cf. J.P. Mallory and V. H. Mair, *The Tarim Mummies*, p.45f.; p.262.

[170] Andronovo type pottery has been found in the early layers of Margiana (see A. Parpola, "The problem of the Aryans and the Soma", in G. Erdosy (ed.), *The Indo-Aryans of Ancient South Asia*, Berlin: Walter de Gruyter, 1995, p.363.

[171] The Hut Grave culture apparently separated into the Timber Grave (proto-Iranian) and Andronovo (proto-Āryan) cultures. The fourth millennium predecessor of the Hut Grave and Catacomb Grave cultures may have been the Yamnaya culture dating from 3500-2800 B.C. (*ibid.*, p.356).

[172] See J.P. Mallory and V.H. Mair, *op. cit.*, pp.260f.

truthfulness, avoidance of theft, celibacy, and avoidance of covetousness. These abstentions are, as we shall see, adopted in Jainism too. The next step consists of five "observances" (niyama's) which include purity of mind, speech, and body, contentment, concentration, study and contemplation of God. These two initial stages are followed by the more practical ones related to the physical postures (āsana's) to be adopted for meditation, breath-control exercises (prānāyama), withdrawal of the senses from external objects (pratyāhāra), concentration (dharana), meditation (dhyāna) and liberation (samādhi).

Yoga seems to have become popular in India especially from around the 9th to the 5th century B.C. judging from the numerous Sanskrit and Prakrit texts of this period which stress the ideology of renunciation in which knowledge (jnāna) is given precedence over ritual action "and detachment from the material and social world is cultivated through ascetic practices (tapas), celibacy, poverty and methods of mental training (yoga)."[173] The doctrine of Jnāna Yoga[174] is enunciated also in the 'Bhagavad Gita', Ch.II:

> The man who, casting off all desires, lives free from attachments, who is free from egoism, and from (the feeling that this or that is) mine, obtains tranquillity. This, O son of Prithâ! is the Brahmic state; attaining to this, one is never deluded; and remaining in it in (one's) last moments, one attains (brahma-nirvâna) the Brahmic bliss.

It is repeated in the treatise on ashtanga (eight-limbed) yoga, *Yoga Sūtras*, by Patanjali, where the state of

---

[173] G. Flood, *An Introduction to Hinduism: The Secret Tradition of Hindu religion*, London: I.B. Tauris, 2006, p.81.

[174] See p.136.

yogic beatitude is understood as "the cessation of mental fluctuations". The final goal is the achievement of a "supreme state" devoid of "mental fluctuations". Consciousness is absorbed in itself, and the self does not becomes "identified with" the Absolute, but, rather, is the Absolute itself, since there is nothing apart from it. The yogi aims to attain the supreme state, as the *Katha Upanishad*, VI, also declares: "That state in which the five sense organs[175] ... remain united with the mind, and where the intuition or the brain remains idle or blank without any thought is the ineffable, supreme state of bliss".

The state of yogic enlightenment is the same as that of the Brahmaloka of the Purānas, since the soul is immobile in its absolute concentration. Once this concentration is relaxed, it is reborn just as the cosmos too is reborn from a disturbance of the perfect balance of the gunas in the first ideal manifestation of the supreme Ātman. The ultimate aim of Yoga thus is to prevent this relaxation in order to achieve a "final liberation from the bonds of action and rebirth".[176] Such a liberation is also described in the *Atharvaveda* X,44:

Desireless, firm, immortal, self-existent, contented with the essence, lacking nothing,

Free from fear of death is he who knoweth that Soul courageous, youthful, undecaying.

---

[175] The action organs are referred to as karma-indriya and the sense organs are referred to as gnāna-indriya.

[176] M. Biardeau, *Le sacrifice dans l'inde ancienne*, Paris: Presses universitaires de France, 1976, p.75.

Jainism

The two major religious traditions that sprang from Yoga-Sāmkhya were Jainism and Buddhism. Both Jainism and Buddhism, along with Chārvāka and Ājīvika, are considered by Brāhmanism as heterodox (nāstika) doctrines.

Nevertheless, Jainism dates its origins to an extremely hoary antiquity. The Jain equivalent of an "avatar", such as the ten incarnated forms of Vishnu, is a "tirthankara", of whom there are twenty-four in each half of a cosmic time cycle.[177] The Jain scriptures maintain that the first Jain Tirthankara, Rishabha, was the father of Bharata, the ruler of India, and that the Vedas originated relatively late, with the son of Bharata, Marichi. So Jainism may well have had its origin outside India. Further, the Vedic doctrines themselves, according to the Jains, were subsequently corrupted by the Brāhmans. According to Jinasena, the author of the 8th century Jain text, *Ādipurāna*, the origin of even the caste system is traced not to the Vedas (that is, the Purushasūkta), but to the Bharata legend, according to which Bharata tested men through a test of "ahimsa" (non-violence), and those who refused to harm any living beings were considered to be *dvija*, twice-born and *deva-Brāhmaṇas*, divine Brāhmans.[178]

Rishabha is supposed to have been born to a queen called Marudevi, the consort of King Nabhi, in Ayodhya, which is also the birthplace of the Ikshvāku avatār, Rāma,

---

[177] In the Brāhmanical tradition there are fourteen Manus in each kalpa (the present kalpa is called the Padma Kalpa, as the earlier one was the Brahma Kalpa), and the beginning of human life on earth is dated to the appearance of Manu Vaivasvata, who is the seventh Manu of our kalpa.

[178] See P. Jaini, *The Jaina Path of Purification*, N. Delhi: Motilal Banarsidass, 1998, p.290.

whose story, as we will see,[179] may well have had an extra-Indian origin. While the early tirthankaras of Jainism seem to be mythological figures, the twenty-third of its tirthankaras, Pārshvanātha, is indeed a historical figure dating back to the ninth century B.C., and the twenty-fourth and last, Mahāvīra, was born in the sixth century B.C. Pārshvanātha was considered to be a prince of the Ikshvāku dynasty[180] who lived in Benares in India while Mahavira was a prince who lived in Bihar. It seems therefore that Jainism, like Buddhism after it, was a religious doctrine developed among kshatriyas.

The canonical scriptures of the Jains are called—as in the Tantra tradition—Āgamas (inherited scriptures), and traced back by the Jains to the first tirthankara, Rishabha, though they were compiled by a certain Gautamaswami around the 6th or 4th century B.C. in Prākrit, rather than Sanskrit. These Āgamas are said to be based on the discourses of the first tirthankara of the present era, Rishabha.

As regards the identity of the first tirthankara, we may note that there is an avatār of Vishnu in the Krita Yuga called Rishaba (*Bhāgavata Purāna*).[181] It is interesting that Rishabha also bears several of Shiva's epithets such as Aghora, Ishana, Sadyojata, and Vāmadeva. Indeed, in the Shaivite *Linga Purāna,* he is considered to be an incarnation of Shiva. According to the *Vishnu Purāna* (II,1,31) the historical Rishabha was an Ikshvāku king and his eldest son is said to have been Bharata, who represents the land of India:

---

[179] See p.92.

[180] Ikshvāku is the son of Manu who begins the Solar dynasty (see p.57). It appears that the Ikshākus, whom we may first locate in West Asia, also moved at some time to India.

[181] See p.32n.

> Rishabha was born to Marudevi, Bharata was born to Rishabh,
>
> Bharatavarsha [India] arose from Bharata, and Sumati arose from Bharata.

In this context, it is interesting to note the evidence of swastika symbols in an ivory carving of a bird from Mezine in the Ukraine dating to ca.10,000 B.C. (that is, long before the rise of the Hamitic cultures of Egypt and Sumer) and the common use of swastikas in the Jain religion. The seventh tirthankara, Suparshvanātha, is indeed designated with the swastika as his 'vehicle'. The evidence of Indic settlement in Bactria, including Brāhmanical, has already been pointed to above, so that we may surmise that both the Shramana traditions and Brāhmanism may have extended from the Pontic Caspian region[182] to Bactria to India.

When we study the Greek writers' accounts of Indian religious sects, we find that both the Hellenistic chronicler, Megasthenes (ca.350-290 B.C.)'s records of India[183] and the geographical histories of Strabo (ca.64 B.C.-A.D.24)[184] distinguish two classes of philosophers in India, the Brāhmans and Sarmanes (Shramanas). Strabo (Geographica, *XV,I,60*) elaborates on the "Sarmanes" in the following manner:

> Of the Sarmanes, the most honourable ... are the Hylobii, who live in the forests, and subsist on leaves and wild fruits: they are clothed with garments made of the bark of trees, and abstain from commerce with

---

[182] This is the Ukrainian steppe, stretching from the northern shores of the Black Sea to the Caspian Sea.

[183] Frag. XLIII.

[184] *Geographica*, XV,1.

women and from wine ... Of the Sarmanes ... second in honour to the Hylobii, are the Physicians, for they apply philosophy to the study of the nature of man. They are of frugal habits, but do not live in the fields, and subsist upon rice and meal, which every one gives when asked, and receive them hospitably. ... Both this and the other class of persons practice fortitude, as well in supporting active toil as in enduring suffering, so that they will continue a whole day in the same posture, without motion.

We may detect in this description of the Shramanas something akin to the Yogic āsanas described in the later, 5th century treatise of Patanjali, the *Yogasūtras*. The Greek Christian convert, Clement of Alexandria (ca. A.D.150-215), even refers to two quite different geographical origins for the early religious sects associated with India. He differentiates the "Gymnosophists" from the Shramanas as belonging to India and Bactria respectively:

Philosophy, then, with all its blessed advantages to man, flourished long ages ago among the barbarians, diffusing its light among the gentiles and eventually penetrated into Greece. Its hierophants—were the prophets among the Egyptians, the Chaldeans among the Assyrians, the Druids among the Galatians [Celts], the Sramanas of the Bactrians, and the philosophers of the Celts, the Magi among the Persians—who announced beforehand the birth of the Saviour, being led by a star till they arrived in the land of Judaea, and among the Indians the Gymnosophists, and other philosophers of barbarous nations. (*Stromata*, 1.15.71)

Porphyry (ca.A.D.234-305) however derives both the Brāhmans and the Shramanas from the "Gymnosophists":

For the polity of the Indians being distributed into many parts, there is one tribe among them of men divinely wise, whom the Greeks are accustomed to call Gymnosophists. But of these there are two sects, over one of which the Bramins preside, but over the other the Samanaeans.[185]

This may explain the association of Bactria with both Brāhmanism and Jainism that we have noted above.

The term 'Jainism' itself is derived from 'jīna', or a human being who has mastered all passions. This bears a resemblance to the Āgamic classification of men in general—according to the predominance of the tāmasic, rājasic, or sāttvic elements in them—as pashu (animal), vira (heroic) or divya (divine).[186] The Jain doctrine of salvation (moksha) is based on the "three jewels" of right belief, right knowledge, and right conduct. These principal moral precepts provide the Jains with the "five vows" of abstinence, or mahāvratas - ahimsa (non-violence), satya (truthfulness), asteya (avoidance of stealth), aparigraha (non-acquisition) and brahmachārya (chastity). It is naturally opposed to the sacrificial rituals of the Brāhmans since these involved animal (and originally also human) sacrifices.[187]

Geoffrey Samuel in his recent work, *The Origins of Yoga and Tantra*, attempts to study two early periods in the development of Indic religions, the early Shramana movements in approximately the fifth to third century B.C. and the growth of Tantra in the seventh to twelfth centuries A.D. Samuel finds in the Vedas themselves "nothing...to imply yogic practice, in the sense of a

---

[185] Porphyry, *On abstinence from animal food*, (tr. T. Taylor) IV,17.
[186] See p.117. This classification roughly corresponds to the vaisya, kshatriya and brāhmanical castes among the Vedic Āryas.
[187] See A. Jacob, *Brahman*, Ch.IX.

developed set of techniques for operating with the mind-body complex".[188] He concludes:

> Our best evidence to date suggests that such practices developed in the same ascetic circles as the early sramana movements (Buddhists, Jainas and Ājīvikas), probably in around the sixth and fifth centuries BCE".[189]

In other words, the Brāhmanical tradition was not yogic as the Jain and Buddhist Shramana traditions were. Monika Shee too distinguishes Brāhmanical ascetiscism (tapas) from yoga:

> As tapas originally lacks any religious aims, it is not primarily connected with ideas of renunciation or salvation—ideas found, for example, in yoga or sanyåsa. Though tapas practices may be called yoga in the epic and a tapasvin is called a yogin sometimes, it is the magical, power-desiring concept of tapas which matters to the authors of these texts [190]

Yoga, on the other hand, focuses on the more ethical notions of karma (action and its moral result) and the cycle of birth, death, and rebirth, which it seeks to overcome through detachment and cessation of all spiritual activity. J. Bronkhurst points to the relative lack of references to the term yoga in the Dharmasūtras as well, though the focus on the realisation of the true nature of the Self is

---

[188] G. Samuel, *The Origins of Yoga and Tantra*, Cambridge University Press, 2008, p.8.

[189] *Ibid*,

[190] M. Shee, *Tapas und Tapasvin in den erzählenden Partien des Mahâbhârata*. Reinbek: Dr. Inge Wezler Verlag, p.405, tr. J. Bronkhurst, "The Brāhmanical Contribution to Yoga", *International Journal of Hindu Studies* 15, 3: 321.

clearly ascribed to the last of the four stages, āshramas, of a brāhman's life.

C.K. Chapple also highlights the yogic aspects of Jainism:

> The term yoga appears in three different usages within the broad tradition of Jainism. The first, and most general coinage of the term yoga, refers generically to the practice of meditation. The second refers to the collection of ascetic disciplines for which the Jaina tradition is famous, including the five great vows beginning with ahimsā. The third, and perhaps the most technical application of the word yoga, refers to the remnants of attachment or yoking that must be abandoned in the highest levels of spiritual ascent. The omniscient being at the thirteenth stage exhibits a connection with karma and hence retains a body; at the fourteenth and final spiritual stage (gunasthåna), all karma is abandoned, resulting in the state of ayoga, which is considered to be the highest state of Yoga in Jainism.[191]

The doctrine of karma too, Chapple points out, is more clearly articulated in the early Jain text, *Tattvārthasūtra* of Umāsvāti (ca.5th c. A.D.) than in the *Yogasūtra* of Patanjali (5th c. A.D.) itself:

> Umåsvåti drew from canonical sources to describe the process through which activity (yoga) draws karmas of various colors to adhere or bind to the soul (jiva). Karma appears in four harming forms and four nonharming forms. The ten chapters of the Tattvårthasutra describe the structure of the cosmos

---

[191] C.K. Chapple, "Recovering Jainism's Contribution to Yoga Traditions", *International Journal of Hindu Studies* 15,3:324.

including the nature and detailed manifestations of karma in 148 prakritis. The text also describes a fourteen-stage process of ascent leading to living liberation (sayoga kevala) and ultimately to total freedom (ayoga kevala), whereby one's soul separates eternally from all remnants of karma (specifically, lifespan, name, feeling, and family: åyus, nåma, vedanīya, and gotra).[192]

However, it must be noted that Jainism itself does not give much evidence of the rigorous discipline of the body and mind that classical Yoga does. Jain philosophers also strove to distance themselves from Tantrism, which experimented with various techniques to achieve union with the divinity. The *Yogadhristhisamucchaya* of Haribhadra Yākiniputra (8th c. A.D.), for example, lists four types of yoga practitioners (family, clan, engaged, and authentic – kula, gotravanta, pravrittracakra, and avañcaka) but makes sure to excoriate Tantra as a licentious cult.

Kali Yuga

A later manifestation of the Shramana tradition is Buddhism, which is based on the doctrines of the Buddha (ca. 6th century B.C.) – who, as we have seen, is an avatār of the Kali Yuga. Buddhism retains notions from the Brāhmanical tradition—which is older than it—such as the Brahmavihāras (the abodes of Brahma) that are invoked to direct righteous thought in the direction of goodwill, compassion, empathy, and equanimity. However, it, like Jainism before it, rejects Brāhmanical rituals, and scholars such as Eraly and Wiltshire believe that Buddhism

---
[192] C.K. Chapple, *ibid.*, 15, 3: 326.

arose from the ascetic Shramana movements of the first millennium B.C.,[193] especially that of the "paccekabuddhas" who are said to have achieved enlightenment independent of the Buddha[194] Wiltshire suggests that paccekabuddhas were kshatriyas who particularly renounced "household" life, which is a life-stage associated with several of the fire-rituals of Brāhmanism.[195]

Buddhism, like Jainism, is based essentially on a pessimistic view of the world (samsāra) where suffering is the characteristic of temporal life. Desire, action, and rebirth are to be overcome through the 'Eightfold Path' of Right Understanding, Right Intention, Right Speech, Right Action, Right Livelihood, Right Effort, Right Thoughtfulness, Right Concentration so that a state of "nirvāna" or liberation from the cycle of earthly lives may be achieved. Buddhism rejected total asceticism as well as hedonistic indulgence in its Middle Path. It advocated five vows of abstinence for its lay devotees, including abstention from killing, stealing, sexual licentiousness, lying and alcohol.

Mahāyāna Buddhism outlined the path of the Boddhisattvas, or those whose minds were "awakened". and on the path to Buddhahood. Hinayāna Buddhism, on the other hand, extolled the path of Arhats, who are considered to have attained a state of nirvāna, like the Buddha. The Mahāyāna Buddhists, however, consider the arhats as occupying an inferior status to that of the boddhisattvas. Buddhism in general rejected both the āstika Brāhmanical and the nāstika doctrines. It denied

---

[193] See A. Eraly, *The First Spring: The Golden Age of India*, N.Delhi: Penguin Books, 2011.

[194] See M. Wiltshire, *Ascetic Figures before and in Early Buddhism: The Emergence of Gautama as the Buddha*, Berlin: Mouton de Gruyter, 1990.

[195] See A. Jacob, *Brahman*, Ch.X.

the permanence of the soul (ātman) as a hindrance to moral conduct and liberation. Indeed, moral conduct, and not rituals, are the only means of liberation according to Buddhism. In the consideration of asceticism, it prefers self-discipline to self-mortification. It not only opposes the theistic and past-life determinism of Brāhmanism but also the quasi-biological determinism of Jainism and posits moral action as the sole determinant of individual destiny. It thus represents a moralistic middle path between the extreme anti-corporealism of Jainism and the immanentist and sublimational doctrines of Tantra and Tantric Buddhists

Indeed, Buddhism did incorporate various Tantric practices from the 7th century A.D. onwards especially in its Vajrayāna branch, which, unlike the Mahāyāna and Hīnayāna schools, emphasises the importance of ritual rather than mere meditation. Scholars such as A. Sanderson and S. Hatley have suggested that Tantric practices may have penetrated Buddhism already in the 5th century from Shaivaite sources.[196] The *Manjushri Mūlakalpa* text attributed to the Boddhisattva Manjushri of the Mahāyāna tradition, and dating from the 6th century A.D., is, for example, based on Shaiva as well as Vaishnava Tantric texts.

***

The Shramana tradition is thus generally an ascetic one. It focuses on the cycle of births and deaths and the liberation (moksha) from it that may be achieved through asceticism and non-violence. Asceticism was more severely practiced

---

[196] See, for instance, S. Hatley, "Converting the Dākini: Goddess Cults and Tantras of the Yoginis between Buddhism and Saivism" in *Tantric Traditions in Transmission and Translation*, (ed.) D.B. Gray and R.R. Overbey, N.Y., NY: Oxford University Press, 2016, Ch.2.

by the Jains than by the Buddhists and one of the major Jain sects, the Digambara, to this day renounces even clothing as an earthly attachment and as a source of violence against the minute organisms present in one's environment.

II. Brāhmana

The Vedas

When we turn to the spiritual traditions of Brāhmanism and Tantra we find that they are much less world-abjuring than the Yogic and Shramana traditions. The Indo-Āryan Brāhmanical tradition venerates the Vedas as the font of its spiritual knowledge. The Vedas are considered to be divinely revealed scriptures that emerged from the original cosmic sacrifice of the Purusha, or Primordial Man, the form in which the divine Soul first imagined itself in the manifest universe.[197] Thus in the Rigveda, X,90 (Purusha Sūkta), we learn that

> 9. From that great general sacrifice, Ṛcas and Sāma-hymns were born: Therefrom were spells and charms produced;[198] the Yajus had its birth from it.

According to the *Manusmriti*, I,23, the Vedas, as liturgical texts to be chanted during sacrifices, were created by the Supreme Soul originally for the performance of the cosmic sacrifice of the Purusha itself:

---

[197] For a full account of the mythology of the Purusha and its significance for an understanding of the Āryan as well as Hamitic religions, see A. Jacob, *Brahman*, and Ch.V below.

[198] This would refer to the contents of the *Atharvaveda*.

22. He, the Lord, also created the class of the gods, who are endowed with life, and whose nature is action; and the subtle class of the sādhyas [lower celestial beings], and the eternal sacrifice.
But from fire, wind, and the sun he drew forth the threefold eternal Veda, called Rik, Yagus, and Saman, for the due performance of the sacrifice.

In *BP* III,12, the Vedas accompany the physical creation of the universe guiding its formation through sacrificial as well as ethical rules:

34. When the creator of all worlds one day wondered how he should create the three worlds the way they were before, the Vedic literature manifested itself from his four mouths.

35. Thus the four functions of [sacrificial] action [the offer, the performer, the fire and the offering] and the supplements of the Veda with their logical conclusions became manifest, as also the four principles of religion [truth, purity, austerity and compassion] and the spiritual stages [*âshramas*] and vocational divisions [*varnas*].[199]

26th Chaturyuga, Dvāpara Yuga

The editing of the Vedas in their present form was undertaken by the sage Vyāsa. Though Vyāsa is mentioned in *BP* I,3, as an avatār of Vishnu in the Treta Yuga, the *Vishnu Purāna*, III,3, declares that the Vedas are edited in every Dvāpara Yuga and the editor of the Vedas that

---

[199] However, we may remember the attribution of the institution of the āshramas to Kapila by the Sāmkhya-Yoga school and that of the caste system to Rishabha by the Jain.

we possess appeared in the Dvāpara Yuga of the twenty-sixth Chaturyuga. The Vedas as we have them are divided into four texts, Rigveda, Sāmaveda, Yajurveda and Atharvaveda. The first three are sacrificial liturgies for the use of the Hotr priest, the Udgātr and the Adhvaryu priest respectively. The Atharvaveda is older in its contents and is meant for the supervising Brahman priest, or Atharvan, a name that is clearly of Indo-Iranian rather than Indo-Āryan origin.

28th Chaturyuga, Treta Yuga

Brāhmanism

Brāhmanism itself traces its origins to the Treta Yuga of the 28th Chaturyuga and the mythic figure of the first man, Manu. A brief account of the beginning of our humanity with Manu may be in order here.

According to the *Bhāgavata Purāna*, the cosmos is said to be ever recreated after a periodic devastation by a "flood", when the supreme deity in the manifest form of Vishnu descends into a deep sleep within the cosmic ocean. Gradually waking, he begins to reproduce the cosmos. The antediluvian epoch, or kalpa, was called Brahmakalpa (*BP* III,11,33ff.), since it was marked by the perfect light of Brahma,[200] and the second, after the cosmic cataclysm, is the present one, called Padmakalpa (the Lotus epoch),[201] in which the divine light is transferred to the material universe. Each kalpa is divided into fourteen "manvantaras" or ages of Manu, a Manu being the type of

---

[200] Brahma is the Purānic form of Brahman.

[201] According to *VP*, I,27-28, however, the first kalpa was called Padmakalpa (the kalpa of the Lotus) and the present one is called Varāhakalpa (the kalpa of the Boar).

enlightened mankind. Each manvantara lasts for 71 odd Chaturyugas, or 310,980,000 years (*BP* III,11,24) and is followed by a deluge lasting as long as a Krita Yuga, or 1,728,000 years (*Sūrya Siddhāntha*, I,18).

According to the *Sūrya Siddhānta*, Ch.I, 22, the Manu of our cosmic cycle is said to have appeared in the 28th Chaturyuga of the [Padma] Kalpa. And, in the *Mahābhārata*, Shantiparva, it is said that Manu manifested himself in the Treta Yuga. This Manu is the seventh and called Manu Vaivaswata [of Vivasvant, the sun]. He is responsible for the transmission of the seeds of life to earth as well as for the mortality (Yama) of the forms that spring from these seeds. *BP* VIII,14,3, informs us that the role of a "Manu" is to maintain the cosmic order at the time of the creation of the universe and in *BP* VIII,24,13 the seventh Manu is called also Satyavrata, and King of Drāvida. So we may assume that Drāvida and its king Satyavrata represent the first fully enlightened post-diluvian mankind. As regards the proto-Dravidians, we may rely on Lahovary's pioneering research into the Mediterranean race, which he identified with the Dravidian, and considered as being the original inhabitants of the ancient Near East "in its largest meaning", that is, including "Anatolia, Syria, Palestine, Caucasia, Persia, Mesopotamia with its extensions towards India, as well as Arabia and the African regions facing Arabia, i.e. from the Nile valley to the high tablelands of East Africa".[202]

Manu is warned of a deluge by a fish (representing Prajāpati in his piscine incarnation Matsya).[203] In the *MBh,* the divine identity of the fish is revealed to be that of Prajāpati/Brahman (the name of the supreme god in his luminous, creative aspect), since the fish declares to the "seven sages"—who accompany Manu in the ship—"I am

---

[202] See N. Lahovary, tr. K.A. Nilakantan, *Dravidian Origins*, p.2.

[203] See the list of Vishnu avatārs.

Brahma, lord of progeny [Prajāpati] ... I in the form of a fish have delivered you from this peril".[204] The fish goes on to state that Manu should create all creatures including "gods, asuras, and men and all the worlds and what moves and what does not move [i.e. animal and vegetable life]."

Manu saves himself in a ship which is tied to the "horn" of the fish[205] and is borne by the latter to the heights of "the northern mountain", which, not being specified as a Himalayan one, may well be Mt. Ararat, which is generally identified as the mountain on which the "ark" of Noah/Manu rested after the deluge.[206] It is important to note that Manu is the divine ancestor of the race that is to inhabit the earth. In the *SB*, Manu is described as offering a sacrifice after the flood recedes, and from this sacrifice arises, first, a "daughter" Idā [a variant of Ilā],[207] and then a son Ikshvāku, from whom the human race is derived.[208]

The Indic Manu is identifiable with the Noah of the Hebrew Bible, and Noah is said to be a descendant of Seth, the son of Adam [Man], who is the same of the Vedic Purusha, or Primordial Man. In the the Ethiopian version of Pseudo-Callisthenes, the brāhmans are said to be the sons of Seth. Josephus identifies the land of Seth as located around "Seiris", which is also the land of Noah, who is said to have preserved the wisdom of Seth.[209] In the Christian *Opus Imperfectum in Matthaeum* of Pseudo-Chrysostom, the books of Seth were supposed to have been hidden

---

[204] *MBh* II,187,2ff.

[205] See *SB* I,viii,1,5.

[206] For the identification of Manu with Noah see below; cf. A. Jacob, *Ātman*, Ch.I; A. Jacob, *Brahman*, Ch.IV.

[207] Ilā and Idā are interchangeable in the *BP* (Ilā: IX,16,22) and other Purānas (Idā: *BrdP* III,60,11, *VP* 85,7).

[208] We have noted the Edda ('The Deluding of Gylfi') records the first human beings as a girl called Embla and a boy called Ask.

[209] See Josephus, *Jewish Antiquities*, I:70-1.

by Noah in the land of Šir, and the so-called "cave of treasures" in which they were hidden is identifiable with Mt. Ararat.[210] In *Genesis* 14:6, the Horites, or Hurrians, are particularly identified with Mt. Seir, and we note here a close identification of the proto-Hurrians with the proto-Dravidians of *BP*, according to which Manu is King of Drāvida. Since Manu/Noah is a Dravidian "king" in *BP*, it seems that Vedic religion itself derives from a proto-Dravidian origin. It may be significant, in this context, that, in the *Mahābhārata*, Āranyakaparva (IX,45, 87ff.), the title "Yogeshvara" (Lord of Yoga) is applied particularly to the chief god of the Dravidians, Muruga/Skanda. F.E. Pargiter maintained that Brāhmanism was not originally Āryan but adopted into Indo-Āryan religion from Dravidian.[211] However, Pargiter did not consider the possibility that both Āryan and later Dravidian may have been derived from a proto-Dravidian/Hurrian[212] spiritual culture.[213]

Manu's daughter Ila, according to the Purānas is the originator of the Lunar Aila dynasty of kshatriyas. According to *Rāmāyana*, Uttarakanda, 100, Ila was the son, rather than daughter, of the Manu Kardama, king of Bāhlika (Bactria). We have already noted the identification of Manu's son with Kapila, the founder of the Sāmkhya-Yoga school. If Bactria should, therefore, be associated with the possible origin of the Shramana sects, we will see that Bactria is equally associated with Brāhmanical fire-

---

[210] See G.G. Stroumsa, *Another Seed: Studies in Gnostic Mythology*, Leiden: E.J. Brill, 1984, p.117.

[211] See F.E. Pargiter, *Ancient Indian Historical Tradition*, London: Milford, 1922, Ch.26.

[212] For a good account of the Hurrians see G. Wilhelm, *Grundzüge der Geschichte und Kultur der Hurriter*, Darmstadt: Wissenschaftliche Buchgesellschaft, 1982; G. Wilhelm, *The Hurrians*, tr. J. Barnes, Warminster: Aris and Phillips Ltd., 1989.

[213] For a detailed discussion of the proto-Dravidian/Druidic origins of Brāhmanism see A. Jacob, *Brahman*, Ch.VI.

worship. In ancient West Asia, the kingdom of Elam in the western part of Iran may well correspond to the Aila dynasty, while the Akshak dynasty of Sumer may represent the Ikshvāku. If so, the entire region from western Iran to Bactria was inhabited by the Aila dynasty. In general, we may assume that the Aila dynasty represents an eastern branch of the same race that is represented in West Asia by the Sumerian/Akkadian Ikshvākus.

Purūravas, a grandson of Chandra and Ila, is said to have acquired the sacred fires of the Āryans from the Gandharvas (Gandharva being a term for heaven as well as for a particular tribe). Purūravas is said to have lived at the end of the Treta Yuga, at the end of which age too there was another flood when the earth was submerged under the waters. However, with the assistance of the sage Agastya the earth was recovered from the depths and life revived on it. The Aila dynasty thus is clearly associated with the Indo-Āryan fire-worshipping peoples, while Agastya represents the transmission of the Vedic religion to the Hamitic peoples of Sumer, Egypt, and India..

Of the Solar Ikshāvku line, Rāma, the famous son of Dasharatha, is said to have been born in the Treta Yuga (*Rāmāyana*, Uttara Kanda, 44). His kingdom is said to be Kosala, which is identified as being a part of present-day Uttar Pradesh, but this might just be a transference of a more westerly original location, perhaps Kish.[214] Although—as we shall see below—the fire-worshipping Āryan tradition is associated specifically with the Aila dynasty of Purūravas and is first evidenced in the Bactria-Margiana Archaeological Complex, the veneration of the Ikshvāku Rāma in Brāhmanical terms in India suggests that his story was equally Brāhmanised by the people who brought the mythological story of Manu and his descendants to the sub-continent.

---

[214] See below p.112.

Both the Brāhmanical religion, which may have had a northerly Indo-Āryan origin in the Pontic Steppe, and the Hamitic religions which begin in eastern Anatolia, around Mt. Ararat – are characterised by a concentration on the Purusha form of the divine Soul in the macrocosmos as well as in the microcosm The fire rituals of the Āryans are magical dramatisations of the cosmic sacrifice of the Purusha and aim at reviving the latter through the force of the ritual fire. The Agnicayana ritual, for instance, is an elaborate example of Vedic ritual conducted for the purpose of reviving the Purusha.[215] These rituals also serve to sustain the entire cosmos through an identification of the chief participants, that is, the sacrificer guided by the brahman priest, with the solar force.

The Vedas in their present form are thus primarily sacrificial liturgies aimed at restoring the creation to its ideal status as the Primordial Man. However, the ethical aspects of Vedic sacrifice too may be gleaned through the description of the evolution of religion provided in the *Manusmrithi*. The aim of all Vedic enlightenment, whether it be through Āryan fire-worship or the later Tantra, is indeed the attainment of the ultimate identity of the individual soul, ātman, with the primal light of the cosmos, Brahman. However, the means of achieving this end apparently varied with the changes in the ages, or yugas, that constitute our present epoch, kalpa. According to *Manusmriti*, I,86, the chief means of enlightenment in the first of the four ages was austerities:

> In the Krita age the chief [virtue] is declared to be [performance of] austerities, in the Treta [divine] knowledge, in the Dvapara [the performance of] sacrifices, in the Kali liberality alone.

---

[215] See A. Jacob, *Brahman*, Ch.IX; cf. Ch.V below.

We see that the Brāhmanical sacrifices are not, like yogic 'tapas' and 'jnana', associated with the Krita Yuga or the Treta Yuga but only with the Dvāpara Yuga. These sacrifices, as we shall see, focus on the macrocosmic elements of the divine manifestation rather more than on the human microcosmic. The esoteric spiritual significance of the Vedas does not emerge in the predominantly liturgical Vedas so much as in the Upanishadic (Vedānta) literature, especially in the Yoga-based Upanishads derived largely from the Krishna and Shukla Yajur Vedas.[216]

It may be mentioned here that later Āgamic texts like the *Tārapradīpa*, Ch.1, state, contrary to the *Manusmriti*, that in the Satya (Krita) age Vaidika Upāsana [meditation] prevailed while in the Dvāpara there were both Smriti[217] and Purāna. Finally, in the Kaliyuga the Tantrika rather than the Vaidika Dharma has come to predominate. The Tantra Shastra was taught at the end of Dvāpara age and the beginning of Kaliyuga. However, we may rely on the *Manusmriti* rather than the Āgamic texts since we find the primacy of Yogic worship over sacrificial maintained also in the *Rigveda* and the epics themselves. *RV* I,84,2, for instance, declares—regarding the forms of worship of the sages and the sacrifices offered by householders— that Indra attended 'eulogies' sung by Rishis and 'yajnas' conducted by humans. So it is apparent that Vedic sacrifices were necessary only for humans. In the *MBh*, VII (Anushāsana Parva), 16, too, Tandi, a sage of the Krita Yuga, is said to have "adored Shiva for 10,000 years with the aid of yogic meditation".

The "divine knowledge" (jnāna) mentioned in the *Manusmriti* as having prevailed in the following Treta Yuga may have been derived from the ascetic disciplines

---

[216] See K. N. Aiyar, *op.cit.*

[217] "Smriti" (=remembered wisdom) refers principally to the epics and the Dharmasūtras.

practiced in the Krita Yuga. In the Treta Yuga, Manu himself is described in the *MP* as practicing tapas, or austerities, on "Mt. Malaya", but also as sacrificing. As for the practice of austerities themselves, the *Rāmāyana*, Uttara Kanda, Sec.87, states that only the Brāhmans practiced austerities in the Krita Yuga. In the following Treta Yuga, Kshatriyas were born and, gaining equal spiritual dignity with the Brāhmans, practiced austerities alongside them, while the Vaisyas and Shūdras served them. Then in the Dvāpara Yuga Vaisyas started to practice austerities as well, just as the Shūdras too began practicing austerities in the Kali Yuga.

Dvāpara Yuga

As regards the geographical origin of Brāhmanism, the *Bhavishya Purāna*, Pratisarga Parva I, maintains that the Dvāpara Yuga was marked by the establishment of three kingdoms, at Pratishthāna (this being related to the Aila dynasty of Purūravas himself), Mathura (associated with Krishna, the lunar/Aila deity)[218] and Marudesh (ruled by Shamashrupal[219] of the Mlecchas,[220] and comprising Iran, Iraq, and Arabia). Marudesh clearly denotes the Hamitic cultures of Mesopotamia and Egypt which must have started at the end of the Dvāpara age since their peak, in the late fourth millennium B.C., coincides with the start of the Kali Yuga, which is traditionally supposed to have begun around 3100 B.C.[221] The Dvāpara age is supposed

---

[218] See p.32n.

[219] Shamash is the Akkadian word for the sun.

[220] In the *Manusmriti*, 'mleccha' is a general term for non-Āryan (see below). However, here it seems to refer particularly to the mostly Semitic Assyrians and Babylonians.

[221] See p.111.

to have lasted for 864,000 years, though there is, as yet, little evidence of the existence of enlightened mankind on earth until the end of the Dvāpara age. The Gandharvas and Purūravas represent the Āryan tradition marked by fire-worship, whereas the Hamitic is marked by temple worship and idolatry.

The fire-rituals which form the backbone of the Brāhmanical religious practice are attested in the typical Indo-Āryan settlement detected in the BMAC. Elaborate fire altars are evident in the ruins of the BMAC which correspond to the Āryan fire-sacrifices. The temples also contain rooms with "all the necessary apparatus for the preparation of drinks extracted from poppy, hemp and ephedra" that may have been used for the soma-rituals.[222] The BMAC may have thus been the centre of cultural contact between the proto-Dravidian/Hurrian peoples of Mundigak and the later Indo-Āryans. It is interesting to note too, in this context, that the Avesta (which is geographically centred in eastern Iran) mentions the Māzanian daevas as worshippers of the Indian gods. According to Burrow, Māzana is known in Iranian sources as the territory between the southern shore of the Caspian Sea and the Alburz mountains.[223] It may be related also to Margiana and the Indo-Āryan culture detected there.

It must be noted that there are indeed fire-altars even in the Harappan sites of Kalibangan, in Rajastan, and Lothal, in Gujarat, which may be dated to around 2500 B.C. So it remains a moot question whether the BMAC fire-altars were introduced from the north or the south, or whether they formed part of an extensive north-south

---

[222] See J.P. Mallory and V.H. Mair, *The Tarim Mummies: Ancient China and the Mystery of the Earliest Peoples from the West*, London: Thames and Hudson, 2008, p.262.

[223] See E.Bryant, *The Quest for the Origins of Vedic culture: the Indo-Aryan Migration Debate,* Oxford: Oxford University Press, 2001, p.130.

Aryan cultural continuum. Indeed the Allchins surmise that there were probably also fire-altars in Harappa and Mohenjo-Daro though these have been missed in the mass-diggings conducted at these sites.[224]

However, it is clear that fire-worship was maintained particularly by the Āryan branch of the Indo-Europeans. For fire-worship is also observed among the Prussian-Lithuanian cult of szwenta (holy fire), as well as among the Greeks and Romans who maintained a cult of hestia or vesta.[225] Plutarch (*Numa*, II) informs us that "Numa is said to have built the temple of Vesta in circular form as protection for the inextinguishable fire, copying not the fire of the earth as being Vesta, but of the whole universe, as centre of which the Pythagoreans believe fire to be established, and this they call Hestia and the monad". The Scythians too worshipped a goddess called Tabit whose name is probably related to the Sanskrit tapti denoting heat.

On the other hand, we must remember Herodotus' statement that the Iranians did not worship fire originally.[226] We have seen that in the Purānas, too, Purūravas, the early Aila [Elamite?] king, is stated, in the *Mbh* I,75, to have obtained sacrificial fire from the "Gandharvas", who also taught him the constitution of the three sacred fires of the Āryans.[227] We have seen that Purūravas is stated

---

[224] See R. and B. Allchin, *The Rise of Civilization in India and Pakistan*, Cambridge: Cambridge University Press, 1982, p.183; cf, also D. K. Chakrabarti, "The archaeology of Hinduism", in T. Insoll (ed.), *Archaeology and World Religion*, London: Routledge, 2001, p.44f.

[225] See M. Sharma, *Fire-Worship in Ancient India,* Jaipur: Publication Scheme, 2002, p.19.

[226] See Herodotus, *Histories*, I,132.

[227] See F.E. Pargiter, *op.cit.*, p.309. The three sacred fires of the Brāhmans are the the circular gārhapatya, representing earth and the world of men (*SB* VII,I,1), the square āhavanīya representing heaven and the world of the gods (*SB* VII,2,2) and the āgnīdhrīya fire representing the air of the Mid-region (*SB* VII,1,2,12).

in the Purānas to be an Aila king of Pratishthāna. The Ailas themselves are designated as Karddameyas, which relates them to Kardama[228] and the river Karddama in Iran, particularly in the region of Balkh, which was called Bactra in Greek.[229]

The fact that the Purūravas are said to have learnt the fire-rituals from the Gandharvas suggests that the early Hurrians of Elam and the earliest Iranians did not worship fire and learnt it from a later Bactrian source, since the Gandhara culture follows the BMAC. However, even the Gandhāras are included among the Aila [Elamite?] dynasties in the Purānas. Herodotus (III,91) mentions the Gandaridae as one of the Indian tribes of the seventh satrapy of Darius I (550-486 B.C.) who can be located near the Bactrians of the 12th satrapy. The term "Gadara", a form of "Gandhara", occurs along with the term "Hindu",[230] in an inscription of King Darius of Iran.

The archaeological evidence of the early Gandharvas may be that found in the Gandhara Grave culture of the Swat settled from 1700-1400 B.C., which followed the BMAC. The occupants of the BMAC may have been related to the same family as the later Gandhara. Since the Gandhara culture also bears the first evidence of cremation rituals in South Asia, we may consider them to have indeed consolidated the Vedic customs of the Indo-Āryans. Cremation is evidenced also in the Andronovo culture. At the same time, the neighbouring Bishkent culture, which is contemporaneous with the Gandhara and is related to the northern BMAC type, exhibits also a curious quasi-Scythian custom of inhumation involving the removal of the entrails and their replacement with

---

[228] See p.71.

[229] See *Rāmāyana* VII,103,21ff.

[230] "Hindu", a form of "Sindhu", is used to denote the people or country on the river Sindhu conquered by Darius.

clarified butter which may have persisted among the Vedic Indians, as is suggested by *SB* XII,v,2,5.[231] The Gandhara culture thus may have had a northern source. The northern and eastern branch of the original Noachidian race may have thus been constituted of "Japhetic" tribes that moved northwards to the Pontic-Caspian steppes and created the Yamnaya culture there[232] which is considered the major source of the Āryan culture.

The Purūravas who adopted fire-worship from the Gandhāras may thus represent an Elamite/Aila branch of the proto-Āryan family, while the Gandaridae, who may have arrived from the south-east Caspian region (since the BMAC culture is apparently derived from the latter)[233] may be a typically Indo-Āryan branch of the same family. It may be noted also that the probability that the Indic Vedic culture itself may have been developed after an original formulation at a proto-Indo-Iranian stage is suggested by the greater elaboration of the name of the god Tvoreshtar amongst the Iranians—representing the older religion of the proto-Āryans—compared to the Vedic Tvashtr.[234] Indeed, many of the characteristic traits of the rituals of ancient India derive from an Indo-Iranian period as is attested by the similarity of the terms, yajna/yaja, soma/haoma, mantra/manθra, nama/nəmô. Even the term atharvan, denoting the originator of the *Atharvaveda*, has only an Iranian etymology âθravâ.[235]

---

[231] See A. Parpola, *op.cit.*, p.365.

[232] W. Bernard suggested that the human remains from Period I of Gandhara bore resemblances to those of Bronze Age and early Iron Age crania of 2500 B.C.–A.D. 500 from the Caucasus and Volga region as well as from Tepe Hissar in Iran (see K.A.R. Kennedy, "Have Aryans been identified", p.49).

[233] See J.P. Mallory and V.H. Mair, *op.cit.*, p.262.

[234] Cf. A. Jacob, "Cosmology and Ethics in the Religions of the Peoples of the Ancient Near East", *Mankind Quarterly* 140, no.1 (Fall 1999), p.96.

[235] The term means "priest" in Avestan (See P. Kretschmer, *Kuhns*

However, it must be remembered that fire-worship is based on a vision of the cosmic creation that formed the basis of the solar religions of the Hamitic Sumerians and Egyptians as well. In the Sumerian religion too, the chief solar god An is equated to Girra, the fire-god (in an Assyrian exegetical text)[236] and Re in Egypt is the same as the solar force, Agni. So that it is possible that the adoration of the solar force as divine fire may have been an integral part of the original proto-Dravidian religion that was shared by Semites, Japhetites, and Hamites. But the worship of cosmic forces through fire-rituals seem to have been characteristic of the Japhetic Indo-Āryan stock that had migrated at a very early date northwards to the Yamnaya and Andronovo cultures whence they moved southwards again later, in the second millennium B.C., towards northern Mesopotamia, Iran, and India. The eastward movement of proto-Dravidians-Hurrians (Ailas as well as Ikshvākus) with Elamite forms of the Brahmanical religion may have encountered the more northerly fire-worshipping Gandaridae tribes to form the typically Indian branch of the Āryan family.

Pargiter has suggested that the Dravidian "brāhmanical" institution was also considerably transformed by the Āryans. While the original [proto-] Dravidian priesthood was characterised by the practice of yogic austerities (tapas) which gave them magical powers, the Āryan was preoccupied with the performance of sacrifices involving the worship of fire.[237] If Pargiter is right, it may be that the Tantric and Brāhmanical traditions were derived from a single proto-Dravidian or

---

Zeitschrift 55, p.80; cf. J. Gonda, *Religionen Indiens*, I, p.107).

[236] RA 62-52,17-8 (see A. Livingstone, *op.cit.*, p.74); cf. K170+Rm520rev. (*ibid.*, p.30ff).

[237] See F.E. Pargiter, *op.cit.*, p.308f.

Noachidian source[238] that split into fire-worshipping and temple-building tribes. We may, in this context, also recall Megasthenes' account of the early Indians:

> The Indians were in old times nomadic, like those Scythians who did not till the soil, but roamed about in their wagons, as the seasons varied, from one part of Scythia to another, neither dwelling in towns nor worshipping in temples;[239] and that the Indians likewise had neither towns nor temples of the gods, but were so barbarous that they wore the skins of such wild animals as they could kill ... they subsisted also on such wild animals as they could catch, eating the flesh raw – before, at least, the coming of Dionysus into India. Dionysus, however, when he came and had conquered the people, founded cities and gave laws to these cities, and introduced the use of wine among the Indians, as he had done among the Greeks, and taught them to sow the land, himself supplying seeds for the purpose ... It is also said that ... the Indians worship the other gods and Dionysus himself in particular with cymbals and drums, because he so taught them ... and that he instructed the Indians to let their hair grow long in honour of the god .[240]

Since Dionysus is the same as the solar god of the Mesopotamians, An, and the Egyptian Horus the Elder-

---

[238] That the biblical Noah, a descendant of Adam's son, Seth, represents the wisdom of Seth is evident from the Gnostic tradition (see G.G. Stroumsa, *op. cit.*, p.107). Josephus' *Jewish Antiquities*, I, 70-71 also makes clear the association of the line of Seth with cosmological learning (see A. Annus, *op.cit.*, p.xxvii).

[239] The fact that the Scythians did not build temples or worship divine images is mentioned also by Herodotus, *Histories*, I,131.

[240] See Arrian, *Indica*, VII (in R.C. Majumdar, *The Classical Accounts of India*, Calcutta: Firma K.L. Mukhopadhyay, 1960. p.220f.).

Osiris,[241] and the earliest evidence of the Dravidian god, Muruga, in India reveals a Dionysiac deity, we may assume that the cultural contact being referred to by Megasthenes is that between the early Indo-Scythian settlers of India and Elamite Dravidians/Hurrians from the Zagros region.[242] The Dionysiac Dravidian religion, associable with the worship of Muruga among the Tamils, may be associated with the Tantric tradition that gradually began to predominate in early historic India. However, it must be remembered also that even the Tantric spiritual tradition is best preserved in Sanskrit, the cultivated [sanskrit=refined] and inflected language of the upper castes of the Indo-Āryans which however retains several Dravidian elements in it.

We have seen that Bactria seems to have been the locus in which the Shramana as well as the Brāhmanical traditions of the Indo-Āryans were consolidated. It is interesting in this context to note also that Herodotus, History of the Persian Wars, III,102, refers to other Indians who "dwell northward of all the rest of the Indians" and describes them as following "the same mode of life as the Bactrians". However, the Indo-Āryans seem to have moved early to India as well, and to have come to consider it their home. For, in the Manusmrithi, Chapter II, the land of the Indo-Āryans is described in fully Indian geographical terms:

> 22. But the tract between those two mountains [Himavat and Vindhya] as far as the eastern and western oceans the wise call Āryāvarta.

---

[241] See A. Jacob, *Ātman*, Ch.XII; cf. A. Jacob, *Brahman*. Ch.I.

[242] The theory that Āryan is pre-Harappan was put forward by A.D. Pusalkar, "Pre-Harappan, Harappan and post-Harappan culture and the Aryan problem", *Quarterly Review of Historical Studies*, 7,4 (1967-8)", p.233ff.

23. That land where the black antelope naturally roams[243] one must know to be fit for the performance of sacrifices; the tract different from that is the country of the Mlecchas.

24. Let the twice-born men seek to dwell in those [lands]; but a Shūdra, distressed for subsistence may reside anywhere.

According to *Vishnusmrithi*, LXXXIV,4, "Those countries are called barbarous (Mleccha) where the system of the four castes does not exist; the others are denoted Āryāvarta." Non-Āryans were in general called Anagni, the fireless.

***

The sacrifice-oriented Vedas are different from Yoga, which encourages the adept to attempt not only a higher Brahmic consciousness but also a total liberation from the bonds of manifestation. The Brāhmanical fire-rituals focus on the sacred fire as part of the solar force that animates the universe and bestows life, and even immortality, on human beings. The fire-rituals were indeed devised to obtain supernatural effects through the control of the sacred fire by means of "tapas", or "fervour". The *Rgveda* (X,154,2), for example, refers to tapas as that by which "one attains the light of the sun". Indeed, in *AV* XI,8, we glimpse the magical power of 'tapas' (fervour/heat) in the formation of the mind and the sense faculties in the macrocosm even before the creation of the gods:

Ten Gods before the Gods were born together in the ancient time.

---

[243] India, which is the natural habitat of the black antelope.

Whoso may know them face to face may now pronounce the mighty word.

Inbreath and outbreath, eye and ear, decay and freedom from decay,

Spiration upward and diffused, voice, mind have brought us wish and plan.

As yet the Seasons were unborn, and Dhātar and Prajāpati,

Both Asvins, Indra, Agni. Whom then did they worship as supreme?

6. Fervour and Action were the two, in depths of the great billowy sea;

Fervour sprang up from Action: this they served and worshipped as supreme.

The Brāhmanās and the Upanishads, however, aim also at the control of the fire within the body. The establishment of Agni within the inner self of the sacrificer is explained in the Shatapatha Brāhmanā as a means of attaining immortality. According to this major Brāhmanical text, in the beginning, not even the gods or their opponents, the asurās, were immortal since they lacked soul, ātman. Only Agni, the fire, was immortal. As Heesterman paraphrases it,

> Fervently chanting and exerting themselves the gods finally beheld the rite of setting up the fire ... They then gained immortality by establishing the fire within themselves, and thereby obtained an ātman, the seat of immortality, as well. And so they overcame the asurās.[244]

---

[244] See J.C. Heesterman, *Broken world*, p.215.

Further, according to the *SB*, "Once the fire has been ritually established in the inner self through the agnyādheya, it is the sacrificer's inalienable true identity, in short, his ātman." The internalisation of Agni within, and as, the individual soul, ātman, is made clear also by *Taittiriya Samhita* III,4,10,5 where, as Heesterman points out, we observe that

> when the sacrificer symbolically has the fire mount the aranis by warming them over the glowing members of the dying fire, he makes it enter into himself ... When churning the fire to reinstall it, he churns it out of himself, exteriorizing, as it were, his own self, for he is himself the yoni, the womb of the fire... For the fire is one's atman.[245]

And *SB* II,2,2,17 declares that "as long as he lives the fire which is established in his inner self does not become extinct in him".

SB III,6,2,16 further reveals that "even in being born, man, by his own self, is born as a debt (owing) to death. And in that he sacrifices, thereby he redeems himself from death." The sacrificer thus has two bodies, one material and the other ritual/spiritual. Through the sacrifice he mounts to heaven to get a divine body and, on earth, he gives his material body to the gods. Thus his material body is sacrificed after purifications such as shaving the hair, cutting the nails, etc. (*TS* VI,1,1,2), although the sacrifice of his material body is performed with a substitute victim. Though this victim was originally a man, it was later replaced by a horse or a bull, while, at the time of the composition of the *SB*, the most common substitute was the goat (*SB* VI,2,1,39).

---

[245] *Ibid.*, p.101.

The importance of Agni as an instrument of the rebirth of man in the heavenly realm is made clear in the *SB*, which declares that Agni entered into a compact with man saying: "I shall enter you; having given birth to me, you must maintain me. As you will give birth to me and maintain me, so I shall give birth to you in yonder world". Indeed, according to *SB* XII,1,3,18,ff., in the last stages of the sacrifice,

> when the sacrificers worship the regions (dishāh) with a sacrifice, they become these deities, the regions. That means that they master the whole of the universe in respect to space ...When they enter upon the mahavrata (day) they worship the deity Prajāpati; they become the deity Prajāpati ... That means that those who now experience intimate union with this god and "residence" in his sphere have reached this ultimate goal ... they establish themselves firmly in the world of heaven.[246]

This is in sharp contrast to the Shramana traditions which do not value fire as a sacred instrument of salvation and do not strive to reach heaven so much as to leave all phenomenal existence behind. Yoga recognises the essence of man as energy (especially in Kundalini Yoga) and yajna too relates it to thermal energy or the vital fire within man. But yajna is external and symbolic worship whereas yoga is more clearly internal and practical.

In the 'Bhagavat Gita' too Yogic exercise is described in terms of fire-worship. It declares that yogis offered their vital force to the cosmic Prāna, which is considered to be a spiritual Havan (offering). 'Bhagavat Gita', 4,24, further states that the self-control aimed at by yogic tapas may become the source of a variety of sacrifices:

---

[246] See J. Gonda, *Prajāpati's Rise to Higher Rank*, Leiden: E.J. Brill, 1986, p.113f.

Others offer up the senses, such as the sense of hearing and others, in the fires of restraint; others offer up the objects of sense, such as sound and so forth, into the fires of the senses. Some again offer up all the operations of the senses and the operations of the life-breaths into the fire of devotion by self-restraint, kindled by knowledge. Others perform the sacrifice of wealth, the sacrifice of penance, the sacrifice of concentration of mind, the sacrifice of Vedic study, and of knowledge, and others are ascetics of rigid vows.

Of all these possible sacrifices the Smārtasūtras consider the sacrifice of the self as the highest.[247] According to the *Prānāgnihotra Upanishad* (derived from *KYV*), 17ff.,[248]

One should meditate on the Atman saying "I offer a sacrifice to Atman through fire" ... In order to set the sacrifice within the motion of the universe, one should make an offering to the interior of one's own body saying "Thus I set the sacrifice into motion".

The *Avyaktopanishad* treats dhyāna or spiritual meditation as a yajna and declares that one should offer one's self as an oblation into the fire in order to attain Brahman. According to the 'Gita', IV, knowledge (jnāna) itself is a supreme sort of sacrifice since "the fire of knowledge reduces all actions to ashes".

The metaphysical constitution of the fire employed in the Brāhmanical rituals is explained in great detail in the Panchāgni Vidya of the *Chāndogya Upanishad*, V,4ff, which identifies the five spiritual fires within the

---

[247] See Vaikhānasa smārtasūtra II,18 (cf. M. Biardeau, *op.cit.*, p.66).

[248] I follow here the French translation of M. Buttex based on the versions of A. G. Krishna Warrier and Paul Deussen.

macrocosm (heaven, the atmosphere, and earth) and the macrocosm (man and woman). The *Prāṇāgnihotra Upanishad* also mentions five fires, but four of these are identified within the human body. The Panchāgni fires of the yajna are also used to clean the five internal fires such as passion, anger, greed, attachment, and jealousy. Similarly, in Kundalini Yoga, Earth is represented by the Mūlādhāra chakra of the yogi and Heaven by the Sahasrara chakra[249] and the Kundalini energy gets elevated to the Sahasrara chakra when it goes through the fire of Agni.

The *Garbha Upanishad* mentions three forms of fire within the human body, koshta agni, darshana agni, and gnāna agni, relating to digestion, sight, and knowledge. These are located in the stomach, face, and heart respectively and correspond to the three fires, gārhaptniyāgni, āhavaniyāgni and dakshināgni, in the fire-ritual. Thus, according to the *Garbha Upanishad*, "There is none living who does not perform yajña (sacrifice). This body is (created) for yajña, and arises out of yajña and changes according to yajña."

Although the sacrifice has more mundane purposes such as the acquisition of offspring, cattle, health, wealth, and the brahmanic splendour,[250] the final aim of the sacrifices is to attain immortality by transfiguring the sacrificer into the solar force. The nectar of immortality that sacrificers seek for by toil and penance is indeed Soma (*SB* IX,5,1,8). The basic meaning of the Soma sacrifice is related to the idea of pressing, or killing the Purusha, as *SB* II,2,2,1 suggests: "in pressing out the king [Soma] they slay him". This may have a special phallic connotation as well since the soma juice is akin to the seminal power of Prajāpati which serves as the source of the sun that

---

[249] The Manipūra chakra is located in the middle – in the stomach. Aum chanting is done from the Manipūrachakra.

[250] See, for instance, *SB* II,3,3,15f; X,1,5,4, etc.

emerges as a result of the castration of the Purusha. Thus the sacrifice, though representing the death of the sacrificer, compensates the latter with his spiritual rebirth.

According to the *Jaiminiya Upanishad Brāhmanā* III,14,8, "As long as a man does not sacrifice, for that long he remains unborn. It is through the sacrifice that he is born". Thus the *Maitrāyani Samhita*, III,6,7, declares that man is indeed born three times, at birth, at the sacrifice, and at death. Indeed *Manusmrithi* V also points out that even lower forms of life, such as plants, animals, trees, birds, which have been killed as sacrificial victims rise to a higher status when reborn. All sacrifice is, like the original sacrifice of the Purusha, a self-sacrifice followed by a spiritual rebirth wherein the sacrificer acquires the essential aspect of his existence, "uniform, undecaying and immortal" (*SB* X,1,4,1).

This rebirth is enacted during the sacrifice in the four-day purification ceremony called dīksha. *SB* III,1,1,8 reveals the importance of the consecration of the sacrificer in the dīksha ceremony whereby the sacrificer is reborn as an immortal: "He who is consecrated truly draws nigh to the gods and becomes one of the deities". The significance of sacrifice as a rebirth is evident in *AB*, I,3, which declares that "the priests transform the one to whom they give the diksha into an embryo." The yajamāna and his wife should be dressed in clothes which correspond to the shell of an egg since they are going to be reborn.[251] Though the sacrificer's wife participates in this ritual, it is principally the sacrificer himself who will be reborn as the sun. *AB* I,1,3, details the process whereby the sacrificer is turned into the embryonic form of Agni in the course of this ceremony and is finally born anew. Interestingly, when the

---

[251] See K.-H. Golzio, *Der Tempel im alten Mesopotamien und seine Parallelen in Indien: eine religionshistorische Studie*, Leiden: E.J. Brill, 1983, p.113.

purificatory rite is completed, the dīkshita is addressed as Brahman, even if he is not a brāhman. So too, in the climactic abhishekam of the rājasūya sacrifice, the king is addressed as "Brahman" by the four priests, which suggests that the sacrifice indeed imbues the sacrificer with the divine Light and Consciousness of Brahman.

***

We see therefore that the fire-rituals of the Brāhmans are essentially magical performances whereby the Brāhmanical "magi" restore the cosmos to its original splendour, and allow the sacrificer who employs them to achieve immortality through the strict observance of the scriptural regulations regarding the sacrifices. The spiritual focus in the Brāhmanical sacrifices on the fire of the macrocosm is complemented by the focus on the microcosm in the Brāhmanās and the Upanishads. The internalisation of Agni within the aspirant's body is also seen to be for the purpose of gaining the vital fluid, Soma, which guarantees immortality. In general, Brāhmanism seeks to control the macrocosm and microcosm through the power of the divine fire, unlike the Shramana religions which seek, through chastity and non-violence and right conduct, to escape from the phenomenal world.

III Tantra

Kali Yuga

The origins of Yoga and of Jainism and Brāhmanism are difficult to date since, as we have seen, they locate their founders in the very remote Treta and Dvāpara Yugas. The Hamitic[252] Tantric religions associated with temple-

---

[252] The Hamitic civilisations include those of Mesopotamia, Egypt

worship that followed them are relatively easier to date since they flourish around the beginning of the Kali Yuga, which is traditionally fixed at the historical date of.3102 B.C.[253] – even though early temple cults are attested already in the sixth millennium B.C., in Ubaid in southern Mesopotamia.[254]

The Indic literary references to the Vedic sage Agastya are of special significance in identifying the sources of the Hamitic spiritual tradition since he is traditionally considered to be the sage who conveyed Vedic wisdom to the Tamils. In the Tamil *Kallatam* (10th c. A.D.), Skanda/ Muruga, or Subrahmanya, is said to have bestowed the Vedic knowledge on Agastya who then transmitted this wisdom to "South India" having crossed the "Vindhya" mountain range. It is quite probable that the sage Agastya is actually a reference to Akkad,[255] and the transmission of Vedic wisdom to "South India" a modern rendering of the traditional memory of a migration of proto-Akkadians from northern Mesopotamia to the Uruk region of southern Mesopotamia. The reference to the "Vindhya" mountain range suggests that this immigration proceeded from a region north-east of Kish, since there are no high mountains south of Kish. Agastya's spiritual instruction of the Tamils also permits a location of the proto-Tamils among the Sumerians of Uruk.

The Dravidians of the "South India" of the *Kallatam* may have been proto-Tamils as distinguished from the proto-Dravidian Manu. These proto-Tamils seem to have been contemporaneous with the rulers of Uruk. An

---

and the Indus Valley.

[253] This is the calculation of the early (ca. 6th c. A.D.) astronomical treatise, Sūrya Siddhānta.

[254] See H. Frankfort, *Archaeology and the Sumerian Problem*, Chicago: Chicago University Press, 1932, p.19.

[255] See A. Jacob, *Ātman*, Ch.I; *Brahman*, Ch.IV.

interesting episode in the Sanskrit poem of Kālidāsa (5th c. A.D.), *Raghuvamsha* (VI,59ff.), refers to Agastya's being the officiating priest of a Pāndya (Tamil) king who is the contemporary of Aja (the grandfather of the Ikshvāku king Rama), and the capital of the Pāndya king here is called not Madurai, as one would have expected if the scene were set in South India, but rather "Uraga",[256] which might indeed refer to the Sumerian Uruk itself. Aja may be represented in the Sumerian king-list as Aka,[257] of the first dynasty of Kish, which preceded the foundation of Uruk. The first rulers of Kish were thus proto-Akkadians from whom the Ikshvākus were derived. Ikshvāku itself seems to be identical to Akshak[258] in the Sumerian King-List.[259] One of the extant Sumerian histories related to "Gilgamesh and Agga" too refers to the initial supremacy of Kish and the north under the king Agga, son of Enmebaraggesi, who demands the submission of Gilgamesh in Uruk.[260] This means that the proto-Akkadian Kish and Kosala are identical and the Treta Yuga date of the story of Rāma, while a chronological exaggeration, an indication of the greater antiquity of this "avatār" to that of Krishna in the following Dvāpara Yuga.

---

[256] See G.S. Ghurye, *Indian Acculturation: Agasthya and Skandha*, Bombay: Popular Prakashan, 1977, p.31.

[257] The "centum" quality of Sumerian is also evident in the Sumerian word for "eye", "igi", which is closer to the Germanic "auge" than to the Sanskritic "akshi".

[258] Akshak was later called Upi (Gk. Opis) and may, like Kish, have been situated in the southern vicinity of modern Baghdad.

[259] See T. Jacobsen, *The Sumerian King-List*, Chicago: University of Chicago Press, 1939, p.107.

[260] See J.B. Pritchard, *ANET*, pp.44-7. In the Sumerian King-List, Aka is a king of the first dynasty (at Kish), though Gilgamesh follows apparently later in the second dynasty (at Uruk) after the fall of Kish (see T. Jacobsen, *op.cit.*, pp.85, 89-91).

Agastya is said to have learned the "difficult language" of the Tamils[261] from either Muruga or directly, from Muruga's father Shiva.[262] The reference in Kālidasa must be to a time when the Uruk Sumerians (speaking an agglutinative language) were still somewhat alien to the Akkadians (speaking an inflected language). The fact that Agastya is said to have crossed the "Vindhya" mountains in order to reach Uraga suggests that the Kish dynasties included peoples who arrived from farther north. These northern Mesopotamians and Elamites may have imparted their spiritual wisdom to the proto-Akkadians who then relayed it to the Sumerians of Uruk, whose political ascendancy seems to have been established first in the south.

The Hamitic religious tradition which came to the fore in the age of temple building is essentially that of Tantra. The term Tantra itself may mean 'essential constitution' or 'doctrine'. It may also be derived from the root "tan" which means "to extend", a concept that is also associated with the Vedic sacrifice.[263] Although the origins of Tantra are obscure it seems most probable that they did not arise among the Āryan Brāhmans.[264] We have seen that Jainism, unlike Buddhism, is averse to Tantric practices. The Āryans who maintained the essentially esoteric Vedic tradition of fire-worship were, likewise, originally opposed to the Hamitic religious tradition centred on temple worship—which they considered to be inappropriately exoteric—just as they were to the various Kundalini Yogic attempts to control the "chakras" in Tantra. The

---

[261] Modern Dravidian languages, like Sumerian, are agglutinative, in contradistinction to the inflected Āryan languages.

[262] See K. Zvelebil, *Tamil Traditions on Subrahmanya-Murugan*, Madras: Institute of Asian Studies, 1991, p.24.

[263] See, for instance, *Rgveda* X,130.

[264] See G. Flood, *ibid.*, pp.161-62.

Manusmriti (III,152), for example, records the aversion of the Āryan brāhmans to the temple priests who followed the Āgamic tradition of Hamitic origin: "Doctors, temple-priests, meat-sellers and such should be excluded from the sacrifices to the gods and manes". Besides, the description of all of Tantra as "liberality" in *Manusmriti*, I,86[265] is a clear indication of the contempt with which it was viewed by the Brāhmans. Heesterman has noted the relative lack of importance of the priestly office in ancient Greece and Iran too.[266] He attributes the rise of the priesthood to the development of the temple cults in the ancient Near East.

Tantra is less focussed on the macrocosm than Brāhmanical yajna and concentrates rather on the microcosm through several symbolistic rituals involving mandalas (yantras that represent larger universal and cosmic structures), yantras (symbolic geometric diagrams), mantras (mystical syllabic chants), nyāsas (invocation of the deity to enter the human body), mudras (symbolic gestures), pūja (worship), yātras (pilgrimages) and dīksha(initiation). Teun Goudriaan defines Tantric practices as a "systematic quest for salvation or spiritual excellence"[267] by realizing and fostering the divine within one's own body, one that is a simultaneous union of spirit-matter and the masculine-feminine and has the ultimate goal of realizing the "primal blissful state of non-duality". Unlike the Shramana doctrines, Tantra is not entirely world-abjuring but maintains that one can realise the divine even in one's corporeal condition.

---

[265] See p.94.

[266] J.C. Heesterman, *The Broken World of Sacrifice: An Essay on Ancient Indian Ritual*, Chicago: University of Chicago Press, 1993, p.184.

[267] T. Goudriaan, S. Gupta, *Hindu Tantric and Shākta Literature*, Wiesbaden: O. Harrassowitz, 1981, p.1.

The Āgamas

Tantra is based principally on Āgama ("inherited scriptures") rather than Vedic texts, though, as the name Āgama implies, it certainly draws on very ancient sources of sacred ritual.[268] The doctrines of the Āgamas are divided into four stages, starting with Charya (selfless conduct and service) and Kriya (esoteric worship and the construction of temples and sculptures) and proceeding to Yoga (spiritual concentration) and Jnāna (supreme knowledge). There is no focus on fire-worship in the Āgamas. The four aspects deal with, first, the rules relating to the observance of religious rites, second, rules for the construction of temples and for sculpting, third, yoga, and mental discipline, and, finally, philosophical knowledge. The lowest form of Āgamic practice, therefore, is that of temple worship and the highest the supreme knowledge of the Supreme Being. The fact that Yoga is included in the Tantra system suggests that it is a more comprehensive one than the Shramana traditions deriving from Sāmkhya-Yoga.

The Āgama texts are normally constituted of speeches made by Shiva to Pārvati, whereas the texts that contain speeches made by the latter to her consort are called Nigama. Yamala texts involve the worship of united deities. The Āgamas are written in Sanskrit using the South Indian Grantha script rather than the Devanāgari. The Āgama texts are divided into three types, Tantra (Sattvaguna – or based on the quality of Sattva), Yamala (Rajoguna – or based on the quality of Rajas) and Damara (Tamoguna – or based on the quality of Tamas). Although drawing

---

[268] According to Flood, the Tantric texts were composed in the 8th century A.D. (see G. Flood, *An Introduction to Hinduism*, p.159) but this may only be the approximate date of the compilation of Tantric doctrines that had an earlier origin.

on the Vedic tradition, Āgama claims to supersede it. As Flood points out,

> The mainstream tantric texts of the Pancharatra and Shaiva Siddhanta maintain a close proximity to the vedic tradition and prescribe a whole way of life that incorporates vedic rites of passage [samksaras] ... along with the supererogatory tantric rites of their tradition.[269]

Āgama considers the universe as a whole whose every single part bears an influence on the others. Thus a system of sympathetic magic was developed out of it in which the final aim of the spiritual adept (sādhaka) is to transform, within his consciousness, his own person as well as cult-objects and rites into that which these phenomena essentially are. Every god is indeed represented by a 'bija' or seminal mantra which embodies the essence of the god. Thus the syllable 'ram' betokens Agni, 'dam' Vishnu, 'horum' Shiva, etc. And the ultimate aim of Tantra, called 'Siddhi' or spiritual perfection, is a practical realisation of the Upanishadic equation of the individual ātman with Brahman ("tat tvam asi"/that art thou).

Men, in general, are classified according to the predominance of the tāmasic, rājasic, or sāttvic elements (terms derived from Sāmkhya) in them, as pashu (animal), vira (heroic) or divya (divine), this classification roughly corresponding to the vaisya, kshatriya, and brāhmanical castes among the Vedic Āryas, though, as we have seen, the Jains trace the caste system to another source than the Vedas. There are only two life-stages (āshramas) recognised by the Āgamic tradition, those of householders and ascetics, for both brāhmans and non-brāhmans,

---

[269] See G. Flood, *The Tantric Body: The Secret Tradition of Hindu Religion,* London: I.B. Tauris, 2006, p.38.

"though the particular practices of the Vipras [brāhmans] and other castes vary" (*Mahānārāyana Tantra*, Ch.8).

In spite of the relatively exoteric aspect of Tantra, the aims of both Brāhmanism and Tantra are not dissimilar, only the means differ considerably. While the Brāhmanical rituals aim at reviving the cosmos through the agency of the divine fire and the construction of elaborate fire-altars, Tantra expands the celebration of the spiritual cosmos from mere fire altars to large temple structures. The Vedic sacrifices do not involve idolatry and the only idol mentioned in the *SB* is the gold man that is placed within the fire-altar.[270] The idolatry employed in Tantra, however, is based on the divinisation of the king as sun-god that is the aim also of the Brāhmanical royal consecration, Rājasuya Yagna.[271] This divinisation resulted in the numerous representations of the king as a god in the Hamitic cultures, and this regal apotheosis is also closely related to the worship of divine idols in the temples. Just as the major focus on Agni in the Vedic rituals is on its creative solar force and the need to preserve this force,[272] in temple worship the deity whose idol is adored is daily created and sustained.

It should be noted also that the Āgama texts on temple worship use Vedic mantras in their Tantric rituals. For instance, the *Bodhayana Shesha Sūtra* and the *Vishnu Pratishtha Kalpa* combine *Grihya Sūtra* rules with Tantric practices to outline the rites for the installation of Vishnu images, etc. The *Grihya Sūtras*, however, do not include the Prāna Prathistāpana ritual (infusing life into the idol) which is taken from Tantra, and the latter is combined, as

---

[270] See A. Jacob, *Brahman*, Ch.IX; cf. Ch.V.

[271] *Ibid.*

[272] For instance, the fire is aroused after its nightly rest in the Agnihotra ritual and put to sleep at the end of the evening (see, for instance A. Jacob, *Brahman*, p.189f).

in Egypt and Sumer, with the ceremony of "opening the eyes of the deity with a needle".

There are clear similarities between the structures of the Vedic fire-altars and those of the temples of the Hamitic traditions. The Gārhapatya fire is represented in the temple by the vedika platform. The cella where the icon is placed is called a garbhagriha (womb chamber), and we may remember that Agni, and the Vedic sacrificer himself, were considered as undergoing a rebirth in the course of the sacrifice. Also, the plinth of the temple is adorned with sculptures of men, horses, and other animals which beings correspond to those of the five heads buried in the foundation of the Vedic altar.[273] The axis on which the temple is built is identical to that of the sacrificial post, yupa, in the Vedic altar which SB III,vii,1,25 describes as rising from the underworld to the heavens. The stambha of the Vedic fire-altar may have later been transformed into the more graphic Shiva Linga of Hindu temples, for Shiva is also called Sthānu or pillar, the *axis mundi*.

The Āgama texts relating to temple worship clearly include Yoga methodology since they consider temple architecture as imitative of the human body and locate the six chakras within the temple structure. Following Yogic correspondences, the mūlādhāra chakra is identified with the platform for the sacrificial food offerings, the svādhishthāna with the flagpole, the manipūra with the vāhana or vehicle of the god, the anāhata with the mahāmandapa or assembly hall, the vishuddha with the antarala or corridor between the mandapa and the cella, the ajna with the cult image, and the brahmarandhra with the amalaka stone.[274]

---

[273] See S. Kramrisch, *The Hindu Temple*, Calcutta: University of Calcutta, 1946, I, 146-7.

[274] See K.-H. Golzio, *op.cit.*, p.127f.; cf. H. v. Stietencorn, *Ganga und Yamuna*, Wiesbaden, 1972, pp.92-4.

Temples are built on a mandala representing a supine Vāstu-Purusha oriented according to the course of the sun. The Vāstu-Purusha is a Purānic variation of the Vedic account of the formation of the Cosmic Man, or Purusha, which coincides with the emergence of the supreme Light and Consciousness of Brahman. The *Agni Purana* LXI, 19-27, for example, declares that the temple is the body of the Purusha, so that the door of the temple is the mouth of the Purusha and the image is his life. In the Vedic fire-altar, the kunda is considered its "mouth".[275] The centre of the mandala, the brahmasthāna, is the most sacred part of it since it denotes the navel of the Purusha whence the universe, or the Mt. Meru which serves as the universal axis, emerged. The spires of Hindu temples, as well as the pyramidal structures of Egypt, are representations of this phallic axis of the universe.

The garbhagriha, or womb-chamber where the idol of the deity is placed, is a square cella where the idol is, as it were, born. Only the priests are allowed into this chamber. There is an ambulatory around the inner chamber for the worshippers' circumambulation of the image of the deity. The steeple of the dome above the sanctuary is called shikhara (summit) and represents Mt.Meru, which represents the central mountain of the matrix of Earth atop which the sun arises.

The erotic sculptures adorning some of the temples of central India are linked to the importance of "kāma" (love) and "mithuna" (sexual union) in Shaktism as well as, earlier, in the Vedic yajna.[276] For Kāma is considered as the root of the universe and the universe is to be reabsorbed into its root through desire.[277] The temple also has a hall held on pillars for meditation, prayer or sacred

---

[275] See A. Jacob, *Brahman*, p.183.

[276] See p.133.

[277] See G. Flood, *op.cit.*, p.86.

dances. The temple tank is outside the temple and used for purificatory purposes.

Temple building was governed by the strictest rules of divine geometry. In the Shāstras and Āgamas, the physical form of the temple is identified with "the laws that govern the movements of heavenly bodies".[278] The plan of the temple is a square which is divided into 64 or 81 smaller squares, each representing a specific deity. These squares are related to yantras, which are specific geometric shapes representing the energies of the devatas, for each devata has his or her own yantra.

The divinisation of the king in ancient India in the rite of anointing during the Rājasūya rituals has already been noticed. In the Tantric tradition, the king's role as a warrior is allied to the shakti (power) of the Goddess which is bestowed upon the king during his consecration.[279] The divinisation of the king is closely related to the divinisation of idols in the temple worship which forms an important part of the Āgama tradition. Idol worship is, as we shall see in the discussion of the divine manifestation in the Pāncharātra system, of special Yogic significance since it allows the devotee to more easily apprehend the formless and quality-less divinity by detaching himself from his own form and quality in the process of admiring those of the idol. Thus, through his adoration of the idol, the devotee is gradually freed from his own ego.

***

Āgama is divided into Vaishnava (215 in all), Shaiva (28) and Shākta Āgama (77). The Shākta Āgama tradition is normally called Tantra, though Tantra is often used to

---

[278] See G. Michell, *The Hindu Temple: An Introduction to its Meaning and Forms*, Chicago: Univeriity of Chicago Press, 1988, p.73.

[279] *Ibid.*, p.78.

describe the Vaishnava and Shaiva traditions as well.

Vaishnava Āgamas

Vaishnava Āgamas are divided into Vaikhānasa and Pāncharātra Āgamas.

Vaikhānasas may have been the first group of professional temple-priests and are more Vedic in their affiliation. Indeed, they are also called Vaidikāgama and Shrutāgama.[280] The principal Vaikhānasa text is the *Vaikhānasa Sūtra* from the 4th c. A.D.

The Vaikhānasas, like the Āryan brāhmans, consider grihasthya as being the best stage of the Hindu's life and worship at home as more important than worship at the temple. Vaikhānasas are devotees of Vishnu and consider Vishnu in four principal forms as Achyuta (the immutable aspect), Satya (the static aspect of the deity), the Purusha (the principle of life), and Aniruddha (the irreducible aspect). The absolute form (nishkala) of Vishnu in the universe is contemplated by the worshipper through the Vishnu form in his own body, and then the worshipper transfers this spirit into the immovable idol. The large immovable image in the temple represents Vishnu's nishkala form and is ritually placed in the sanctuary and consecrated. The smaller moveable images in the temple represent the sakala forms that represent the manifest emanations of the divinity.

Pāncharātra is a later form of Vaishnava worship associated with Rāmānuja and his teacher Yāmuna (ca. 918-1038 A.D.), who wrote the *Āgamaprāmānya* in defence of the Pāncharātra tradition.[281] In the Pāncharātra,

---

[280] Shruti ("revealed") is the term used for the Vedas.

[281] For an interesting study of Pāncharātra Tantrism, see G. Flood, *The*

yajnas are less valued than idol-worship whereas, in the Vaikhānasa tradition, idol-worship is only a development of the yajnas. Also, among the Southern Indian Pāncharātra followers, more Tamil hymns are recited and more festivals are organised involving all sections of the community. Shūdras and ascetics are given an important role in the performance of rituals. Although Vaikhānasa is generally considered to be the first and principal Vaishnava Āgamic tradition, Abhinavagupta (ca.975-1025 A.D.),[282] however, maintained that the Pāncharātra is superior to the Vaikhanasa since it is meant for the spiritually advanced.

The Pāncharātra doctrine of divine manifestation: is of special importance in understanding the crucial correspondence between the macrocosm and the microcosm. According to the *Jayākhya Samhita* written before the 10th c. B.C. and based on Sāmkhya philosophical categories, the Absolute Being (Brahman) is equated with the personal being of Vāsudeva (Vishnu). From Vāsudeva emanate lower forms as vyūhas. The description of the transformations of the ultimate reality in this work is worth noticing for its spiritual insight into the Purusha cosmology of the Vedas and Purānas:

> Having a hundred-fold radiance of fire, sun, and moon, Vāsudeva is the Lord, the truth of that [absolute], the supreme Lord. Agitating his own radiance through his own energy (tejas), the Lord whose form is light manifests the god Achyuta, like lightning ... [Then] that Achyuta of firm radiance spreads his won form, depending on Vāsu as a wisp of cloud [depends] on the summer heat. Then shaking himself he [in turn] produced the god Satya, whose body is shining, as the

---

Tantric Body, p.99ff.

[282] See p.127.

ocean [produces] a bubble. He is called the light mode of consciousness who produces himself by means of himself [as the god] called Purusha, who is great, an unending stream of light. That supreme Lord is [in turn] the support of all the [lower] gods, their inner controller,[283] as the sky [is the support] of the stars.[284]

We see that the Pāncharātra employs the same hypostases of Aniruddha, Achyuta, Satya and Purusha that the Vaikhānasas also do. And we note also the very elaborate understanding of the Purusha cosmology that the Āgamic traditions display.

After the initial ideal creation comes a lower material phase characterised by Māyā Shakti along with the cosmic body of Purusha. During this phase emerge the individual souls "contaminated by the dust of beginningless karmic traces ... and to which they return during the periodic destruction or reabsorption of the lower creation".[285] From Māyā then emanates Prakrti, the material creation which emanates from the Mahat (the Great). From the Mahat, in turn, is generated the Ahamkāra (the Ego) and thence the mind (for dealing with worldly transactions), the five senses, the five organs of action, the five subtle elements and the five material elements (space, air, fire, water, and earth). The individual soul is wrapped in these Shakti emanations and entrapped in them. Liberation consists of the extraction of the soul from its Shakti envelope.

The Pāncharātra, much like the Vaikhānasa, maintains that the deity manifests himself in a five-fold manner, as Para, Vyuha, Vibhava (or Avatāra), Antaryāmin (or Aniruddha), and Archa. The first four detail the process of divine emanation from macrocosm into microcosm. The

---

[283] Antaryāmin (see below).
[284] Quoted in G. Flood, *op. cit.*, p.102.
[285] *Ibid.*

last two are the manifestations of the lord within humans and in idols.

Para is the first immanent manifestation of the Lord. This is the "best of the Purushas", "the highest Light". The *Padma Tantra* describes the Lord as dividing himself and becoming with one half the Vyuha Vasudeva and with the other Nārayana, creator of the primal waters.

Vyuha is the process of emanation itself marked by the appearance of six guna's in Nārāyana and his consort Lakshmi.

Avatāra (descent) is the next manifestation of the Lord, also called Vibhava (human manifestation). All the avatāras spring from Aniruddha, or some from Vāsudeva and the others from the other three vyuhas. The supreme Being, however, remains transcendent and indifferent to the manifestation.

Antaryāmin is Aniruddha as the inner ruler of all souls seated in the lotus of the heart.

Archa is an inanimate object which is duly consecrated and possessed of miraculous power when the shakti of Vishnu descends into it. It is used as an object of daily worship since the devotee feels the very presence of God in it. The non-initiated devotee in the Pāncharātra tradition adores the Vibhava form of the Lord, the incarnation of the deity, as Rāma, etc., in the temple and then moves on to the worship of His more subtle Vyuha forms.

The rituals detailed in the *Jayākhya Samhita* are interesting for the yogic complexity they point to in the divine worship that is to be undertaken by an adept.[286] The rituals consist of 1. purificatory ablutions (snāna), 2. purification of the elements within the body (bhūtashuddhi), 3. divinisation of the body through

---

[286] This account of the rites prescribed in the *Jayakha Samhita* is derived from G. Flood, *op.cit.*, p.106ff.

imposing mantras upon it (nyāsa), 4. internal worship of the deity (antara-yoga) performed in the mind, 5. external worship of the deity (bahya-yoga) with offerings. The aim of the rituals is to allow the adept to purify the physical or elemental body (bhautika sharira) and induce the soul to ascend from the heart through the body (and simultaneously through the cosmos) to the Lord Nārāyana located at the crown of the head. .

During these rituals the adept performs the divinisation of his own body through imposing mantras upon it, followed by mental sacrifice (mānasayāga) and external sacrifice (bāhyayāga). The divinisation of the adept's body is undertaken through the imposition of mantras upon it by touching the various parts of the body while reciting the appropriate mantras.[287] When the adept is thus fully divinised he is identified with Nārāyana and his ego is transformed into the absolute subjectivity of Vishnu. He can say at the end of this process, "I am the Lord Vishnu, I am Nārāyana, Hari, and I am Vāsudeva, all-pervading, the abode of beings, without taint".

In the internal worship that follows, the adept seeks to establish the supreme Lord within his heart, which is envisaged as a throne. The adept visualises the hierarchical cosmos in the forms of the deities located within his own body. First, he situates the power of Earth on his penis, above that the fire of Time, then the Tortoise incarnation of the Lord bearing the insignia of Vishnu, the discus, and the club. Above that are situated the cosmic snake, Ananta, and, above Ananta, Prithvi, the Earth-goddess. Above her, at the navel, is located an ocean of milk from which arises a white lotus. On this lotus are situated the sun, moon, and fire. Above these is the throne of being

---

[287] As Gonda points out (*Die Religionen Indiens II: Der jüngere Hinduismus*, Stuttgart: Kohlhammer, 1963, p.47), there are Vedic precedents for these tactile rites (for example, in *SB* III,1,3,25); cf.

upon which rests Garuda, the solar vehicle of Vishnu, and the boar Varāha. The area from the navel to the heart is divided into five sections and the adept finally worships the mantra-throne in the heart. We note the similarity that this ritual of divinisation bears to the identification of the various parts of the fire-altar with those of the Purusha in the Vedic Agnicayana ritual.[288]

Shaiva Āgamas

The Shaivāgama consists of four different schools, the Shaiva, Pashupata, Soma, and Lakula. Of these, the Shaiva is said to have had three branches: Vāma, Dakshina and Siddhānta. The Vāma branch includes Kapala, Kālamukha, and Agora.

The Dakshina branch includes Kashmir Shaivadarshanas, Svachanda Bhairavam, etc., making up a total of 18 Āgamas. Of the Dakshina branch, Kashmir Shaivism is mostly monistic in its metaphysics and its principal exponent is Abhinavagupta (10th century A.D.), author of the *Tantraloka*. Other texts include the *Shiva Sutras* of Vāsugupta (ca. 875-925) and Jayaratha's 12th century commentary on the *Tantraloka*.

Kashmir Shaivism considers Shiva as the only Reality and infinite Consciousness. By his own will and energy (Shakti) he appears as the phenomenal universe. Shakti has five qualities, chit, ānanda, ichcha, jnāna, and kriya. To this is added māyā, or the agent of phenomenal manifestation, which in turn gives rise to five kanchukas – kala (power), vidya (knowledge), rāga (attachment), kāla (time) and niyati (space). One of the major doctrines developed by Vāsugupta is that of spanda, or

---

[288] See A. Jacob, *Brahman*, Ch.IX; cf. Ch.V.

vibration, which is manifest as a sound within the divine consciousness, rather like the Vedic Vāk.[289] The individual soul is essentially the pure consciousness of Shiva and must strive towards recognition of its real divine self, as in Shankara's Advaita Vedantic philosophy. One key feature of this school is 'krama' meaning progress wherein the stages prior to spiritual realisation are understood in a monistic-dualistic (bhedābhedopāya) manner, though the underlying metaphysical doctrine remains monistic.

The Shaiva Siddhānta branch[290] was most probably a Kashmiri school in its original form, for Satyajyothi Shivāchārya (ca. 7th century) is a well-known Siddhānta scholar from Kashmir who is extensively quoted in the pre-Meykandar Shaiva texts. The Siddhānta doctrines of the Kashmiris were continued in southern India by Aghorashiva of Chidambaram (12th century), who is considered one of the most authoritative representatives of southern Indian Siddhānta. Indeed, from the 12th century, the school is evidenced only in southern India. In the 13th century, Meykandar, who is famous for his treatise *Sivajnānbodham*, formulated a dualistic form of Siddhānta based on Aghorashiva's.

The Siddhānta Āgamic texts, which number 28, are said to have been authored by the Seven Sages themselves who received them from the five "faces" of Shiva. According to another tradition, Shiva revealed the Āgamas to Pārvati and Nandi, the bull that serves as Shiva's vehicle and assistant. Parvati revealed it to her son Lord Muruga, while Nandi, for his part, revealed it to his eight disciples, Tirumalar, Patanjali, Vyaghrapada, Sanatkumar, Sivayogamuni, Sanakar, Sanadanar, and Sanandanar, all of whom are given Tamil names, though these may be Tamil

---

[289] See p.130.

[290] For an excellent study of Shaiva Siddhānta see G. Flood, *op.cit.*, p.120ff.

forms of Sanskrit ones. We note here also the inclusion of Patanjali, the Yogic scholar. Tirumular, who propounded a monistic Shaivite doctrine that is redacted in his yogic compendium, *Tirumantiram*, is considered by some to have lived in the third millennium B.C., even though the actual redaction of this work may have been made only as late as the 8th century A.D.

For the followers of Shaiva Siddhānta, as for the Vaishnavas, worship of Shiva is graded through charya, external worship such as cleaning the temple, offering flowers, etc., kriya, which is internal worship related to the actual rituals, yoga, seeking identity with Shiva and jnāna, or wisdom in which the devotee and Shiva are one. The Shaivāgama texts on pūja, such as the 17th century *Pūjaprakāsha* of Mitramishra, make clear that the devotee must purify himself internally so that he becomes similar to the deity he is about to worship since "only Śiva may worship Śiva".[291]

Shiva is understood in Shaiva Siddhānta as the totality of all, consisting of three perfections: Parameshvara (the Personal Creator Lord), Parashakti (the substratum of form) and Parashiva (Absolute Reality which transcends all). Souls and world are identical in essence with Shiva, yet also differ in that they are evolving. A pluralistic stream arose in the middle ages from the teachings of Aghorasiva and Meykandar. For Aghorasiva's school (ca 1150), Shiva is not the material cause of the universe, and the soul attains perfect "sameness" with Shiva upon liberation. Meykandar's (ca 1250) pluralistic school denies that souls ever attain perfect sameness or unity with Shiva. Thus some followers of the Shaiva Siddhānta system maintain a distinction between the self, the Lord and the universe. The Lord is considered as the Pati, or Lord of

---

[291] See A. Michaels, *Hinduism Past and Present*, NJ: Princeton University Press, 2004, p.243.

animals, the soul as Pashu, or an animal, and the bonds of the universe are called pāsha. The bond is constituted of five components – egoism (anava), action (karma), illusion (māyā), the illusory universe, and the power of concealing reality.

The unfolding universe is made up of 36 tattvas (the constituents of matter and of the incarnate soul) which allow the soul to experience the results of their actions. Through ritual reabsorption of the tattvas, the soul may be liberated. The first ideal manifestation of the Shiva-tattva is called Bindu, the next Māyā, which produces the mixed creation and the last is Prakrti tattva which produces the lower categories of Nature described in the Sāmkhya.

Siddhānta recognises three types of souls, sakalas are those that have become free from all the three pashas, vijnanakalas are those that have freed themselves from māyā and karma, and pralayakalas are those that would become free from māyā only when Shiva withdraws his entire māyā-shakti finally into himself as a part of the dissolution of the worlds. Indeed, the soul's bond within the universe can be broken only by the grace (prasāda) of Shiva whereby the soul is able to become like the Lord, though ever remaining distinct from Him, for Shiva alone is always free (anādimukta).

The initiation rites of the Shaiva Siddhānta system interestingly include a ritual called vishesa-dīkshā whereby the guru transports the soul of the disciple into the womb of the goddess Vāk, consort of Shiva, who has been installed in the fire. The disciple is then reborn from her, exactly as the Vedic sacrificer is reborn during the fire-rituals studied above. Vāk here is Aditi, consort of Varuna/Vishnu in the underworld and gives birth to Agni, the underworld form of the sun which later emerges in our universe as Āditya.[292] So the process of rebirth in the Shaiva Siddhānta is essentially identical to that of the sun.

In the next ritual, nirvāna-dīksha, the master installs in the body of the disciple the totality of the subtle elements of the cosmos. He then envisages himself as entering the central channel of the disciple's body through the aperture at the crown of the head and going down to the chakra at the heart. Next, the master leaves the disciple's body by the same route taking his disciple's soul as well as the subtle constituents of the universe with him. He brings the soul and the universal elements into his own heart through the aperture at the crown of his own head, and finally emits them from there establishing the disciple's soul and the subtle cosmos on a cord that symbolizes the spinal cord of the disciple. These are purified by the master on the cord and then replaced in the disciple's body as in a new birth.

These major rituals are then followed by daily (nitya karman) rites which burn up the remaining karma in the disciple so that, at death, he may achieve final liberation.

Shākta Āgamas

Shākta Āgamas, which are popular in Bengal, and are generally called Tantras, consider Shiva's consort, Shakti, as the supreme deity. Shakti is the divine energy of Becoming while Shiva is the divine Being. Shakti is therefore regarded as the real power of all creation, maintenance, and destruction. It is maintained that from the divine Shakti emerges first a Bindu, or mystic drop which calls to life the diverse components of the universe. Shakti creates through her power of Māyā the multiplicity of the phenomenal world. The mystic seed-syllables used

---

[292] See p.259.

in Tantrism are considered as forms of Shakti and are called "mātrkā's" in yantras.

Shākta Tantra divides spiritual development into seven stages. The first four stages are constituted of the lowest stage, that of Vedic sacrifices, followed by the Bhakti stage practiced by the Vaishnavites, and the highest stage of the Jnānamārga (the path of knowledge) followed by Shaivites. The fourth stage is called Dakshināchāra (the right-sided, or male) which leads the sādhaka into the nature of the Devi and makes him a shākta. These first four stages are together called "pravrtti", an emergence from the eternal maternal womb. As in the Vedic sacrifices, the adept has to undergo a "dīksha" and obey his guru to the last moment of salvation. Indeed the dīksha consists of the transference of the vital force of the guru into the adept.

The following three stages are termed 'nivrtti'. During these, the sādhaka seeks to neutralise his newly acquired powers in such a way that he realises a universal life. The fifth stage is called Vāmachāra (the left-handed, or female) and aims at the self-destruction of the powers of pravrtti. Vāmachāra tantras are considered to be non-Vedic since they include ritual practices involving meat-eating and sexual union. The sixth stage is called Siddhāntachāra which aims at freeing one from darkness and all the bands in order to establish the universe in macrocosm and microcosm. The seventh stage is called Kaulāchāra, where the adept prepares his own funeral rites. At this stage the adept has gone beyond time and space, having acquired gnosis, Brahmagnāna, and the great mother, Shakti, dwells in his heart.

Since stress is laid on the shakti (energy) of the divinity and this shakti is characterised as female, personified as the consort of Shiva, women are in this tradition given a much more important role as images of the great goddess, and they serve as teachers as well. Also, unlike in the Vedic society, widows are allowed to remarry and the practice of sati is forbidden.[293] Generally, unlike in the Vedic system, there is much less focus on asceticism in Shākta Tantra, which rather emphasises the female principle.

The Smārta[294] literature, particularly the Dharmashāstras, had given more emphasis to brahmachārya, while sexual union was permitted only to the grihastha and that only for reproduction. The Shākta Tantric tradition, on the other hand, stresses kāma in such a way that bhoga (pleasure) becomes identified with yoga and bhukti (pleasure) with mukti (salvation).[295] In the secret nocturnal rite called Shrichakra indiscriminate coitus takes place to recreate the marriage of Shiva and Shakti. The Panchatattva rites involve the use of mada (alcohol), matsya (fish), mamsa (meat), mudrā (grains) and maithuna (coitus). But these rites are not entirely unbridled orgies but rather aim to control the instincts so that carnal activities are given a cosmic, divine dimension. This has precedents in Vedic religious doctrine as well, as, for instance, in *BAU* VI,4.

Ch.29 of Abhinavagupta's *Tantraloka* details the 'kula prakriya' rite which involves the unorthodox consumption of meat, alcohol, fish and the performance of ritual sex.[296] However, as Flood points out, the *BAU* (IV,3,21) too describes the realisation of the self as the Absolute in sexual terms, while the *Chāndogya Upanishad* (II,13,1-2) identifies Vedic recitation itself with the sexual act. As Brajalal Mukherji also explained,[297]

---

[293] See *Mahānirvāna Tantra* 1,79-80.

[294] i.e. derived from Smriti (see p.94n)

[295] See G. Flood, *op.cit.*, p.82.

[296] *Ibid.*, p.154ff.

[297] In 'Arthur Avalon' (Sir John Woodroffe), *Shakti and Shākta: Essays and Addresses on the Shâkta Tantrashâstra,* London: Luzac and Co.

All Vedic yajnas are based on the idea that Maithunikarana (coitus) leads to spiritual happiness. Sexual intercourse is Agnihotra (*SB* XI, 6,2,10). Maithunakarana is consecration (*SB* III, 2,1,2, etc.) ... [Yajnas] direct the observance and performance of Maithuna as a religious rite or part of a religious rite ... and they direct that Mantras are to be uttered during the observance of this rite ... One of the articles of faith of the Vaidik people, therefore, was that sexual union led the way to bliss hereafter and must be performed in a true religious spirit to ensure spiritual welfare, wanton indulgence being severely deprecated ...

Those who have studied Vedic sacrificial rituals will also remember the dramatic performance of copulation between the king's wife and the dead horse in the Ashvamedha sacrifice and may reasonably suppose this to have been a part of the original Purushamedha as well. However, it is important to observe here that, in the Vedic sacrifice, the stress is always on the phallus and its power to create the sun as well as our ordered universe, whereas in the Shākta Āgama the female aspect of coition is given special stress.

According to Mukherji, many of the other aspects of Tantra are also derived from the Vedas themselves:

The Vaidik people performed their Somayajnas and Haviryajnas which included the Sautramani, with libations and drinks of intoxicating liquor ... The Vaidik people used to offer to their Devatas at their sacrifices animal and vegetable food ... They offer animal sacrifices ... which include the horse, goats, sheep, oxen ... and human beings (*TB* III,4,1). They believe that by performing animal sacrifices the

---

1918, 'Note to Ch.IV'.

sacrificer ransoms himself ... or wins all these worlds ... The animal is the sacrificer himself (*AB* II, 2,1).

Mukherji pointed out further similarities between the divinisation rituals of the Āgamic tradition and some of the Vedic rituals:[298]

> The worship in both Vaidik and Tantrik rites begins with Acamana, which is a form of ablution in which certain parts of the body are touched with water .... They purify themselves by uttering some Mantras as Bijas while contemplating the Deities of certain parts of their bodies and touching such parts with their fingers ... They make use of certain sounds for removing unclean spirits, e.g., Khat, Phat, Hum ... They attribute a Deity to each letter in a Mantra ... They make gestures with their fingers as part of their religious rites ... and locate the Devatas of particular sounds in particular parts of their bodies ...

Indeed, Āgamic practice also includes sacrifices which are called yāga, rather than yajna, and are mostly impersonal, in the spirit of the bhakti cult of the *Gita*. Further, Biardeau has pointed out, "le 'sacrifiant' du culte agamique—qui est toujours, par la force des choses, un notable, au moins local—se rapproche ainsi beaucoup plus au roi que du maître de maison ordinaire".[299] This suggests that the Tantric sacrifices retain the public significance of the early sacred rituals of the Indo-Europeans rather more than the rituals of the later Vedic Āryans, which tended to be more domestic, and exclusive, affairs.

---

[298] *Ibid.*

[299] See M. Biardeau, *Le sacrifice dans l'inde ancienne*, Paris: Presses universitaires de France, 1976, p.139.

Shākta Tantra places a special emphasis on Kundalini Yoga since Kundalini represents Shakti while the Purusha is located in the Sahasrāra lotus in the crown of the head. In Shākta Tantra, as in the Vaishnava Pāncharātra, the deities are identified within the adept's body. However, in the Shākta system, within the calyx of the heart (lotus) are visualised Shiva and his consort locked in sexual union, which indicates the non-differentiation of consciousness and the phenomenal world.[300] The ritualised sexual acts performed in Shākta Tantric rituals reflect this union of Shakti and Shākta. As Flood points out, in the ecstasy of this union, the body of the adept becomes filled with an awareness of its equivalence to the cosmos and its identity to Shiva, the supreme subject of consciousness, which is "inseparable from his energy and containing within it the totality of manifestation". Here again we note that the enlightenment offered by Shākta Āgama is described in terms of the union of male and female principles, or in the terminology of the Sāmkhya philosophy, of Purusha and Prakrti, whereas, in the other Āgamas, the Vedic image of the Purusha is located by itself in the heart and the highest Bliss is the Light of Brahman to be attained at the crown of the head.

The highest stage of the entire Āgamic system is Jnāna, or perfect knowledge of divinity. This is the philosophical stage of the more practical disciplines of Yoga and the jnāna sections of the Āgamic texts contain various discussions of cosmogony and the individual self. Similar to the precepts of the Vedānta (i.e., of the Upanishads), the jnāna doctrine of the Āgamic schools is one which aims at achieving identity with Shiva. According to the *Tirumantiram,* of Tirumalar, in charya, the soul forges a kindred tie in "God's world" (salokya), in kriya it attains

---

[300] Shiva is envisioned within the heart as united with his consort Uma also in the *Kaivalya Upanishad*.

"nearness" (samipya) to Him, in yoga it attains "likeness" (sarupya) with Him and finally, in jnāna, the soul enjoys the ultimate bliss of identity (sayujya) with Shiva.[301] The Siddhi who has become one with the deity sheds blessings on mankind even while remaining in his body.

***

We see therefore that the Brāhmanical fire-rituals and the Tantric psychosomatic ones are related to each other through the same cosmological insights that gave rise to the earliest Indo-European spirituality. The adoration of the Purusha form of the supreme Godhead in the fire-worship of the Āryans is transformed into worship of divinised idols in the Tantric tradition that culminates in the divinisation of religious adepts themselves. The religious traditions of Brāhmanism and Tantra are indeed contiguous in several aspects and, though Tantra is more exoteric than Brāhmanism, it is at the same time more elaborate in its worship of the divinity as Purusha. On the other hand, the Shramana tradition deriving from Sāmkhya-Yoga sees no value in performing rituals in its effort to abjure the world altogether. Consequently, neither the severe world-abjuration of Jainism nor the less ascetic and more ethical heterodoxy of Buddhism exhibits the *prisca theologia* in its full cosmological complexity as the Brāhmanical and Tantric traditions do. And of the latter two traditions, it is clear also that it was the Hamitic Āgamic tradition—with its elaborate temple structures, idolatry, and sacred music- and dance forms—that crystallised the later 'Hindu' culture of India just as, in the West (through Anatolia and Egypt), it informed the powerful 'Humanism' of Graeco-Roman civilisation.

---

[301] See the summary of Jnāna Yoga in the 'Bhagavad Gita' quoted above.

IV. VEDIC AND TANTRIC RITUALS
A Comparison

WE HAVE SEEN in our survey of the earliest religious forms of the ancient Indo-European wisdom that, among the Krita Yuga avatārs of Vishnu listed in the *Bhāgavata Purāna* I,3,[302] Kapila (the name of the historical founder of Sāmkhya Yoga) precedes Yajna (representing Vedic sacrifice), who in turn precedes Rishabha (the name of the historical founder of Jainism). The avatārs of the Krita Yuga are of course cosmic phenomena rather than earthly, but the sequence of these names suggests that Sāmkhya-Yoga may indeed have preceded Vedic Brāhmanism, which in turn preceded Jainism. While the origins of Yoga and of Jainism and Brāhmanism are difficult to date since they locate their founders in the very remote Treta and Dvāpara Yugas, the Tantric religions associated with the temple-worship of the Hamitic[303] cultures that followed them are relatively easier to place since they flourish around the beginning of the Kali Yuga, which is traditionally fixed at the historical date of.3102 B.C.[304] – even though early

---

[302] See p.70n.

[303] The Hamitic civilisations would include those of Mesopotamia, Egypt and Dravidian India.

[304] This is the calculation of the early (ca. 6th c. A.D.) astronomical

temple cults are attested already in the sixth millennium B.C., in Ubaid in southern Mesopotamia.[305]

As regards Buddhism, which is the last of the ascetic, as opposed to sacrificing, sects, it must be noted that it too incorporated various Tantric rituals from the 7th century A.D. onwards especially in its Vajrayāna branch, which, unlike the Mahāyāna and Hīnayāna schools, emphasises the importance of ritual rather than mere meditation. Scholars such as A. Sanderson and S. Hatley have suggested that Tantric practices may have penetrated Buddhism already in the 5th century from Shaivaite sources.[306] The *Manjushri Mūlakalpa* text attributed to the Boddhisattva Manjushri of the Mahāyāna tradition, and dating from the 6th century A.D., is, for example, based on Shaiva as well as Vaishnava Tantric texts.

Jainism too adopted Tantric practices to a certain extent but mostly focused on the use of mantras and yantras rather than visualisation or meditation.[307] Jain Tantra, unlike Buddhist, does not aim at liberation but rather at achieving worldly gains such as health, wealth, and power. Nevertheless, it must be noted that the canonical scriptures of the Jains are called—exactly as in the Tantra tradition—Āgamas (inherited scriptures), and traced back by the Jains to the first tirthankara, Rishabha, though they were compiled by a certain Gautamaswami

---

treatise, *Sūrya Siddhānta*.

[305] See H. Frankfort, *Archaeology and the Sumerian Problem*, Chicago: Chicago University Press, 1932, p.19.

[306] See, for instance, S. Hatley, "Converting the Dākini: Goddess Cults and Tantras of the Yoginis between Buddhism and Saivism" in *Tantric Traditions in Transmission and Translation*, (ed.) D.B. Gray and R.R. Overbey, N.Y., NY: Oxford University Press, 2016, Ch.2.

[307] See John E. Cort, 'Worship of Bell-Ears the Great Hero, a Jain Tantric Deity', in D.G. White (ed.), *Tantra in Practice*, Princeton: Princeton University Press, 2000, p.417.

around the 6th or 4th century B.C. in Prākrit, rather than Sanskrit These Āgamas are said to be based on the discourses of the first tirthankara of the present era, Rishabha.

In all of the most ancient religions of the Āryan as well as of the Hamitic peoples of Mesopotamia and Egypt the understanding of the relation between the macrocosm and the microcosm may be traced back to a Yogic source. For instance, the Tantric Yogic notion of the Kundalini serpent and the awakening of this serpentine form to the light of Brahman lies at the basis of the Egyptian drama of Osiris in the underworld, as well as of the concept of the universal Tree of Life which features in the cosmologies of all the ancient Indo-European cultures. All of the ancient Indo-European religions are, furthermore, based on a vision of the Godhead as a Supreme Soul (Ātman) that manifests itself first as an Ideal and then as a Cosmic Man, or Purusha. This Purusha is castrated by his son (Chronos/Shiva/Time), though his seminal force is restored in our universe as the sun by a son of Chronos (Zeus/Dionysus/Muruga).[308] This Purusha, as we shall see, is the same as the Self of the human microcosm as well.

While the Purusha cosmology informs all the early religious forms of the Indo-Europeans, Brāhmanism, Zoroastrianism, and Tantra employ this mythology in their various rituals mostly in order to recover the divine dimensions of both the macrocosm and the microcosm. Sāmkhya-Yoga and the ascetic Shramana traditions following it, on the other hand, use it mostly as a theoretical background for ethical systems that seek to escape from cosmic manifestation and earthly incarnation

---

[308] For a full discussion of this cosmology see A. Jacob, *Ātman: A Reconstruction of the Solar Cosmology of the Indo-Europeans*, Hildesheim: G. Olms, 2005, and A. Jacob, *Brahman: A Study of the Solar Rituals of the Indo-Europeans*, Hildesheim: G. Olms, 2012.

altogether. In this focus on the escape from the cycle of birth, death and rebirth they take special care to stress the importance of the precept of non-dualism which was particularly crystallised in the Advaita Vedanta [Non-Dualistic Upanishadic] school of Indian philosophy associated with the sage Shankara (8th c. A.D.).

The aim of all enlightenment, whether it be through the fire-worship of the Āryans or the forms of worship evident in Tantra, is, however, the ultimate identification of the individual soul, ātman, with Brahman. The term "yoga" itself means "yoking" and may signify the union of the individual soul to the supreme which is brought about through several strict physiological and mental austerities. However, the means of achieving this end apparently varied with the changes in the ages, or yugas, that constitute our present epoch, kalpa. According to *Manusmriti*, I,86, the chief means of enlightenment in the first of the four ages was austerities:

> In the Krita age the chief [virtue] is declared to be [performance of] austerities [tapas], in the Treta [divine] knowledge [jnānam], in the Dvapara [the performance of]sacrifices [yajnam], in the Kali liberality [dānam] alone.

We see that the Brāhmanical sacrifices are not, like yogic 'tapas' and 'jnāna', associated with the Krita Yuga or the Treta Yuga but only with the Dvāpara Yuga. It may be mentioned here that later Āgamic texts like the *Tārapradīpa*, Ch.1, state, contrary to the *Manusmriti*, that in the Satya (Krita) age Vaidika Upāsana [Vedic meditation] prevailed. In the Treta age, worship followed the Smriti prevailed. while in the Dvāpara there were both Smriti and Purāna. Finally, in the Kaliyuga the Tantrika rather than the Vaidika Dharma has come to predominate. The Tantra Shastra was taught at the end of Dvāpara age and the beginning of Kaliyuga. However, we may assume that the meditation associated with the Krita age was indeed yogic meditation since we find the primacy of yogic worship over sacrificial maintained also in the *Rigveda* and the epics themselves. *RV* I,84,2, for instance, declares – regarding the forms of worship of the sages and the sacrifices offered by householders – that Indra attended 'eulogies' sung by Rishis and 'yajnas' conducted by humans. So it is apparent that Vedic sacrifices were necessary only for humans. In the *MBh*, VII (Anushāsana Parva), 16, too, Tandi, a sage of the Krita Yuga, is said to have "adored Shiva for 10,000 years with the aid of yogic meditation.

The "divine knowledge" (jnāna) mentioned in the *Manusmriti* as having prevailed in the following Treta Yuga may have been derived from the ascetic disciplines practised in the Krita Yuga. In the Treta Yuga, Manu himself is described in the *MP* as practising tapas, or austerities, on "Mt. Malaya", but also as sacrificing (*BP* VIII,24). Manu, the survivor of the "flood" and the counterpart of Noah is also called Satyavrata, King of Drāvida. In the Biblical account of the 'deluge', Noah is the counterpart of Manu and said to be a descendant of Adam's son, Seth. That Noah represents the wisdom of Seth is evident from the Gnostic tradition.[309] Seth himself is described by Josephus as one who

> strove after virtue and, being himself excellent, left descendants who imitated the same virtues. All of these, being virtuous, lived in happiness in the same

---

[309] See G.G. Stroumsa, *Another Seed: Studies in Gnostic Mythology*, Leiden: E.J. Brill, 1984, p.107. Josephus' *Jewish Antiquities*, I, 70-71 also makes clear the association of the line of Seth with cosmological learning.

land without civil strife, with nothing unpleasant coming upon them until after their death. And they discovered the science with regard to the heavenly bodies and their orderly arrangement.[310]

Josephus identifies the land of Seth as located around "Seiris", which is also the land of Noah. In the Christian *Opus Imperfectum in Matthaeum* of Pseudo-Chrysostom, the books of Seth were supposed to have been hidden by Noah in the land of Šir, and the so-called "cave of treasures" in which they were hidden is identifiable with Mt. Ararat.[311] In *Genesis* 14:6, the Horites, or Hurrians, are particularly identified with Mt. Seir, and we note a close identification of the proto-Hurrians with the proto-Dravidians of *BP*, according to which Manu is King of Drāvida. The brāhmans who are considered to be the "sons of Seth" must have originally constituted the priesthood of the proto-Hurrian/proto-Dravidian population, though it is true that the Āryan (Indo-Iranian), and particularly Indo-Āryan, line deriving from this original population, as well as the later Dravidians of India, seem to have retained the Brāhmanical tradition best of all.

We have noted that all the accounts of the religious practice characteristic of the Krita Yuga declare it to have been marked by austerities and tapas, or internal heat. As for the practice of austerities themselves, the *Rāmāyana*, Uttara Kanda, Sec.87, states that only the Brāhmans practiced austerities in the Krita Yuga. In the following Treta Yuga, Kshatriyas were born and, gaining equal spiritual dignity with the Brāhmans, practiced austerities alongside them, while the Vaisyas and Shūdras served them. Then in the Dvāpara Yuga Vaisyas started to practice austerities as well, just as the Shūdras too began

---

[310] See Josephus, *Jewish Antiquities*, I:70-1.

[311] See G.G. Stroumsa, *op.cit.*, p.117.

practicing austerities in the Kali Yuga.

The statement in the *Rāmāyana* that these austerities were originally the privilege of Brāhmans contrasts with the general view that 'yajna' or sacrifice was the typical custom of the Āryan Brāhmans. Yajna appears only in the Dvāpara Yuga, according to the *Manusmriti*, and were followed by Puranic beliefs and Tantric. However, some maintain that fire-worship began already in the Krita Yuga. Shriram Sharma, for instance, has suggested that "yajnas" were performed intensively already in the Krita Yuga:

> The yajnas were ... performed in the divine Krita Yuga, by the rishis [i.e. the seven sages] and the demigods since the demigods themselves were manifest on earth.[312]

These "yajnas" of the Krita Yuga performed by the seven sages and demigods may, however, have been different from the human fire-sacrifices which appeared after Manu Vaivasvata. Shriram Sharma[313] points out that "In comparison to what man attains via yajnas, great Rishis attain much more via sankalpa/strength of resolve and eulogy to God (*YV* 17,28)." However, he suggests that "this power of eulogy was attained by the Rishis via fire worship (*AV* IV,23,5)".[314] The Atharvavedic reference he gives represents Indra as being aided by Agni in his battle against the sources of resistance (Panis) which obstruct the rise of the solar force into our system. It is possible that both yoga and fire-worship may have originally

---

[312] Shriram Sharma, *Scientific Basis of Yajnas along with its wisdom aspect*, ed. A.N. Rawal and tr. H.A. Kapadia, Ch.20.

[313] S. Sharma, *Ibid*.

[314] *AV* IV,23,5:"With [Agni] as friend the Rishis gave their power new splendour, with whom they kept aloof the Asuras' devices".

developed from a focus on the thawing power of fire required to release the solar force in microcosm as well as macrocosm. In the former, it is manifest as the "heat" of yogic austerities or "tapas". Fire-worship, on the other hand, is a more external dramatic recreation of the macrocosmic solar force.

It is interesting to note in this context that Pargiter suggested that Brāhmanism was originally a Dravidian religious institution and that it was considerably transformed by the Āryans. While the original Dravidian priesthood was characterised by the practice of yogic austerities (tapas) which gave them magical powers, the Āryan was preoccupied with the performance of sacrifices involving the worship of fire.[315] Pargiter may indeed have been right if he were referring to a 'proto-Dravidian', rather than a later Dravidian, source, for it is not improbable that the Brāhmanical and Tantric traditions may have been derived from a single proto-Dravidian/Noachidian source that split into fire-worshipping and Tantric temple-worshipping cultures.

***

The Vedas in their present form are primarily sacrificial liturgies aimed at restoring the creation to its ideal status as the Primordial Man. These sacrifices focus on the macrocosmic elements of the divine manifestation rather more than on the human microcosmic. The esoteric spiritual significance of the Vedas itself does not emerge in the predominantly liturgical Vedas so much as in the Upanishadic (Vedānta) literature, especially in the Yoga-based Upanishads derived largely from the Krishna and Shukla Yajur Vedas.[316]

---

[315] See F.E. Pargiter, *Ancient Indian Historical Tradition*, p.308f.

[316] See K.N. Aiyar, *Thirty Minor Upanishads,* Madras: Vasanta Press,

Indeed, the Upanishads, and particularly the yoga-based ones, give a clear account of the actual spiritual basis of the identification of the individual self with the universal. The power of 'tapas' (fervour/heat) in the formation of the mind and the sense faculties in the macrocosm before the creation even of the gods is vividly depicted in *AV* XI,8:

> 3. Ten Gods before the Gods were born together in the ancient time.
>
> Whoso may know them face to face may now pronounce the mighty word.
>
> 4. Inbreath and outbreath, eye and ear, decay and freedom from decay,
>
> Spiration upward and diffused, voice, mind have brought us wish and plan.
>
> 5. As yet the Seasons were unborn, and Dhātar and Prajāpati,
>
> Both Asvins, Indra, Agni. Whom then did they worship as supreme?
>
> 6. Fervour and Action were the two, in depths of the great billowy sea;
>
> Fervour sprang up from Action: this they served and worshipped as supreme.

The descriptions of the Light of Brahman and the inner fire of the tapasvin [practictioner of austerities] in the yoga-based Upanishads provide further clues to the cosmic significance of the Vedic deities invoked during the fire-rituals of the Indo-Āryans. We may, for instance, recall the extraordinary description that is to be found in the yoga-based *Mandalabrāhmana Upanishad*, I of the different forms of primal light that the enlightened yogi is able to perceive:

> In order to cross the ocean of samsara ... one should adhere to the subtle path and overstepping tattva and other gunas should look out for Taraka. Taraka is Brahman which, being in the middle of the two eyebrows, is of the nature of the spiritual effulgence of Sachchidananda. The (spiritual) seeing through the three lakshyas (or the three kinds of introvision) is the means to It (Brahman). Sushumna which is from the muladhara to brahmarandhra has the radiance of the sun. In the centre of it is kundalini shining like crores of lightning and subtle as the thread in the lotus-stalk. Tamas is destroyed there ... When the mind is fixed on it, it sees a blue light between the eyes as also in the heart. (This is antarlakshya or internal introvison). In the bahirlakshya (or external introvision) one sees in order before his nose at distance of 4, 6, 8, 10, and 12 digits, the space of blue colour, then a colour resembling syama (indigo-black) and then shining as rakta (red) wave and then with the two pita (yellow and orange red) colours. Then he is a yogin. When one looks at the external space, moving the eyes and sees streaks of light at the corners of his eyes, then his vision can be made steady. When one sees jyotis (spiritual light) above his head 12 digits in length, then he attains the state of nectar. In the madhyalakshya (or the middle one), one sees the variegated colours of the morning As if the sun, the moon, and the fire had joined together in the Ukas that is without them.

Then he comes to have their nature (of light). Through practice, he becomes one with akas, devoid of all gunas and peculiarities. At first akas with its shining stars becomes to him Para-akas as dark as tamas itself, and he becomes one with Paraakas shining with stars and deep as tamas. (Then) he becomes one with Maha-akas resplendent (as) with the fire of the deluge. Then he becomes one with Tattva-akas, lighted with the brightness which is the highest and the best of all. Then he becomes one with Surya-akas (sun-akas) brightened by a crore of suns. By practicing thus, he becomes one with them. He who knows them becomes thus.

As regards the physiological constitution of the human microcosm, the *Yogatattva Upanishad*, for instance, specifies the parts of the human body governed by the several cosmic deities:

83b: There are five elements: Prithvi, Apas, Agni, Vāyu, and Ākāsha.

84-87a: To the body of the five elements, there is the fivefold Dharana. From the feet to the knees is said to be the region of Prithvi

87b. The region of Apas is said to extend from the knees to the anus.

91. From the anus to the heart is said to be the region of Agni.

94b: From the heart to the middle of the eyebrows is said to be the region of Vāyu.

97-98. From the centre of the eyebrows to the top of the head is said to be the region of Ākāsha.

In the *Brahma Upanishad*, the macrocosmic Man, or Purusha, itself is revealed to be entirely concentrated within the human microcosm:

> 2: This being or Self is fully self-extended (into world-forms), he is the indwelling controller of things and beings, he is the Bird, the Crab, the Lotus, he is the Purusha, the Prana, the destroyer, the cause, and the effect, the Brahman, the Atman, he is the Devata making everything known.

> 3: Now this Purusha has four seats, the navel, the heart, the throat, and the head. In these shines forth the Brahman with four aspects: the state of wakefulness, of dream, of dreamless sleep, and the fourth or transcendent state.

--

> 21: The heart (i.e. the inner chamber of the heart) resembles the calyx of a lotus, full of cavities and also with its face turned downwards. Know that to be the great habitat of the whole universe.

> 22: Know the wakeful state to have for its centre the eyes; the dreaming state should be assigned to the throat; the state of dreamless sleep is in the heart, and the transcendent state is in the crown of the head.

The *Katha Upanishad* II,4,12, identifies the Purusha with the Self in the following manner: 'The person (Purusha), of the size of a thumb, stands in the middle of the Self, as lord of the past and the future, and henceforward fears no more'. *SB* X,6,3,2 and understands the Purusha as the Self:

this golden Purusha in the heart [is] even as a smokeless light, it is greater than the sky, greater than the ether, greater than the earth, greater than all existing things;–that self of the spirit (breath) is my self: on passing away from hence I shall obtain that self.

The *Garbha Upanishad* outlines part of the yogic method to be employed in the realisation of the individual self as the Supreme Self or Purusha:

Through yoga, it should be brought from the middle of the eyebrows to the end of sushumnā (*viz.*, the pineal gland), when he becomes the cognizer of the Real like the child in the womb. In the body of this nature, Ātmā is latent and deathless and is the witness and Purusha. It lives in this body, being enveloped (by māyā). Prānī (or the jīva having prāna) has abhimāna (identification with the body) on account of avidyā. Ajñāna [ignorance] which surrounds it is the seed; the antahkarana (internal organ) is the sprout and the body is the tree.

The jīva or personal ego is deluded by the illusory power of māya into thinking that it is identical to the body and it is this error that is sought to be corrected through yoga. By contemplating the Yajna Purusha as the Supreme Soul, Ātman, however, we may acquire the cosmic consciousness of Brahman. The identification of the individual ātman with Brahman is the same as the attainment of the abode of the Purusha/Vishnu, which is informed by Brahman, and hence equal to Brahmaloka, from which one is not reborn. As Biardeau explains, il y a une hiérarchie de plans qui va des organes sensoriels au Purusa suprême, nommé ... Visnu ... L'atman est au-delà de l'ego limitateur et fait accéder à un stade où le Réel est non manifesté, l'atman lui-même se trouvant absorbé dans ce Réel informe avant d'accéder au Purusa Visnu, en qui il trouve la délivrance finale.[317]

***

The esoteric significance of the various components of the Vedic fire-rituals is explained in detail in the Upanishads. The 'Vaishvānara Vidya (knowledge of the soul of the universe)' at the conclusion of Ch.V of the *Chāndogya Upanishad* points to the different forms of the divine Soul in the individual body as well as in the All (Vaishvānara). Of particular interest is the association of the heart, mind and mouth with the three sacrificial fires of the Āryans:

> Of that Vaisvânara Self the head is Sutegas (having good light),[318] the eye Visvarûpa (multiform),[319] the breath Prithagvartman (having various courses),[320] the trunk Bahula (full),[321] the bladder Rayi (wealth),[322] the feet the earth,[323] the chest the altar, the hairs the grass on the altar, the heart the Gârhapatya fire, the mind the Anvâhârya fire, the mouth the Âhavanîya fire.

---

[317] See M. Biardeau, *op.cit.*, p.75.

[318] i.e. Heaven (V,12,1).

[319] i.e. the sun (V,13,1).

[320] i.e. air (V,14,1).

[321] i.e. ether (V,15,1).

[322] i.e. water (V,16,1).

[323] Prathishta (V,17,1)

The Vaishvānara, however, is the same as the Purusha within the human soul "as a span long and as identical with [oneself]" (V,18,1).

Indeed, the Vedic texts reveal a more than scientific understanding both of the several forms of heat that pervade the human microcosm and of the different parts of the flames of external fire. The metaphysical significance of the fire-rituals is detailed in the Panchāgni Vidya of the *Chāndogya Upanishad,* V,4ff, which identifies the five spiritual fires within the macrocosm (heaven, the atmosphere, and earth) and the macrocosm (man and woman). Such an understanding is clearly due to the supernatural yogic discipline that informed the original religion of the brāhmans and identifies them not just as wise men but indeed as "magicians". This is, of course, the reason why the term "magi" used for their Iranian counterparts has long been equated with "magicians".

The *Prānāgnihotra Upanishad* similarly mentions five fires, four of which are within the human body:

> 19.The fire of the sun in the form of the solar disk whence millions of rays are diffused is found in the head corresponding to the Ekarshi fire.
>
> The fire of vision is found ... in the mouth corresponding to the Ahavaniya fire.
>
> The gastric fire which supports the digestive function is found ... in the heart, corresponding to the Dakshinagni.
>
> Then there is the intestinal fire which cooks that which has been eaten, drunk, licked and masticated and is found towards the navel, corresponding to the Garhapatya fire.

20. Finally, there is the expiatory fire which is found under [the navel] and shares with it the three principal nadis (ida, pingala, and sushumna) as its common spouses and activates the process of procreation by means of the lunar light which circulates through them.

The Panchāgni-vidya includes not only knowledge of the fires within the body but also that of the different intensities within the flames of fire. According to the *Mundaka Upanishad* (I,2,4), Agni contains seven flames, Kâlî (black), Karâlî (terrific), Manogavâ (swift as thought), Sulohitâ (crimson), Sudhûmravarnâ (purple), Sphulinginî (sparkling), and brilliant Visvarûpî (having all forms), which, like the sun-rays bear the sacrificer to the world of the gods. Agni is thus the vital link between Heaven and Earth. Within the body itself the ancients identify the following fires:

Durgarshatā = bodily strength

Jyoti = aura

Tāpa = body temperature

Pāka = digestive fire

Prakāsh = wisdom

Shauch = fire that destroys bodily dirt

Rāg = fire that possesses magnetic attraction

Laghu = fire that makes the body light

Taishnya = fire that raises the mental powers

Urdhwagaman = fire that joins the mental powers to the divine powers (demigods)

As Shriram Sharma points out,[324] these ten qualities and functions of fire are related to the five prānas and five sub-prānas of the body.

The *Garbha Upanishad* mentions three forms of fire within the human body, koshta agni, darshana agni, and gnāna agni, relating to digestion, sight, and knowledge. These are located in the stomach, face, and heart respectively and correspond to the three fires, gārhaptniyāgni, āhavaniyāgni and dakshināgni, in the fire-ritual:

And of how many kinds is that agni? It has three bodies, three retas (seeds or progeny), three puras (cities), three dhātus, and three kinds of agni threefold. Of these three, Vaiśvānara is bodiless. And that agni becomes (or is subdivided into) Jñānāgni (wisdom-fire), Darśanāgni (eye-fire), and Koshthāgni (digestive fire). Of these Jñānāgni pertains to the mind; Darśanāgni pertains to the senses; and Koshthāgni pertains to dahara and daily cooks (or digests) equally whatever is eaten, drunk, licked, or sucked through prāna and apāna. Darśanāgni is (in) the eye itself and is the cause of vijñāna and enables one to see all objects of form. It has three seats, the (spiritual) eye itself being the (primary) seat, and the eyeballs being the accessory seats.

This Upanishad also describes in great detail the internal heat within the human body in terms of an internal fire-ritual:

Dakshināgni is in the heart, Gārhapatya is in the belly, and in the face is Āhavanīya. (In this sacrifice with the three agnis), the Purusha is himself the sacrificer;

---
[324] S. Sharma, *op.cit.*, Ch.9.

buddhi becomes his wife; santosha (contentment) becomes the dīkshā (vow) taken; the mind and the organs of the senses become the sacrificial vessels; the karmendriyas (organs of action) are the sacrificial instruments. In this sacrifice of the body, the several devas who become the rtvijas (sacrificial priests) perform their parts following the master of the sacrifice, (*viz.*, the true individuality), wherever he goes. In this (sacrifice), the body is the sacrificial place, the skull of the head is the fire-pit, the hairs are the kuśa grass; the mouth is the antarvedi (raised platform in sacrifice); kāma (or passion) is the clarified butter; the period of life is the period of sacrifice; nāda (sound) produced in dahara (heart) is the sāmaveda (recited during the sacrifice); vaikharī is the yajus (or yajurveda hymns); parā, paśyanti, and madhyamā are the rks (or rgveḍa hymns); cruel words are the atharvas (atharvaveda hymns) and khilas (supplementary texts of each veḍa); true words are the vyāhrtis. Life, strength, and bile are the paśus (sacrificial creatures) and death is avabhrta (the bath which concludes the sacrifice). In this sacrifice, the (three) fires blaze up and then according to (the desires of) the worldly the devas bless him.

We see therefore that the fire rituals of the Āryans involve magical evocations of the macrocosmic fire through manipulation of the fire within the ritual-altar (represented by the three sacred fires) and that within the human microcosm. These rituals serve to sustain the entire cosmos as well as the sacrificer, who, guided by the brahman priest, becomes identified with the solar force, Brahman.

***

We may briefly compare here the Zoroastrian understanding of and reverence for the sacred fire, Atar, which is symbolic of Ahura Mazda himself and of the Truth. The *Greater Bundahishn*, a describes the process whereby Ahura Mazda manifests himself materially. First, he draws forth, from his own Endless Light, Fire, and then Ether (the Sky) out of Fire, Water out of Ether, and Earth out of Water. Then he produces "the Tree" (which corresponds to the Tree of Life representing our universe), followed by "the Beneficent Animal" (the Cow) and "the Holy Man" (Gayomaretan/the First Man). The Fire derived from the Endless Light is called Khvarag (4).

In the *Greater Bundahishn* Ch.XVIII and the *Lesser Bundahishn* Ch.XVII, mention is made of five fires, the Berezi-savang, Vohufryan, Urvazisht, Vazisht (one of the sages in the Indian tradition), and Spenisht. The Berezi-savang is "the fire which glitters before Ohrmazd the Lord". The fire Spenisht is that which is lit in the material world. The Vohufryan is "that which is in the bodies of men and animals", the Urvazisht is that which is in plants, and Vazisht that which is in clouds. Of Spenisht, the three principal fires are Farnbag, Gushnasp and Burzin Mihr. Descriptions of the various fires worshipped by the Zoroastrians are given also in the *Greater Bundahishn*, Ch. VIG, where the fire Vasisht is said to facilitate the production of rain, and the fires Farnbag, Gushpasp and Burzin Mihr the protection of the world and the preservation of the creatures. Other fires such as those within the plants, men and beneficent animals maintain and increase the life of these species.

The *Greater Bundahishn* Ch.XVIII also provides an account of the fires Burzen Mihr, Adar Gushnasp, and Farnbag. Of these, the fire Farnbag is considered to be the "athravan" (priest) of the fires, the fire Gushnasp the warrior, and the fire Birzin Mihr the husbandman. "They are the protectors of the world until the renovation of the universe" (17). Thus Farnbag has the ritualistic eminence of Agni as the brāhmanical god among the Indo-Āryans. He is assisted by the two other fires, representing the warrior and the peasant, in his protection of the world.

Regarding the kinds of fire-rituals practiced by the Zoroastrians, the Avesta mentions three consecrated fires, a household fire, a communal fire and a national. The ritual employing the domestic hearth fire, called Ātash Dādgāh, is the lowest, for this fire is turned into a more significant cult fire by putting it in an appropriate place, i.e. a fire-temple. The fire room in the temple was itself constructed in the form of a dome recalling the dome of heaven.[325] The Avesta (Yasna 62,5) values most of all the national fire, the Ātash Bahram, the fire of victory. This was the cult fire of the royal house of the Sassanians. The king himself is believed to be endowed with khvarena, the sacred victory-giving glory that is dispensed by Mithra.[326] The consecration of the Atash Bahram is conducted with a collection of the sixteen fires mentioned in the *Vendidad*, Ch.8. The hymns used for its consecration are mostly directed to Srosh, the assistant of Mithra[327] and the guardian of all that is pure and sacred in the world. The sacred fire of the second grade is called Ātash Adarān, meaning fire of [different] fires, i.e. taken from the embers of the hearth fires of the various castes, priests, warriors, farmers, and artisans.

We see that the primary focus in Zoroastrian fire-worship is on the external and macrocosmic forms of fire. There is little yogic understanding of the internal

---

[325] See J. Darmsteter, *Zend Avesta*, I, 152f; 169.

[326] Sol Invictus takes the place of the Avestan khvarena in the later Mithraic religion. All the Roman emperors after Commodus (161-192 A.D.) assumed this title.

[327] Cf. Mihir Yasht XXV.

thermal energies that inform the human microcosm. However, Grether, who has attempted to demonstrate the close resemblances between the Tantric homa and the Zoroastrian fire-rituals, points out that, at least in the case of the Zoroastrian chief priest, there is a clear correlation between the deity and the fire.[328] The Lord of Wisdom is believed to be present in the form of fire as well as in the body of the priest. Thus the Zoroastrian priest's role is that of a representative of the Lord of Wisdom, of Ahura Mazda, who has become visible to the worshippers in the form of the ritual fire.

***

When we turn to the fire-rituals that were conducted within the Tantric tradition we find that they reflect a more pristine system of ritual practice than even the Indo-Āryan Vedic fire-rituals. As Grether has pointed out,

> None of the elements common to homa are exclusively Vedic. However, all of the quintessential portions—structure and efficacy—do have parallels in the Iranian cultural paradigm. Therefore, tantric homa rites are more properly characterized as Indo-Iranian in origin.[329]

As she suggests, 'the ritual efficacy common to all homa rites can be found in the Central Asian culture dating back to the pre-Vedic period but re-articulated in the tantric period.' Further, Biardeau too has pointed out that "le 'sacrifiant' du culte agamique—qui est toujours, par la force des choses, un notable, au moins local—se rapproche ainsi beaucoup plus au roi que du maître de maison

---

[328] See Holly Grether, "Tantric Homa Rites in the Indo-Iranian Ritual Paradigm," *Journal of Ritual Studies* 21.1 (2007), pp.16-32.

[329] *Ibid.*, p.28.

ordinaire".³³⁰ This suggests that the Tantric sacrifices retain the public significance of the early sacred rituals of the Indo-Iranians rather more than the rituals of the later Vedic Āryans, which tended to be more domestic, and exclusive, affairs.

However, it is not likely that the original sacrificial rituals of the Tantric or the Vedic Indians were derived directly from those of the Iranians. The Iranians are represented in Herodotus as worshipping the "circle of heaven" (Ahura, from Ashur/Anshar=circle of heaven) as well as the heavenly bodies. The incantation that the priest utters during the animal sacrifice is supposed to evoke the creation of the heavenly bodies. The Iranians discussed by Herodotus, however, did not build temples or worship statuary representations of their deities (I,131), and this emphasises their ancient affiliation with the Scythians, while the Mitanni – and the Hittite-Hurrians, however, were certainly not averse to such representations.

Besides, the Iranian rituals are described by Herodotus as not involving fire, even though the later Zoroastrian religion—like the Indic—is indeed typified by its worship of fire, Atar. More recently Mary Boyce has pointed out that "no actual ruins of a fire temple have been identified from before the Parthian period [i.e. before the 3rd c. B.C.]".³³¹ This suggests once again that the Iranians, like their Mitanni kinsmen, must have come into contact in the south with the Purūruva Ailas [Elamites/Hurrians], who, as we shall see, derived their worship of fire from the Gandharvas, or the inhabitants of the Gandhara Grave culture (ca. 1700-1400 B.C.), which followed the Bactro-Margiana Archaeological Complex (ca. 2200-1700 B.C.).³³²

---

[330] See M. Biardeau, *op.cit.*, p.139.

[331] See Mary Boyce, "On the Zoroastrian temple-cult of fire", *JOAS*, 95/3, p.454.

[332] See A. Parpola, "The Problem of the Aryans", in G. Erdosy,

Indeed the Iranians seem originally to have been nomadic peoples, as is attested by the imagery of the Old Avesta, wherein the cosmos is viewed as an enormous tent.[333]

The relatives of the Iranians, the ancient Scythians, also do not exhibit any developed form of religious worship that may be ascribed to yogic understanding. The royal hearth was the most sacred place in the Scythian domain and solemn oaths were sworn there (Herodotus IV,68). This may be related to the veneration of the Royal Fire, the Ātash Bahram, among the Iranians. When the king died, the royal funeral cortege travelled throughout the Scythian kingdom for forty days in order to receive the homage of the people, some of whom even mutilated themselves in partial self-sacrifice.

Other practices that link the Scythians to the Indo-Iranians is their custom of soma-drinking which accounts for their ancient designation as "hoamavarga", or "soma-drinking", Scythians. However, Eliade's researches in Central Asian shamanism, which may be a vestige of ancient Scythian religious practice, point to a rather rudimentary practical application of the spiritual basis of the cosmological religion of the ancients in the shamanistic rituals.[334] The use of intoxicants for the acquisition of transcendental states is, according to Eliade, a relatively inferior path in comparison to the inner spiritual discipline advocated by yoga,[335] and the reduction

---

(ed.) *The Indo-Aryans of Ancient South Asia*, Berlin: Walter de Gruyter, 1995, p.366.

[333] See P.O. Skjaervo, "The Avesta as source for the early history of the Iranians", in G. Erdosy (ed.), *The Indo-Aryans of Ancient South Asia*, Berlin: Walter de Gruyter, 1995, p.168.

[334] Cf. M. Eliade's discussion of shamanism among the Scythians, *Shamanism: Archaic Techniques of Ecstasy*, N.Y.: Pantheon Books, 1964, pp.394ff.

[335] See M. Eliade, *op.cit.*, p.401.

of yogic knowledge to ecstatic flights among the shamans is an indication of a certain degeneration of the wisdom of the ancient Near East in its transmission to the north. As Eliade pointed out, let us emphasize once again the structural difference that distinguishes classic Yoga from shamanism. Although the latter is not without certain techniques of concentration ... its final goal is always ecstasy and the soul's ecstatic journey through the various cosmic regions, whereas Yoga pursues entasis, final concentration on the spirit and "escape" from the cosmos.[336]

To discern the original tradition of the Indo-Iranians from whom the Tantric, Vedic, and Zoroastrian rituals were all derived, we may turn once again to the Indic Purānas, where we find that Purūravas, the early Aila [=Elamite?] king, is said to have obtained sacrificial fire from the "Gandharvas", who also taught him the constitution of the three sacred fires of the Āryans.[337] Purūravas is stated in the Puranas to be an Aila king of Pratishthana, Aila itself designating a descendant of Ila, the offspring of Manu and originator of the Lunar dynasty of kshatriyas, while Manu's son, Ikshvāku is the author of the Solar dynasty. The Ailas are designated as Karddameyas, which relates them to the river Karddama in Iran, particularly in the region of Balkh.[338] The kshatriya ruler of the lunar dynasty, Purūravas, is, according to the *Bhavishya Purāna*, Pratisarga 3, the son of Budh, the son of the Moon, Chandra,[339] who himself was the son of the sage Atri born of Brahma. The rise of both Chandra and Purūravas is dated to the Treta Yuga. Fire-worship

---

[336] *Ibid.*, p.417.

[337] See F.E. Pargiter, *op.cit.*, p.309. In the *Mbh* I, 75, too Purūravas is said to have brought the three kinds of sacrificial fire from the Gandharvas.

[338] See *Rāmāyana* VII,103,21ff.

[339] Budh was married to Ila, the daughter of Manu Vaivaswat.

was thus perhaps not universal among the earliest Āryan tribes.

The fact that the Purūravas are said to have learnt the fire-rituals from the Gandharvas suggests that the early Hurrians of Elam and the earliest Iranians did not worship fire and learnt it from another group of Āryans who must have, at a very early date, moved eastwards from their Anatolian/Armenian homeland. However, even the Gandhāras are included among the Aila [=Elamite?] dynasties in the Purānas, which suggests that these Āryans too were a branch of the original Noachidian family that we have called proto-Dravidian/Hurrian.

***

Given the intimate relationship between Yoga, Upanishadic Brāhmanism and Tantra and the reference in *Manusmriti*, I,86, to the fact that austerities marked by tapas preceded the development of fire-rituals, it is important to descry the relations between the Vedic and Tantric rituals. That Tantra is closely related to Brāhmanism is clear from the many similarities in their respective ritual practices. In fact, even the apparently unorthodox practices of the Shaiva Tantric Kaula [non-dualistic but liberal] sect are a practical application of Advaita Vedic knowledge, as Woodroffe pointed out:

> The *Kularnava* (III.113) says that there is no knowledge higher than that of Veda and no doctrine equal to Kaula. Here a distinction is drawn between Veda which is Vidya and the Kaula teaching which he calls Darshana [school of philosophy].[340]

---

[340] See John Woodroffe ("Arthur Avalon"), *Shakti and Shâkta: Essays and Addresses on the Shâkta Tantrashâstra*, London: Luzac and Co. 1918.

Ch.29 of Abhinavagupta's *Tantraloka* details the 'kula prakriya' rite as involving the unorthodox consumption of meat, alcohol, fish and the performance of ritual sex.[341] However, as Flood points out, the *Brihadāranyaka Upanishad* (IV,3,21) also describes the realisation of the self as the Absolute in sexual terms, while the *Chāndogya Upanishad* (II,13,1-2) identifies Vedic recitation itself with the sexual act.[342] Yael Bentor has also recently noted that

> The brahmanas and upanisads contain various passages linking the fire offering to sexual intercourse and conception. The milk offered into the fire has been related to semen and the boiling of the milk to orgasm ... Also, the kindling of the fire from the friction of the two fire sticks (arani) is correlated to sexual intercourse.[343]

Those who have studied Vedic sacrificial rituals will also remember the dramatic performance of copulation between the king's wife and the dead horse in the Ashvamedha sacrifice and may reasonably suppose this to have been a part of the original Purushamedha (human sacrifice) as well. As Brajalal Mukherji also explained,

> All Vedic yajnas are based on the idea that Maithunikarana (coitus) leads to spiritual happiness. Sexual intercourse is Agnihotra (*SB* XI, 6,2,10). Maithunakarana is consecration (*SB* III, 2,1,2, etc.) ... [Yajnas] direct the observance and performance of Maithuna as a religious rite or part of a religious

---

[341] *Ibid.*, p.154ff.

[342] See G. Flood, *The Tantric Body: The Secret Tradition of Hindu Religion*, London: I.B. Tauris, 2006.

[343] Yael Bentor, "Interiorized Fire Rituals in India and in Tibet." *JAOS* 120.4 (2000), p.600.

rite ... and they direct that Mantras are to be uttered during the observance of this rite.[344]

What is interesting is that many of the other aspects of Tantric ritual also have counterparts in Vedic ritual. Mukherji highlighted similarities between the divinisation rituals of the Āgamic tradition and some of the Vedic rituals:

> The worship in both Vaidik and Tantrik rites begins with Acamana, which is a form of ablution in which certain parts of the body are touched with water .... They purify themselves by uttering some Mantras as Bijas while contemplating the Deities of certain parts of their bodies and touching such parts with their fingers ... They make use of certain sounds for removing unclean spirits, e.g., Khat, Phat, Hum ... They attribute a Deity to each letter in a Mantra ... They make gestures with their fingers as part of their religious rites ... and locate the Devatas of particular sounds in particular parts of their bodies ... [345]

However, a closer study of the Vedic and Tantric rituals will reveal certain significant differences between them. We may for the purpose of such a comparison consider the Tantric fire rituals or 'homa' sacrifices performed by both the Indians and the Asiatic Buddhists who adopted these Indian rituals in Tibet and the Orient. The primal deity in the homa is indeed the god of fire, Agni. The Tantric Shaiva Siddhānta sacrificial ritual envisages a symbolic birth of the deity into the ritual enclosure. As Richard Payne has pointed out,

---

[344] In John Woodroffe, *op.cit.*, 'Note to Ch.IV'.
[345] *Ibid.*

This involves the full range of sexual imagery, that is, impregnation, gestation, and birth, as well as the other rituals of childhood: Two deities (identified as Brahmā and Sarasvatī) are installed in the hearth altar, and burning coals identified as Śiva's semen are then poured in while the practitioner visualizes the act of impregnation. By these ritual actions, Agni is born as the ritual fire in the hearth-altar.[346]

The identification of the forms of Agni, or Agni Vaishvānara, with the three sacrificial fires used in the Kālachakra Tantric rituals of Vajrayāna Buddhism—just as they are in the Vedic—has been noted by Vesna Wallace:

The first is the southern fire (dakshinagni), identified with lightning that resides in a bow-shaped firepit in the heart cakra. The second is the domestic fire (garhyapatya), which is identified with the sun that dwells in a circular firepit within the throat cakra; the third is the consecrated fire taken from the perpetual domestic fire (ahavaniya), or the flesh-consuming fire (kravyada), which is located in a quadrangular firepit within the navel cakra. Above these three fires, at the edge of darkness, where neither the light of lightning, the sun, the moon, or the planets shine, there is an additional fire, the fire of gnosis (jnanagni). This fourth fire is of the nature of joy (ananda) located in the secret and forehead cakras, and it has been there since beginningless time.[347]

---

[346] See R. Payne, 'Homa: Tantric Fire Ritual', *Oxford Research Encyclopedia of Religion*, p.7.

[347] Vesna Wallace, 'Homa Rituals in the Indian Kālacakra Tradition', in R.K. Payne and M. Witzel (ed.), *Homa Variations: Ritual Change across the Longue Durée*. Oxford: Oxford University Press, 2015, p.260.

We see that the sacrificial fires are simultaneously identified with the thermal energies located within the chakras of the human body. The internal homa of the Tantric Tibetans is even more illustrative of the movement of Agni or termal energy within the chakras of the human body in such a way that the practitioner transforms his sexual energy into a source of enlightenment. For example, in the Tibetan yoga of the subtle body (linga sharīra),

> inner heat (gtum-mo) is generated in the navel (or in the junction of the central channel with the ro-ma and rkyang-ma below the navel) and blazes up through the central channel. As a result of the bodhicitta, the white drop located at the head's center, melts and meets with the red drop, the gtum-mo fire. The practice culminates in the realization of supreme nondual enlightened wisdom.[348]

In Tantric worship, the virtual creation of Agni in the fire-altar and the worship of Agni through oblations and entreaties are accompanied by the divinisation of the priest. This aspect of Tantric worship will be observed also in the adjunct to the homa, the pūja, where the sādhaka is divinised before he can venerate the deity manifest in temple idols. The fire that is created in the fire-altar is in fact created by the priest from within his own heart. This is evident especially in the Kālachakra Tantra rituals studied by Vesna Wallace.[349] Grether too has noted that

> Vedic priests may identify parts of their bodies with a variety of gods, but "there is no unified nor even consistent parallel of worshipper and god" … Tantric rites, on the other hand, tend to focus on a direct

---

[348] See Y. Bentor, *op.cit.*, p.597.

[349] See V. Wallace, *op.cit.*

correlation between a singular divine being—who becomes present in the fire—and the worshipper.[350]

Thus we may agree with Bentor that 'Tantric rituals, external rituals included, are in fact ritualized meditations'.[351] Indeed, the entire office of the brahman priest in the Vedic ritual stresses the internal significance of the external fire-rituals:

> The role of the brahman priest in vedic rituals also points to the importance of the mental aspect in outer vedic sacrifices. While the other priests, such as the adhvaryu and hotr, perform the ritual actions and recite, the brahman follows the ritual mentally. Whenever an error in the performance occurs he corrects it not by ritual actions, but through his mental powers.[352]

Heesterman's conjecture that yogic asceticism was an "internalisation" of the Vedic sacrifices is thus clearly inaccurate in its suggestion of the priority of sacrifice.[353] The fire-rituals of the brāhmans may more likely have been an externalisation of the thermal disciplines of yoga since the *Rgveda* (X,154,2) itself mentions [yogic] tapas as that by which "one attains the light of the sun".

As regards the use of mantras in these various rituals, Grether points out that the recitation of Vedic mantras merely narrates the defeat of evil while the tantric mantras, on the other hand, actually effect the destruction. Another indication that the Vedic fire-rituals were not prior to

---

[350] See H. Grether, *op.cit.*, p.21.

[351] See Y. Bentor, *op.cit.*, p.605.

[352] *Ibid.*, p.605.

[353] See J.C. Heesterman, *Broken world: An Essay on Ancient Indian Ritual*, Chicago: University of Chicago Press, 1993, p.186.

yogic practices among the earliest Indo-Europeans is that the implements used in the latter often have a sexual significance, as when the ladle symbolises a penis and the hearth a vagina. This significance is derived from Tantric symbolism, as Wheelock reminds us:

> [In the Tantric ritual] not only the worshipper is made identical to the central deity ... but all of the components of the ritual as well.[354]

Wheelock also notes that, in the system of correspondences between the external objects of the ritual and their cosmic referents, the Vedic practice is not so comprehensive as the Tantric:

> the transformations of objects in the Vedic ritual arena does not generate a precisely ordered mandala that replicates the divine powers in a one-to-one fashion. Rather, one finds a more variegated and constantly changing amalgam of divine resonances.[355]

Whereas

> The Tantric ritual in an even more systematic fashion transforms a mundane setting into a precisely and minutely conceived replica of a sacred cosmos. The purification and cosmicisation of ritual components covers everything from the individual worshipper (sadhaka), whose body becomes an image of the deity in both transcendent and manifest form, to the altar on which the offerings are made, which is changed into a mandala housing the entire retinue of divine beings, the manifold body of the supreme deity.

---

[354] See Wade T. Wheelock, 'The Mantra in Vedic and Tantric Ritual', in H.P. Alper (ed.), *Understanding Mantras*, Albany, NY: SUNY Press, 1989, p.108.

[355] *Ibid.*, p.105.

The imprecision in the correspondences noted above is further highlighted by a comparison of the Tantric 'pūja', which is, apart from 'homa', the other common form of Tantric worship, with the Vedic fire-ritual. As Wheelock states:

> One noteworthy difference from the Tantric ritual is that the Vedic priest ... identifies parts of his body with parts of a variety of different gods. There is no unified nor even consistent parallel of worshipper and god.[356]

In the 'pūja', on the other hand, there proceeds a process of divinisation of the worshipper that follows a series of steps that steadily recall the macrocosmic dimensions of the human microcosm. These steps have been well studied by Wheelock,[357] whom I shall cite here. The first step is 'bhūtashuddhi':

> Bhutashuddhi, as the name implies (purification of the elements) involves visualising the refining of the worshipper's own body by a process inwardly re-enacting the destruction of the cosmos and the reabsorption of the basic elements into primal, undifferentiated matter ... With some variation in different texts, the worshipper proceeds to visualise the cosmic fire being extinguished with earth and the resulting ashes finally being washed away with wáter, completing the process of purification.

Bhūtashuddhi is followed by the recreation of the worshipper's body, now as an image of the cosmos. This is accomplished through the process of 'nyāsa' (placing):

---

[356] *Ibid.*

[357] Wheelock, *op.cit.*, p.102ff.

Like bhutashuddhi, nyāsa involves the use of nonsentence mantras but with an accompanying physical act, touching various parts of the body. The mantras, in effect, are applied to the body manually. Two basic types of mantras are used. First, the letters of the Sanskrit alphabet are placed in order on different parts of the body (matrka-nyasa) providing the worshipper's body with the fifty basic elements of the Tantric cosmogony.

Next, a series of essentially reverential mantras are offered to the parts of the body (anga-nyāsa) to consecrate them as implicitly identical to those of the supreme deity. The mantras of the anga-nyasa then transmute the purified body of the worshipper into the fully manifest form of the supreme deity.

The entire Tantric ritual is thus viewed 'as god offering worship to god'.

In the idol-worship section of Tantra, the liturgy begins with an invocation of the deity and moves to providing the deity with a detailed manifest form.[358] This begins with the establishment of the life breaths in the image (yantra, statue) that the invoked deity has just entered. This is the rite of 'prāna pratishtha'. However, as Wheelock points out:

> the deity is not descending from the distant heaven of the Vedic cosmology but is drawn out from the very heart of the worshipper and asked to become manifest in some concrete object in the ritual. For example, Siva is invoked into the temple's lingam.

---

[358] For a further account of the divinisation of idols in the Tantric tradition, see A. Jacob, *Brahman: A Study of the Solar Rituals of the Indo-Europeans*, Hildesheim: G. Olms, 2012, Ch.XV.

In the deity's acquisition of a manifest form, the worship of the limbs of the divine body is conducted using a set of mantras employed in the Tantric worshipper's rite of nyāsa. As with the rite of nyāsa, the point of these mantras is to identify parts of the mandala with parts of the deity's body. This focus on the physical aspect of the deity is different from the Vedic ritual, as Wheelock points out:

> that an important part of the homage expressed in the Tantric puja concerns the physical traits of the deity. This is certainly not the case in the Vedic ritual, where one mentions the deeds and functions of the god with almost no mention of his physical appearance.

Further, the fact that the idol-worship prescribed as part of Tantric worship corresponds closely to the original yogic meditation is made clear in the description of such worship in the *Mandalabrāhmana Upanishad* II:

> Not being troubled by any thoughts (of the world) then constitutes the hyāna. The abandoning of all karmas constitutes āvāhana (invocation of god). Being firm in the unshaken (spiritual) wisdom constitutes āsana (posture). Being in the state of unmanī constitutes the pāya (offering of water for washing the feet of god). Preserving the state of amanaska (when manas is offered as sacrifice) constitutes the arghya (offering of water as oblation generally). Being in state of eternal brightness and shoreless nectar constitutes snāna (bathing). The contemplation of Ātmā as present in all constitutes (the application to the idol of) sandal. The remaining in the real state of the dṛk (spiritual eye) is (the worshipping with) akshaa;(non-broken rice). The attaining of Chiṭ (consciousness) is (the worshipping with) flower. The real state of agni

(fire) of Chiṭ is the hūpa (burning of incense). The state of the sun of Chiṭ is the īpa (light waved before the image). The union of oneself with the nectar of full moon is the naivēya (offering of food, etc.). The immobility in that state (of the ego being one with all) is praakshia (going round the image). The conception of 'I am He' is namaskāra (prostration). The silence (then) is the sui (praise). The all-contentment (or serenity then) is the visarjana (giving leave to god or finishing worship). (This is the worship of Āṭmā by all Raja-yogins). He who knows this knows all.

Another index of the original quality of Tantric ritual is the importance of mantras in it. Every god is indeed represented by a 'bīja' or seminal mantra which embodies the essence of the god. Thus the syllable 'ram' betokens Agni, 'dam' Vishnu, 'horum' Shiva, etc. A connected series of bīja mantras in the form of a mūla, or root, mantra of the deity is used in the climactic rite of 'japa' at the end of the pūja in such a way that the multiple repetitions of the mūla-mantra serve as a means of producing a concrete sonic manifestation of the deity. As Wheelock points out:

> In the Tantric ritual] the deity becomes manifest as the world first by taking on Sonic form, the concrete objects or referents (artha) of those primordial words following afterward in the course of cosmic evolution.

By contrast,

> the orthodox formulation of the Vedic tradition, the Purva-Mimamsa, virtually ignores mantras. Its key task is to determine a valid means (pramana) for ascertaining dharma ... Only the set of explicit injunctions to action (vidhi) found in the brahmana section of sruti are to be counted as relevant to defining dharma.

***

We see therefore that Tantric worship is much more detailed in its divinisation of the worshipper than the Vedic. Tantric Āgama indeed considers the universe as a whole whose every single part bears an influence on the others. Thus a system of sympathetic magic was developed out of it in which the final aim of the spiritual adept (sādhaka) is to transform, within his consciousness, his own person as well as cult-objects and rites into that which these phenomena essentially are. And the ultimate aim of Tantra, called 'siddhi' or spiritual perfection, is a practical realisation of the Upanishadic equation of the individual ātman with Brahman ("tat tvam asi"/that art thou).

Thus it is not surprising that, although drawing on the Vedic tradition, Āgama claims to supersede it. As Flood points out, "The mainstream tantric texts of the Pancharatra and Shaiva Siddhanta maintain a close proximity to the vedic tradition and prescribe a whole way of life that incorporates vedic rites of passage [samskaras] ... along with the supererogatory tantric rites of their tradition".[359] Kulluka Bhatta, the celebrated commentator on Manu, for instance, says that Shruti is of two kinds, Vaidik and Tantrik, while the Niruttara Tantra also calls Tantra the Fifth Veda.

We have noted that the Vedic fire-rituals do not exhibit the correspondences between the elements of the external altar and the thermal energies within the body so closely as the Tantric homa rituals do. The sexual connotations of the fire-ritual also point to the fact that the latter was an externalisation of the yogic understanding of the forces within the chakras of the human body rather than vice-versa. Besides, the Tantric homa as practiced by certain

---

[359] See G. Flood, *op.cit.*, p.38.

Tibetan Buddhists display a greater understanding of the internal sexual transformations that are meant to take place in the sacrificer during a fire-ritual. The divinisation process detailed in Tantric pūjas also demonstrates a stricter adherence to the yogic mode of transcendence through the chakras than the temporary elevation of the sacrificer with the help of the officiating priests in the Vedic ritual does. Finally, the utilisation of mantras in the Vedic rituals is less forceful than in the Tantric, where the chanting effectively reproduces the primal sonic aspect of the divine creation.

Given the complexity of the rituals whereby the Tantric priest and worshipper transform their human forms as well as those of idols into divine ones, employing the fires within themselves as well as without, it would appear that the Tantric rituals of India—as well as those of the other idol-worshipping cultures of Mesopotamia and Egypt[360]—are indeed closer to the original yogic wisdom of the proto-Dravidian/Hurrian family of Manu/Noah than the Vedic or Zoroastrian fire-rituals are.

---

[360] Cf. A. Jacob, *Brahman*, Chs.XIII-XV.

V. REVIVING ADAM

The sacrificial rituals of the Indo-Āryans &the Early Christians

FROM THE BEGINNING of the nineteenth century, the historicity of the Christian story has been questioned by several scholars who have preferred to consider it as the historicisation of a primordial myth. This is hardly surprising given the scientifically impossible details of the Christ story. Though it must be added that it is precisely its value as myth that endows this story with a numinous power that is lacking in the more sociologically oriented cults of the Jahvist and Arab tribes who formulated and follow the related Semitic religions of Judaism and Islam.

I have myself recently[361] argued for an understanding of this story as a transformation of an Indo-European myth by certain groups of Jews who must have been exposed to the Indo-European cosmological views during their exile in Babylon in the sixth century B.C. The similarity of the passion, death, and resurrection of Christ to those

---

[361] See A. Jacob *Ātman,* Hildesheim: Georg Olms Velag, 2005, and *Brahman* , Hildesheim: Georg Olms Verlag, 2012.

of Dionysus, Marduk, Osiris is too obvious to need emphasis.[362] It may be somewhat more instructive now to observe the similarities between the original religious rituals that were employed by groups following the Āryan and the Semitic traditions.

In my study of Indo-European ritual, *Brahman*, I have suggested that the Āryan cosmological religion is indeed older than those of the Hamites (Egyptians/Sumerian),[363] since, although the earliest attested religions are those of the Hamites, Ham is, in the early Jahvist version of Genesis, considered to be the "youngest son of Noah".[364] However, it is possible that both the Āryan and Hamitic religions may have derived from a proto-Dravidic/Druidic source,[365] since Manu, the first man in the Sanskritic Purānas, is considered to be a King of Drāvida.[366] The proto-Dravidians themselves may have been part of an antique proto-Hurrian branch of the Indo-Europeans.[367]

It is likely also that the cosmological and philosophical insights that inform all the ancient Indo-European religions (Japhetic, Semitic and Hamitic) were developed originally through yogic meditation, as the *Brahmānda Purāna* I,i,3,8, for instance, declares. It is significant in this context that, in the *Mahabhārata*, Shalyaparva, 44, Skanda or Muruga, the Dionysiac god of the Dravidians,

---

[362] For a quick survey of scholars who have pointed this out see the Wikipedia article, 'Christ myth theory'.

[363] I use Indo-European to designate the Noachidian race that includes Āryans, Semites and Hamites and not just the first of these.

[364] See *The Interpreter's Bible*, I:560.

[365] For the identification of Dravidic with Druidic see A. Jacob, *Brahman*, pp.134ff.

[366] See *Bhāgavata Purāna* VIII,24.

[367] For the Hurrians, see E. Speiser, *Mesopotamian Origins* (1930), A. Ungnad, *Subartu* (1936), I. Gelb, *Hurrians and Subarians* (1944), G. Wilhelm, *The Hurrians* (1989).

is described as being endowed with yogic powers while his father Shiva is in *Mbh*, Anushāsanaparva, 14, is addressed as the "soul of yoga" and the object of all yogic meditation. Since it is most likely that the original Indo-European Noachidian race was indeed a proto-Dravidian/proto-Hurrian one, it is probable that this profound yogic knowledge of the universe is characteristic of it.

Āryan Origins and Fire-Worship

The Japhetic Āryans, however, are distinguished by their adherence to the worship of sacred fire. The chief branches of the eastern Āryans are the Iranians, Indians, and Scythians.[368] Of these, the Indians and Iranians seem to have preserved best, in their oral hieratic linguistic tradition, the philosophical import of the ancient cosmology of the proto-Dravidians/Hurrians. So it would be helpful to consider here the conduct and significance of their particular sacred rituals.

A brief account of the beginnings of fire-worship among the Indians and Iranians may be in order. We may recall Herodotus' statement that the Iranians did not worship fire originally.[369] In the Purānas, too, Purūravas, the early Aila [=Elamite?] king, is said to have obtained sacrificial fire from the "Gandharvas", who also taught him the constitution of the three sacred fires of the Āryans.[370] Purūravas is stated in the Puranas to be an Aila king of

---

[368] The Scythians form an integral part of the Indo-Iranian group, but their spiritual tradition seems to have been less developed (see A. Jacob, *Ātman,* p.41f).

[369] See Herodotus, *Histories,* I,132.

[370] See F.E. Pargiter, *Ancient Indian Historical Tradition,* London: Milford, 1922, p.309. In the *Mbh* I, 75, Purūravas is said to have brought the three kinds of sacrificial fire from the Gandharvas.

Pratishthana and the Ailas themselves are designated as Karddameyas which relates them to the river Karddama in Iran, particularly in the region of Balkh.[371]

The fact that the Purūravas are said to have learnt the fire-rituals from the Gandharvas suggests that the early Hurrians of Elam and the earliest Iranians did not worship fire and learnt it from a more northerly wave of Āryans who must have, at a very early date, moved eastwards from their Armenian homeland. However, even the Gandhāras are included among the Aila [=Elamite?] dynasties in the Purānas, which suggests that these Āryans too were a northern and eastern branch of proto-Hurrians identifiable with the Japhetites. The Japhetic tribes that moved northwards to the Pontic-Caspian steppes created the Yamnaya culture there[372] which is considered the major source of the Āryan tribes.[373]

The Gandaridae are also mentioned by Herodotus (III,91) as one of the Indian tribes of the seventh satrapy of Darius I (550-486 B.C.) and can be located near the Bactrians of the 12th satrapy. The archaeological evidence of the early Gandharvas may be that found in the Gandhara Grave culture of the Swat settled from 1700-1400 B.C., which followed the Bactria-Margiana Archaeological Complex (BMAC). The occupants of the BMAC may have been related to the same family as the later Gandhara. Since the Gandhara culture also bears the first evidence of

---

[371] See *Rāmāyana* VII,103,21ff.

[372] W. Bernard suggested that the human remains from Period I of Gandhara bore resemblances to those of Bronze Age and early Iron Age crania of 2500 B.C.–A.D. 500 from the Caucasus and Volga region as well as from Tepe Hissar in Iran (see K.A.R. Kennedy, "Have Aryans been identified in the preshistoric skeletal record from South Asia?" in G. Erdosy, (ed.) *The Indo-Aryans of Ancient South Asia*, Berlin: Walter de Gruyter, 1995, p.49).

[373] See A. Parpola, "The Problem of the Aryans and the Soma" in G. Erdosy, *op.cit.*, p.356.

cremation rituals in South Asia, we may consider them to have indeed consolidated the Vedic customs of the Indo-Āryans. Cremation is evidenced also in the Andronovo culture.[374] At the same time, the neighbouring Bishkent culture, which is contemporaneous with the Gandhara and is related to the northern BMAC type, exhibits also a curious quasi-Scythian custom of inhumation involving the removal of the entrails and their replacement with clarified butter which may have persisted among the Vedic Indians, as is suggested by *Shatapatha Brāhmana* XII,v,2,5.[375]

Elaborate fire-altars are evident in the ruins of the BMAC complex which correspond to the Āryan fire-sacrifices. The temples also contain rooms with "all the necessary apparatus for the preparation of drinks extracted from poppy, hemp and ephedra" that may have been used for the soma-rituals.[376] The BMAC may have thus been the centre of cultural contact between the proto-Dravidian/ Hurrian peoples of Mundigak and the later Indo-Āryans. It is interesting to note too, in this context, that the Avesta (which is geographically centred in eastern Iran) mentions the Māzanian daevas as worshippers of the Indian gods. According to Burrow, Māzana is known in Iranian sources as the territory between the southern shore of the Caspian Sea and the Alburz mountains.[377] It may be related also to Margiana and the Indo-Āryan culture noted there.

The Purūravas who adopted fire-worship from the Gandhāras may thus represent an Elamite branch of the proto-Āryan family, while the Gandaridae, who may have arrived from the south-east Caspian region (since

---

[374] *Ibid.*, p.366.

[375] *Ibid.*, p.365.

[376] *Ibid.*, p.262.

[377] See E.Bryant, *The Quest for the Origins of Vedic Culture: The Indo-Aryan Migration Debate*, Oxford: OUP, 2001, p.130.

the BMAC culture is apparently derived from the latter)[378] may be a typically Indo-Āryan, north-eastern branch of the same family.

It is clear that fire-worship was maintained particularly by the Japhetic branch of the Indo-Europeans. For, fire-worship is observed also among the Prussian-Lithuanian cult of szwenta (holy fire), and the Scythians too worshipped a goddess called Tabit whose name may be related to the Sanskrit 'tapti' denoting heat. The Greeks and Romans also maintained a cult of hestia or vesta. Plutarch (*Numa*, II) informs us that "Numa is said to have built the temple of Vesta in circular form as protection for the inextinguishable fire, copying not the fire of the earth as being Vesta, but of the whole universe, as centre of which the Pythagoreans believe fire to be established, and this they call Hestia and the monad".

That the Indic Vedic culture itself may have been developed after an original formulation at a proto-Indo-Iranian stage is suggested by the greater elaboration of the name of the god Tvoreshtar amongst the Iranians—representing the older religion of the proto-Āryans—compared to the Vedic Tvashtr. Indeed many of the characteristic traits of the rituals of ancient India derive from an Indo-Iranian period as is attested by the similarity of the terms, yajna/yaja, soma/haoma, mantra/manθra, nama/nəmô. Even the term atharvan has only an Iranian etymology âθravâ.[379]

In the literary record of the Vedic scriptures, the Indo-Āryans are fully identified with fire-worship. Indeed, the

---

[378] See J.P. Mallory and V.H. Mair, *The Tarim Mummies: Ancient China and the Mystery of the Earliest Peoples from the West*, London: Thames and Hudson, 2008, p.262.

[379] See P. Kretschmer, *Kuhns Zeitschrift* 55, p.80; cf. J. Gonda, *Religionen Indiens I: Veda und älterer Hinduismus*, Stuttgart, 1960, p.107.

Āryans designated the Dasyus or non-Āryans as Anagni, the fireless. The reference in *Manusmrithi* X:43-45 to "the Dravidas, the Kāmbojas, the Yavanas [Ionians], the Sakas [Scythians], etc." as Kshatriya races which have sunk to the level of Shūdras on account of their neglect of the sacred rites and the authority of the Brāhmans suggests that Brāhmanism, though based on the spiritual insights of the proto-Dravidians, was formulated by the Indo-Āryans as an exclusively fire-worshipping cult.

However, it should also be noted that this Āryan fire-worship is employed in a religion which formed the basis of the solar religions of the Sumerians or Egyptians as well. In the Sumerian religion too, the chief solar god An is equated to Girra, the fire-god (in an Assyrian exegetical text)[380] and Re in Egypt is the same as the solar force, Agni. So that it is possible that the adoration of the solar force as divine fire may have been an integral part of the original proto-Dravidian religion that was shared by Semites, Japhetites, and Hamites.

Pargiter suggested that the Dravidian "brāhmanical" institution was perhaps considerably transformed by the Āryans. However, Pargiter did not consider the possibility that both Āryan and later Dravidian may have been derived from a proto-Dravidian/Hurrian spiritual culture.. While the original [proto-] Dravidian priesthood was characterised by the practice of yogic austerities (tapas) which gave them magical powers, the Āryan was preoccupied with the performance of sacrifices, especially revolving around the worship of fire.[381] The Indo-Āryan religion thus seems to have combined the ancient proto-Dravidian wisdom of the Elamite/Mesopotamian

---

[380] RA 62-52,17-8 (see A. Livingstone, *Mystical and Mythological Explanatory Texts of Assyrian and Babylonian Scholars*, Oxford: Clarendon Press, 1986, p.74).

[381] See F.E. Pargiter, *op.cit.*, p.308f.

Hurrians with more northerly fire—and soma—rituals and horse-sacrifices. And the original proto-Dravidian or Noachidian wisdom[382] is also mostly preserved in Sanskrit, the cultivated [sanskrit=refined] and inflected language of the upper castes of the Indo-Āryans which however retains several proto-Dravidian elements in it.[383]

The Prisca Theologia

The original religion of the ancients was based on a spiritual vision of the formation of the cosmos. According to this cosmogonic scheme—which I reconstructed in my work *Ātman*[384]—after the cosmic deluge which marks the end of the first cosmic age (kalpa), the Divine Soul, Ātman, within the cosmic ocean (the Abyss) gradually recreates the cosmos assuming the form of an Ideal Macroanthropos, or Cosmic Man. The breath or life-force (Vāyu/Wotan) of the cosmic Man first unites with matter (Earth) to form a closely united complex of Heaven (the substance of the Purusha) and Earth. But the temporal aspect (Kāla, Chronos) of the rapidly moving breath or wind also separates the two elements, an event

---

[382] That the biblical Noah, a descendant of Adam's son, Seth, represents the wisdom of Seth is evident from Josephus' *Jewish Antiquities*, I, 70-71, which makes clear the association of the line of Seth with cosmological learning.

[383] Aurobindho Ghose pointed out that some of the obsolete or "high" Sanskrit words were indeed common Dravidian ones such as "sodara" for brother (instead of the typical Sanskritic "bratha") and "akka" for sister (see A. Ghose, "The Origins of Aryan Speech", *Sri Aurobindo Birth Centenary Library*, vol.10, p.560). Interestingly, the common Germanic word for son, "sohn", is similarly cognate with a high Sanskrit word, "sūnuh", rather than with the typical Sanskritic "putra" (*ibid.*). This confirms the relative lateness of the formation of Sanskrit.

[384] See A. Jacob, *Ātman*.

represented as a castration of the Purusha. The semen that falls from the castrated phallus impregnates the Purusha himself with a Cosmic Egg from which emerge the manifest cosmos comprised, again, of Earthly substance and Heavenly light (Brahman). This luminous Brahman is also represented anthropomorphically as a Cosmic Man.

However, this light, again represented in anthropomorphic form, continues to possess a stormy quality which is a persistence of Chronos in the manifest cosmos. This force, represented as Zeus/Seth/Ganesha, shatters the light and forces it to descend to the lower regions of Earth, where it lies moribund as, for instance, Osiris. However, the same storm-force has, in its assault on the manifest light, swallowed the divine phallus and it eventually revives the moribund light in the underworld with its potency. Separating the substance of Earth, into which the cosmic light has sunk, into the earthly regions and heaven of our universe, it emerges through the cleft between the two into the mid-region of the stars as a universal Tree of Life, or Phallus. The seed of this newly formed universe is then emitted within our galaxy, first as the moon, and then the solar force finally emerges above the top of the Tree (Phallus) as the sun.

Āryan Rituals

The fire-based rituals of the Indo-Āryans are based on the original sacrifice of the Ideal cosmic macroanthropos, Purusha, as well as on its repetitions in the manifest cosmos and in the underworld, for it is these sacrifices that result in the formation of the sun.[385] The primary aim of the Vedic ritual is thus to restore the disintegrated

---

[385] For a detailed study of the ancient Indo-European rituals, see A. Jacob, *Brahman*.

Purusha and, especially, his solar energy. As Gonda pointed out with regard to the construction of the Vedic fire-altar,

> In building the great fireplace one restores and reintegrates Prajāpati [Purusha], whose dismemberment had been the creation of the universe, and makes him whole and complete. At the same time and by means of the same ritual act, the sacrificer, who is identified with Prajāpati (cf. *Shatapatha Brāhmana* VII,4,15) constructs himself a new social personality and secures the continuance of his existence.[386]

The sacrifice of the Purusha which initiated the formation of the universe was most probably imitated in the ancient Indo-European religions by a human sacrifice.[387] Human sacrifice is indeed archaeologically evidenced in the early Bronze Age (fourth millennium B.C.) Luhansk site in the Ukraine which forms part of the Yamnaya culture associated with the Āryans. It is attested among the ancient Germanic peoples too and discernible (in Caesar's writings) among the Celts, as well as among the Scythians, and Thracians.[388] Among the Indo-Āryans the human sacrifice is naturally called a Purushamedha (sacrifice of the Purusha).

The primary purpose of a sacrifice is, however, self-sacrifice and the sacrifice of a human involved in the proto-Vedic Purushamedha must originally have been conducted as a substitute for the sacrifice of the sacrificer himself, since the sacrificer is, in all Vedic sacrifices,

---

[386] See J. Gonda, *Prajāpati's rise*, p.16f.

[387] See A. Jacob, *Brahman*, Ch.I.

[388] K. Rönnow, ("Zur Erklärung des Pravargya") pointed to the significant evidence of human sacrifice among the Germans, Celts, Scythians and Thracians and suggested that it must have been practised even by the Greeks and Indians, in spite of the dearth of such evidence among them (see B. Lincoln, *Myth, Cosmos and Society*, p.172).

identified with the victim. As Heesterman states, "self-sacrifice is an all-but-ubiquitous theme in the ritual brāhmana texts, the victim as well as the other offerings being regularly equated with the sacrificer".[389] That is why the victim in the Purushamedha was originally exclusively a brāhman or a kshatriya, since only these two castes were qualified to act as representatives of the Purusha and to conduct sacrifices.

The sacrificial victim is also always a male[390] since only his energy can substitute for the phallic force of the Purusha that fills the universe with its life. We have observed in our survey of the cosmological bases of sacrifices that the entire evolution of the material universe arises from repeated castrations, and preservations, of the divine phallus, first in the Ideal realm of the Purusha, then in the early cosmos of Brahman and, lastly, in the material universe, as the Tree of Life that arises from the underworld and extends to the heavens. If what is most important in the Purusha is his phallic power, as is evident also in the Hesiodic account of the castration of Ouranos by Chronos,[391] it is probable that the sacrifice originally focussed on the victim's phallus, as we observe, for example, in the veneration of the penis of a slaughtered stallion noted among the ancient Nordic peoples.[392] Similarly, in the Equus October ceremony in ancient Rome, a race-horse was slaughtered and its tail (standing no doubt for its penis) was brought to the regia.[393]

---

[389] J.C. Heesterman, *The Broken World of Sacrifice: An Essay on Ancient Indian Ritual*, Chicago: University of Chicago Press, 1993, p.173.

[390] This is reflected even in the Hebrew Paschal sacrifice (see below), where the lamb necessarily has to be a male one.

[391] See Hesiod, *Theogony*, I, 170ff.

[392] See 'Volsa pattr' in *Óláfs saga helga*.

[393] See J. Mallory and D.Q. Adams, *Encyclopedia of Indo-European Culture*, p.330.

Over time, however, the human victim was substituted with animals that equally represented the energy of the divine phallus, thus a horse or a bull, and finally with lesser animals such as sheep and goats. Indeed, at the time of the composition of the *Shatapatha Brāhmana*, the most common substitute was the goat (*SB* VI,2,1,39). In all cases, however, the original significance of the sacrifice as a self-sacrifice is never forgotten, as many of the processes of the Vedic sacrifices as well as many of the accompanying Vedic chants reveal. *SB* I,3,2,1, for instance, identifies the sacrifice (also frequently called Vishnu) with the Purusha: "Now the sacrifice is the man".

Just as the death of Osiris is followed by his revival in our universe as the sun, the Indo-European religious sacrifices also betoken not only a self-sacrifice of the sacrificer but also a solar rebirth that they allow the sacrificer to undergo as a brāhman, or one who has realised the solar virtue of his soul. In the Indian horse-sacrifice, Ashvamedha, for instance, the horse represents the sun which has been lost and must be recovered. Thus *SB* XIII,3,1,1 declares:

> Prajâpati's eye swelled; it fell out: thence the horse was produced; and inasmuch as it swelled (ashvayat), that is the origin and nature of the horse (ashva). By means of the Aśvamedha the gods restored it to its place, and verily he who performs the Aśvamedha makes Prajâpati complete, and he (himself) becomes complete; and this, indeed, is the atonement for everything, the remedy for everything.

This is the same significance that attaches also to the Osirian funereal rites, especially the mouth-opening ritual.[394] For the assault on the solar force by Seth is

---

[394] See A. Jacob, *Brahman*, p.211f.

referred to as the damage or robbing of the "Horus eye" [the sun] which must be restored to Horus the Elder/Osiris.

By transfiguring the sacrificer into the solar force, the sacrifice simultaneously bestows immortality on him. The nectar of immortality that sacrificers seek for by toil and penance is indeed Soma (*SB* IX,5,1,8). The underlying motif of the Soma sacrifice is one related to the pressing, or killing of the Purusha, as *SB* II,2,2,1 suggests: "in pressing out the king [Soma] they slay him". This may have a special phallic connotation as well since the soma juice is akin to the seminal power of Prajāpati which serves as the source of the sun. Thus the sacrifice, though representing the death of the sacrificer, also signifies the production of Soma, the nectar of immortality. The sacrificer's spiritual rebirth is essentially akin to that of the solar force Agni that we have observed above.

The ultimate aim of the original Indo-European sacrifices, modelled after the cosmic sacrifice of the Purusha, however, must have been the liberation of the self from the illusions of the material fabric in which it is entangled and the direction of the energy of man into the divine consciousness. This is indeed the principal aim of yogic ascesis as well, which, according to Heesterman, is an internalisation of the sacrifice. However, since yoga is likely to have preceded fire-sacrifices since it is the basis of the cosmic vision that informs both, it is more probable that the fire-sacrifices were a later externalisation of yogic practice rather than that the latter was an internalisation of the former.

Agnicayana

One of the most important of the rituals of the ancient Indians is the Agnicayana, which recreates the birth of the universe in the form of Prajāpati as well as the birth of Agni as Agni (the fiery solar force)-Vāyu (the life-force)- and Āditya (the sun).[395] The first rites of this ceremony are dedicated to the engendering of Agni as the elemental solar fire. This is done through an initial sacrifice of five forms of animal life, starting with a human. These five victims also symbolise the five layers of the altar that is to be built in the course of this ceremony (*SB* VI,2,1,16). After the initial animal sacrifices, the fire-pan (ukha) is fashioned, which is considered to be the "ātman" (soul) of the fire-altar. It is four-sided to represent the four quarters of the universe. The first major step in this ceremony (*SB* VI,2,2,27) is the symbolic pouring of his seed by the sacrificer into the fire-pan representing a womb. As *SB* VI,2,2,22 declares "there is seed here in the sacrifice". *SB* X,4,1,1-2 explains that the pouring of the seed of the sacrificer into the fire-pan as into a womb is the same as the pouring of the seed of Prajāpati.

Agni is later looked for in the clay (*SB* VI,3,3) and dug up (*SB* VI,4,17) and then deposited on an antelope-skin representing Earth (also called the "sacrifice") and a lotus-leaf representing the Sky ("the womb"), for the first birth of Agni is from the Heavens, the second from Earth and the third from the Waters surrounding Earth.[396] Agni is poured as seed into the lotus-leaf (*SB* VI,4,3,6). Then Agni is created for a second time from Earth, represented now by the fire-pan (*SB* VI,5,1,11-12), which is the "earthen

---

[395] The Agnicayana rituals are described in *SB*, Books VI-X (cf. also *KYV* V-VI). They are also detailed in the Shulba Sutras.

[396] For a detailed description of the Indo-European cosmology underlying the rituals see A. Jacob, *Ātman;* A. Jacob, *Brahman.*

womb for Agni" (*SB* VI,5,2,21). Milk is poured into it and Agni is generated as Vishnu (*SB* VI,6,6,2,16). The sacrificer now fashions the "seed" of Agni in the form of a winged solar bird (*SB* VI,7,2,5). Next, he takes the Vishnu strides which formed the universe (*SB* VI,7,2,10). The ashes of the fire in the fire-pan are then thrown into water (*SB* VI,8,2,2), since the last birth of Agni is from the Waters.

Then follows the construction of the three hearths, the circular gārhapatya, representing earth and the world of men (*SB* VII,I,1) and the square āhavanīya representing heaven and the world of the gods (*SB* VII,2,2). The air of the Mid-region is represented by the āgnīdhrīya fire (*SB* VII,1,2,12). During the building of the gārhapatya hearth, the fire-pan is again impregnated with sand to conceive Agni a second time (SB VII,1,1,41-42). In addition, a Nirriti hearth is built representing the corruption and evil that have to be removed from the sacrifice (*SB* VII,2,1). This is followed by the construction of the vedi, also representing earth, and the mahāvedi, representing heaven (*SB* VII,3,1,27). The catvala (pit/womb) represents the original site of the sun before it moved to the heavens of our universe (*Jaiminiya Brāhmana* I, 86,7). The area on which the fire-altar is to be constructed is scattered with sand representing seed in order to fill Prajāpati with seed (*SB* VII,3,1,42).

The construction of the fire-altar is begun a year (suggesting a year's gestation period) after the ukha is prepared. The process of constructing the five layers of the fire-altar is described in *SB* VII,4,1-VIII,5,1. A lotus leaf representing Earth is placed in the centre of the altar site and on it a gold plate that the sacrificer has been wearing for a year. On top of this plate, which represents the orb of the sun, a gold man representing the Purusha finally manifest within the sun (*SB* X,5,2,6) is placed facing the east. The sacrificer sings over the gold man to transfer his virility or semen into it (*SB* VII,4,1,24). *SB* X,4,1,6 equates the gold plate with Indra symbolising kshatra (sovereignty) and the gold man with Agni symbolising brahman (priesthood). The identification of the yajamāna with the gold man stresses the identification of the sacrificer with Agni as the Purusha.

Then the Purusha sāman is sung and the laying of the bricks is begun, the first being the svayamātrrina ('the naturally pierced') placed on the gold man to allow him to breathe. Within the first layer of the altar are buried the fire-pan (representng a womb), a living tortoise and a mortar and pestle (representing a penis in a womb). The tortoise, an avatār of Vishnu, represents the form of the universe, comprising heaven and earth.[397] Thus the fire-pan and the lotus leaf are considered to be "female"[398] and the "womb" which the sacrificer impregnates in order to generate Agni, the solar force, as Āditya, the sun.

Next, after a square mortal (ulūkhulaka) made of udumbara wood is installed at the 'northern shoulder' of the fire-altar, the fire-pit (ukhā) is placed in the middle. The fire-pan that was used by the sacrificer for carrying around the fire for a year is buried in the first layer, and the heads of the five sacrificial victims are placed in it, the human head in the middle of the fire-pit, the head of a horse towards the west, of a bull towards the east, of a ram towards the south, and of a goat towards the north, while seven pieces of gold are laid in the seven orifices of the human head.[399] The bricks of the altar are animated by

---

[397] See M. Biardeau, *Le sacrifice dans l'Inde ancienne,* p.18.

[398] See H.W. Tull, *The Vedic Origins of Karma*, Albany: SUNY Press, 1989, p.87f.

[399] See H.T. Bakker, "Human sacrifice (Purushamedha), construction sacrifice and the origin of the idea of the 'man of the homestead (Vāstupurusha)" in H.N. Bremmer (ed.) *The Strange World of Human Sacrifice*, Leuven: Peeters, 2007, p.183.

vital breaths represented by certain bricks called "breath-holders" (prāna-bhrt). The altar indeed represents the cosmic body of Agni as Purusha, and the brick-layers represent the various breaths of the Purusha.

Macrocosmically, Purusha's feet represent earth, legs intermediate space, waist the mid-region, chest intermediate space, and head heaven.[400] The lowest level of the altar in which the image is embedded represents the Svarloka (Heaven), the third level the Bhuvarloka (the Mid-region of the stars), the fourth level Brahman and the immortal regions, and the fifth the Bhurloka (Earth). However, although vertically the altar represents the Purusha, horizontally, it represents the solar force in the form of a sun-bird with outstretched wings facing the east. The fire-altar in the form of a sun-bird that may fly to the heavens[401] represents the phallic force of the Purusha that generates the sun.

After the completion of the five layers, the altar is sprinkled with gold-chips to confer a golden form to the "body" of the Purusha (SB X,1,4,9)[402] as well immortality on Agni (SB VIII,7,4,7). Layers of soil are then scattered in between the brick-layers to represent the Purusha's marrow, bones, sinews, flesh, fat, blood, and skin (SB X,1,4).

Then a hymn to propitiate the fierce form of Agni, Rudra, is chanted (SB IX). This is followed by the chanting of sāman hymns representing the immortal vital airs (SB IX,1,2,32). The chanting of these hymns is said to make

---

[400] H.J. Tull, *op. cit.*, p.93.

[401] See A. Michaels, *Hinduism Past and Present*, Princeton, NJ: Princeton University Press, 2004, p.249.

[402] We see that although there is very little idolatry among the ancient Āryans, the geometric form of the Vedic altar nevertheless possesses a palpable anthropomorphic quality that is manifest more fully in the worship of sacred idols among the Hamites - the Egyptians, Sumerians and later Indians (see A. Jacob, *Brahman*, Chs.XIII,XIV,XV).

the priests who chant as well as the sacrificer "boneless and immortal" (*SB* IX,I,2,34). Then follows a chanting of the Gāyatri hymn which makes the head immortal (*SB* IX,1,2,35). The right wing of the sun-bird which represents earth is then made immortal by the chanting of the Rathanthara hymn (SB IX,I,2,36), the left wing representing the sky is made immortal by the chanting of the Brhat hymn (*SB* IX,1,2,37), the breath of the sun-bird is made immortal by the chanting of the Vāmadevya hymn (*SB* IX,1,2,38), the tail representing the moon is made immortal by the chanting of the Yagnyayagnīya hymn, and the heart representing the sun is made immortal by chanting hymns about Prajāpati and progeny (*SB* IX,1,2,40-42).

After the generation of Agni as the sun-bird Āditya, Agni is led to the fire-altar (*SB* IX,2) and installed there (*SB* IX,3). The aim of the Agnicayana ritual is the flight of Āditya, the sun, to the heavens.403 The sacrificer too is thereby borne by the altar, or the sun-bird, to heaven. However, the sacrificer does return to the earth (represented by the gārhapatya hearth) after his journey to the otherworld. As Tull points out, the purpose of the construction of the fire-altar is "to reunify man's material being with the essential aspect of existence and thereby regain the original state of wholeness".[404]

Jewish Origins

The elaborate sacrificial ritual we have just studied gives us an idea of the magico-symbolic nature of the religious

---

[403] See H.W. Tull, *op.cit.*, p.95f. In *SB* X,2,1 the contraction and expansion of the wings of the sun-bird are depicted as being incorporated into the construction of the fire-altar.

[404] See H.W. Tull, *op.cit.* p.101; cf. *SB* X,1,4,1.

worship of the ancient Indo-Europeans. The *prisca theologia* of the Indo-Europeans informing these Indo-Āryan rituals was a polytheistic one in which the various transformations of the divine Soul Ātman through its fiery energy Agni are worshipped as individual deities. This is in stark contrast to Hebrew monotheism, which should more properly be designated as a mono-nationalism based on the tribal cult of Yahve, the god of the Hebrews. The Hebrews are a branch of the Semitic Arameans who are recognisable in the nomadic "habiru" of the ancient Near East who were considered as dangerous and subversive mercenaries and brigands.[405] The radical difference between Hebraic monotheism and ancient henotheism is that the latter is a genuinely universal religion based on the scientific and philosophical understanding of the cosmos, whereas the Abrahamic revolution represents a repudiation of this religiosity for a obscurantist anthropocentric ethics.

The Jewish aversion to cosmological religion is indeed confirmed in the references to Abraham's career as a religious leader in Josephus' *Jewish Antiquities*, I,157:[406]

[Abraham] began to have higher notions of virtue than others had, and he determined to renew and to change the opinion all men happened then to have

---

[405] See J. Bottero, *op.cit.*; cf. S. Smith, *op.cit.*, p.192. The equation of "habiru" with "Hebrew" is confirmed by Philo the Jew's explanation of the latter term as "migrant" (*De Migratione Abrahami*, 20).

[406] The Abrahamic Hebrews were probably forced to leave Mesopotamia, as Josephus' further statement suggests: "For which doctrines, when the Chaldeans, and other people of Mesopotamia, raised a tumult against him, he thought fit to leave that country; and at the command and by the assistance of God, he came and lived in the land of Canaan. And when he was there settled, he built an altar, and performed a sacrifice to God." Cf. Philo the Jew's *De mutatione nominum*, 72-6.

concerning God; for he was the first that ventured to publish this notion, That there was but one God, the Creator of the universe; and that, as to other [gods], if they contributed anything to the happiness of men, that each of them afforded it only according to his appointment, and not by their own power.

However, as Renan pointed out in his *Histoire Générale et Système Comparé des Langues Sémitiques* (1863), monotheism, far from representing a higher stage of religious consciousness, is

> en realité, le fruit d'une race qui a peu de besoins religieux. C'est comme minimum de religion, en fait de dogmes et en fait de pratiques extérieures, que le monothéisme est surtout accommodé aux besoins des populations nomades".[407]

The historical record of the Jews itself was completed as the Hebrew Bible (Old Testament) by around the third century B.C., though it may have been begun shortly after the Babylonian exile of the sixth century B.C. In its monotheistic glorification of the history of the Jewish tribes, the Hebrew Bible naturally ignores the spiritual bases of the older polytheistic cosmogony.

The Kabbalah

However, some evidence of cosmological mysticism appears even among the Jews in their Kabbalistic works such as *Sepher Yetzirah* (The Book of the Creation) and the *Zohar* (The Book of the Light), which were composed in

---

[407] E. Renan, *Histoire Générale et Système Comparé des Langues Sémitiques*, Paris: Levy, 1863, p.432.

the first centuries A.D. In all probability these works too, like the Gnostic ones and the early notions of a Christian messiah, were derived from the Assyrians among whom the Hebrews were exiled in the 6th century B.C.[408] and contain some insights into the original cosmological bases of the first few sections of *Genesis*.

The Kabbalah begins with the ineffable Deity Ein Sof (corresponding to Ātman) and posits two trinities emanating from him, representing the Ideal Man (Adam Kadmon) and the Cosmic Man. The first, ideal trinity is constituted of

1. Being (Eheieh) also called Kether or the Crown, conceived of as a point Arich Anpin,
2. the ideal light constituted of a Father, Chokmah (also called Yahweh) and a Mother, Binah (also called Elohim), and their progeny,
3. a male hypostasis called Chesed (also called El) and a female one called Geburah (also called Eloh).

The last two together produce the second, cosmic trinity ruled by

1. Tiphereth or the King (also called Eloha), who corresponds to the brilliant divine Consciousness of Brahman and also to the cosmic Christ. The King rules over
2. a male hypostasis Netzah (also called Yahweh Sabaoth)

---

[408] The *Sepher Yetzirah* dates from around the 2nd century A.D. and contains Babylonian, Egyptian and Hellenic cosmogonic notions. The *Zohar* was first published in 13th century Spain by Moses de Leon, who attributed the work to Rabbi Shimon bar Yochai of the 2nd c. A.D. However, much of it may date back to the time of the Babylonian Talmud.

and a female Hod (also called Elohim Sabaoth) who in turn produce

3. Yesod (also called El Chai), corresponding to Re as Osiris, and the female world of matter Malkuth (also called Shekinah) corresponding to Isis.

The final effect of this cosmic evolution which is the creation of the sun is not elaborated upon in the Kabbalah. However, we note that the Kabbalistic conception of Yahweh is indeed loftier than the biblical one where Yahweh is considered as the creator of the earthly Adam and god of only the Jewish tribes.

Unfortunately, Judaism has, by and large, subordinated the Kabbalistic exegeses to the literal study of the Torah and Talmud, which are mundane records of early Jewish political and social life quite lacking in spirituality. The lack of any strong development of the Kabbalah as a mainstream Jewish cult indeed confirms the foreign origins of the system and its quasi-polytheistic cosmogonical model.

Christian Origins

As regards the Christian cult, the fact that it too was derived from Indo-European cosmogonical notions, and dates back, like the Kabbalah, to the time of the Babylonian exile, is clear from the contemporary Gnostic cosmological descriptions of the Christ as the cosmic macro-anthropomorphic manifestation of the Idea of God,[409] as well as in the extraordinary story of the death

---

[409] A philosophical explanation of the Gnostic Adamas, the First Man, and the Son of Man is provided by the second century document of the Gnostic Naassenes that is cited by Hippolytus of Rome (170-235)

and resurrection of the Christ himself, since this can only be a historicisation of the cosmic drama of the descent of the solar force (Osiris) into the underworld and its later emergence as the sun (Horus the Younger) of our solar system. Another proof of the mythological basis of the Christ story is the employment of a "carpenter" as the father of Jesus, since this figure corresponds exactly to the formative force Tvashtr (Tuisto among the Germans) of the cosmic Man, Purusha, for the Indo-Iranian name Tvoreshtar also signifies a carpenter. It is Tvashtr who forms the seed of the light of the universe which appears as Brahman, whereas the impregnation of the material substrate of the cosmos is undertaken by the breath of the Purusha, represented as the wind-deity Vāyu (Wotan), who corresponds to the Christian Holy Spirit. As we know, at the Council of Ephesus of 431 A.D., the Virgin Mary too was confirmed as the mother not of a human son but, rather, of God (that is, of the Cosmic Christ), while the Lateran Council of 469 clarified that Mary conceived Jesus through the Holy Spirit.

The translation of this cosmological myth of Jesus, which is the same as that of Helios/Brahman, into a historical tale set in Roman times in Judaea is perhaps the work of a certain group of Jews called the Essenes who later called themselves Evangelists and, more particularly, of Paul, who wished to make the Christian cult an international Jewish one by adding a final chapter to the Jewish history of the Old Testament. The Essenes are described by Josephus (1st c. A.D.) as being a philosophical group that believed in the immortality of souls, a doctrine not adhered to by Jews in general and who were ruled by severe ideals of simple and righteous communal living.410 The Essenes, according to the bishop Epiphanius of

---

in his *Philosophumena*.

[410] See Josephus, *The Wars of the Jews*, Bk.II, Ch.8.

Salamis (4th c. A.D.),[411] included the Nazarenes whose practices retained many of the old Jewish ones except that they did not believe that the Laws that Moses received were those followed by the Jews.[412]

The originators of the Christian religion were probably also related to the authors of the Dead Sea Scrolls[413] who maintained a belief in a "Teacher of Righteousness" dated to the second century B.C. who would guide the erring Jews in "the hidden things in which Israel had gone astray".[414] Evidence that the Dead Sea Scrolls may have been the work of the Essenes is particularly provided in the repeated references in these scrolls to the Jews as "the breakers of the Covenant".

As for the contribution of the Jew Saul of Tarsus, who converted to Christianity and called himself Paul, it must be noted that he was, contrary to common belief, not more Judaic than his counterpart Peter but less. For, whereas the latter insisted on obedience to the Mosaic Law, Paul advocated a degree of freedom from it.[415] This is evident in the dispute regarding circumcision in Acts 15, wherein Peter maintained the need for adherence to this

---

[411] See Epiphanius, *Panarion*, I, 19.

[412] Some of whom migrated to India along with St. Thomas to found the Syriac Orthodox Church of Malabar, whose members are to this day called "Nasrani" or Nazarenes.

[413] Pliny the Elder (*Historia Naturalis* V, 17) refers to the Essenes as living a monastic life along the northwest shore of the Dead Sea, close to where the Scrolls were discovered.

[414] See the Cairo Damascus Document, 3, 12-15.

[415] This view of the conflict between Peter and Paul was first presented by Ferdinand Baur (1792-1860) of the Tübingen School of theology in his *Kritische Untersuchungen über die kanonischen Evangelien, ihr Verhältniss zu einander, ihren Charakter und Ursprung* (1847). For Paul's rejection of the Jewish Law see James Parkes, *The Conflict of the Church and the Synagogue: A Study of the Origins of Antisemitism*, N.Y.: Meridian, 1964, p.53ff.

custom whereas Paul argued against it. The early Christian thinker, Marcion of Sinope (2nd c. A.D.),[416] too pointed out that the reference to false apostles in Galatians was indeed directed to Peter, James, and John, the so-called "Pillars of the Church". Irenaeus and Tertullian, however, argued against Marcionism's elevation of Paul and stated that Peter and Paul were equals among the apostles.

Marcion himself manifested a deep-seated aversion to the materialism and nationalism of Judaism. He was revolted by the Hebraic conception of Yahwe as a tribal god who sanctions all manner of crimes to his chosen Israelites and so he, like the Gnostics, differentiated the supreme deity (whom he identified with the Heavenly Father of Christianity) from a demiurge identified with Yahwe. The sins of the mankind created by Yahwe had to be expiated by the sacrifice of the Incarnate God, Christ, in order that all men may inherit eternal Life. Unfortunately, Marcion was excommunicated by the Petrine Roman Church, which reinforced its Judaic connections in forming an orthodox "Catholic" (universal) Church.

Christian Ritual

Although the Jews rejected the cosmological religions of Mesopotamia, there is continuing evidence of their regular performance of sacrificial rituals (korban) using animal victims, especially in the Temple at Jerusalem. The sacrifice of Christ celebrated in the Christian mass is indeed the culmination of this long tradition since it restores to the Jewish sacrifices the cosmological significance that they had lacked. That the Christian eucharist (thanksgiving)

---

[416] Most of Marcion's doctrines are to be gleaned from Tertullian's tract *Adversus Marcionem*, which rejects the dualism of Marcion's in favour of a strict monotheism.

ceremony or 'mass'[417] is actually a sacrificial ritual is made clear by the appellation employed for it by the East Syriac and West Syriac Churches. "qurbana" or "qurbono", which is the equivalent of the Jewish "korban". The Christian sacrifice is derived from the Paschal sacrifice of the Hebrews which was first performed on the night of the exodus from Egypt. For it was the blood of the sacrificed lamb sprinkled on the door-posts of the Israelites in Egypt that allowed the Lord to pass over these houses while conducting His massacre of the first-born of the Egyptians. However, the substitution of Christ for the sacrificial lamb constitutes a revolution against the Jewish religion since, by proclaiming Christ as the Messiah who gave his life for the world, it makes the Christians the redeemed Jews while the Jahvist Jews continue unredeemed in their constant expectation of a saviour. This is one reason why the Christian liturgy often uses passages from the Hebrew Bible—such as the *Sanctus* borrowed from Isaiah 6:3—without sensing any contradiction.

The mass was undoubtedly the principal sacrament among the early Christians. The resurrection of Christ celebrated in the Mass is indeed a revival of the heavenly nature of the first Adam (Purusha) whose "fall", as we have seen, was occasioned by his intimacy with Earth. Thus, in the first Epistle to the Corinthians 15:21-22 we read: "For since by man *came* death, by man *came* also the resurrection of the dead. For as in Adam all die, even so in Christ shall all be made alive." The epistle goes on to explain the cosmic drama at greater length but simplifying the original Adam into an "earthly" entity on account of his association with Earth:

---

[417] The term 'mass' is derived from the conclusion of the Latin liturgy which states "Ite, missa est" (go, this is the dismissal).

44 ... There is a natural body, and there is a spiritual body.

45 And so it is written, The first man Adam was made a living soul; the last Adam was made a quickening spirit.

46 Howbeit that was not first which is spiritual, but that which is natural; and afterward that which is spiritual.

47 The first man is of the earth, earthy: the second man is the Lord from heaven.

...

49 And as we have borne the image of the earthy, we shall also bear the image of the heavenly.

The earliest Christian rite that is attested is that of the St. James Liturgy,[418] which was used originally in Jerusalem, perhaps in the Greek language, and then transferred to the patriarchate of Antioch when it was translated into Syriac. An important section of this rite is that where the priest, making the sign of the cross on the gifts, says:

Holy art Thou, King of eternity, and Lord and giver of all holiness; holy also Thy only-begotten Son, our Lord Jesus Christ, by whom Thou hast made all things; holy also Thy Holy Spirit, which searches all things, even Thy deep things, O God: holy art Thou, almighty, all-powerful, good, dread, merciful, most compassionate to Thy creatures; who didst make man from earth

---

[418] James is said to have been a "brother" of Christ, though it is not clear if this is a familial or fraternal appellation.

after Thine own image and likeness;[419] who didst give him the joy of paradise.

This is a reference to the creation of Adam/the Purusha, who is also, as we have seen, formed of a union of heavenly substance with material substance of "earth". The "fall" of Adam is a reference to the castration of the Purusha effected by Chronos on account of his aversion to his father's lascivious union with Earth. The priest then continues:

> and when he transgressed Thy commandment, and fell away, didst not disregard nor desert him, O Good One, but didst chasten him as a merciful father, call him by the law, instruct him by the prophets; and afterwards didst send forth Thine only-begotten Son Himself, our Lord Jesus Christ [Tiphereth], into the world, that He by His coming might renew and restore Thy image;

This is a description of the production of the supreme Light of Consciousness that is Brahman, who is identifiable with the Cosmic Christ and the Kabbalistic Tiphereth.

We know from our reconstructed scheme of the Indo-European cosmogony that Brahman is indeed felled by the continuing stormy aspect of Chronos in the manifest cosmos called Zeus/Ganesha. The result of this assault is the descent of the Heavenly Light to the underworld, which is described thus in the Christian rite:

> Who, having descended from heaven, and become [Osiris] flesh of the Holy Spirit [Yesod] and Virgin Godmother Mary [Malkuth],

---

[419] My italics.

This earthly incarnation of Christ actually corresponds to the beginning of the ordeal of Osiris/Dionysus in the underworld that we have already observed in the pagan myths:

> and having sojourned among men, fulfilled the dispensation for the salvation of our race; and being about to endure His voluntary and life-giving death by the cross, He the sinless for us the sinners, in the night in which He was betrayed, nay, rather delivered Himself up for the life and salvation of the world.

The ordeal represented in the Christian rite as an earthly historical one meant to improve humanity is, in fact, an ordeal that the heavenly light undergoes in order to purify itself of its material dross and emerge in the atmospheric space between the Earth and Heaven of our own universe as the sun. However, the reference to the "power of the precious and life-giving cross" in this liturgy[420] brings to mind the import of the cross as an Indo-European phallic symbol. In Germanic mythology the tree also serves as the locus of the great self-sacrifice of the god Odin/Wotan/Wata to himself, which is a repetition, as it were, of the original killing of Ymir, the First Man/Purusha:[421]

> I know that I hung on a windy tree
> nine long nights,
> wounded with a spear, dedicated to Odin,
> myself to myself.[422]

It is as a result of this sacrifice—akin to the ordeals of Osiris, Marduk, Tammuz, and Christ—that Odin achieves knowledge of the magical runes.

---

[420] "Exalt the horn of Christians by the power of the precious and life-giving Cross".

[421] See, for instance, 'Vafþrúðnismál' in the *Poetic Edda*.

[422] 'Havamal', 138.

An even more precise understanding of the crucifixion and the of the significance of the cross itself emerges in one of the early Syriac hymns, the Haw Nurone hymn,[423] which demonstrates the significance of the Christian sacrifice in considerable detail. The Haw Nurone hymn first declares that the Christian altar

> is fashioned like the chariot of the cherubim. And is surrounded by multitudes of the heavenly hosts. On this altar is laid the Body of God's Son and Adam's children in their hands administer It. Instead of a man clad in silk, stands the (priest), and distributes alms among the needy. If envy existed among the angels the cherubim would envy human beings.

The Christian altar, therefore, has the same significance as the altar constructed by the brāhmans in the Agnicayana ritual which seeks to restore the mutilated Purusha. The reference to the shape of the altar as resembling "the chariot of the cherubim" should be glossed by the instructions given to Solomon by his father David in 1 Chron. 28:18:

> And, for the altar of incense, refined gold by weight; and gold for the pattern of the chariot of the cherubims that spread out their wings, and covered the ark of the covenant of the Lord.

The Ark of the Covenant itself is the one that preserves the stone tablets bearing the Ten Commandments (Exod.25:10ff). However, in the Roman Catholic and Eastern Orthodox Churches,[424] Mary is referred to as

---

[423] See the translation of this hymn at http://newandoldmonks.blogspot.ca/2009/09/syriac-hymn-nurone.html

[424] See, for instance, the 16th century Litany of Loreto, where Mary is addressed as the "Ark of the Covenant".

the "Ark" in that she bore Christ, just as the original Jewish ark bore the Mosaic Law. So the reference in the Christian hymn to the "chariots of the cherubim" and the Ark here suggests that the Christian sacrifice, unlike the Jewish ones, is aimed at producing not the Law of the Old Testament but the Christian solar god who is also the god of Love, since his original form as the Cosmic Christ is the same as that of the Indo-European Brahman/Helios, who is regularly identified with Eros.[425]

More interestingly, the hymn now directly refers to the cross as the "Tree", which is of course the "tree" or "axis" of the universe that is now being formed from the restored phallus of the Purusha/Adam so that the sun which it bears within it may emerge at the top:

> Where Zion set up the Cross to crucify the Son, there grew up the Tree which gave birth to the Lamb.

The final value of the manifestation of Christ therefore—after his original appearance as the cosmic Light (Tiphereth/Brahman), and then as a suffering victim in the underworld (represented by the early Christians as the passion of the "human" Christ among the Hebrews and Romans)—is as the "resurrected" sun of our universe. The reference to the "Lamb" in this passage is to the Old Testament sacrifice of Isaac by his father Abraham, which is considered by the Christians as a prototype of the sacrifice of the Christ:

> Where the nails were firmly driven in the Son's hands, there Isaac's hands were bound for an offering. Welcome priest who carries his Lord's Mysteries, and with thy right hand, life is given to mankind.

---

[425] See A. Jacob, *Brahman*, pp.7,34.

The solar nature of the resurrected Lamb of Christianity may itself be observed in the frequent Christian use of the term "sun of righteousness"[426] for Christ.[427]

The climactic point of the Christian sacrifice is the magical transformation of the bread and wine of the Holy Communion into the body and blood of Christ. Already in the second century A.D. St. Irenaeus of Lyons made it clear that "the bread which is produced from the earth is no longer common bread once it has received the invocation of God; it is then the Eucharist consisting of two realities, earthly and heavenly."[428] This is due to the inspiration of the Word of God, "When the ... cup and the man-made bread receive the Word of God, they become the Eucharist of the blood and body of Christ".[429] The vivifying principle of the Word of God is the Holy Spirit, as Clement of Alexandria (ca.150-215) declared: "To drink of the blood of Jesus is to partake in the Lord's immortality for the Spirit is the vital principle of the World, as blood is of flesh".[430]

This participation in the Christian mass endows an individual with eternal life, as St. Irenaeus continues to explain: "So also our bodies, when they receive the Eucharist, are no longer corruptible but have the hope of the resurrection to eternity".[431] This is, of course, an exegesis of the Gospels, for, as Jesus declares in John 6:54, "Whoso

---

[426] This term is taken from the last OT book of Malachi 4:2: "the Sun of Righteousness shall arise with healing in its wings".

[427] See for instance the blessing, "Christ the Sun of Righteousness shine upon you, scatter the darkness from before your path" used in certain Anglican Prayer Books.

[428] St. Irenaeus of Lyons, 'Against Heresies', 4.17.5-4.18.6, quoted in Mike Aquilina, *The Mass of the early Christians* (2007), p.98.

[429] 'Against Heresies', 5.2.2, in Aquilina, *op.cit.*, p.98.

[430] Clement of Alexandria, 'The Teacher', 2.2, quoted in Aquilina, *op.cit.*, p.135.

[431] St. Irenaeus of Lyons, 'Against Heresies', 4.17.5-4.18.6.

eateth my flesh, and drinketh my blood, hath eternal life; and I will raise him up at the last day". Jesus particularly contrasts the nourishment he offers with the manna that the Hebrews were said to have received from their God while they travelled in the desert (Exod 16): "This is that bread which came down from heaven: not as your fathers did eat manna, and are dead: he that eateth of this bread shall live forever". This gift of immortality is stressed by the early Christian father St. Ignatius of Antioch (d. 107 A.D.) who stated that the sacrament is "the medicine of immortality and the antidote to prevent us from dying".[432]

Indeed, the mass is meant to even physically transform the individual who participates in it. As the fourth century bishop St. Cyril of Jerusalem declared in his *Mystagogical Lectures*, after receiving the wine during the Communion, the participant should: "while the moisture is still upon [his] lips, touch it with [his] hands and bless [his] eyes and forehead and the other organs of sense."[433] And he further exhorts his reader: "And make your face shine so that, having it unveiled with a pure conscience, you may, like a mirror, reflect the glory of the Lord and proceed from glory to glory, in Jesus our Lord."[434] This illumination may have something to do with the common Levantine practice of ritual purification with water and the contemporary Christian use of "holy water" to bless supplicants, but it also resembles practices in Tantric Hinduism (derived from Yogic and Vedic rituals) where the adept, after elaborate yogic purification of his bodily elements, undertakes a divinisation of his body through

---

[432] St. Ignatius of Antioch, 'Ephesians' 20, in Aquilina, *op.cit.*, p.72.

[433] St. Cyril of Jerusalem, *Mystagogical Lectures*, 5, quoted in Aquilina, *op.cit.*, p.202.

[434] *Ibid.*, 4, quoted in Aquilina, *op.cit.*, p.195. Cf. also Rom 12:1: "Present your bodies a living sacrifice, holy and acceptable to God, which is your reasonable service."

the utterance of magical mantras at the same time as he touches various parts of his body.[435]

We see from this comparison of the religious rituals of the Āryans and the early Christians that, in spite of the apparent geographical and cultural differences between the religions of the eastern Indo-Āryans and the middle-eastern Christians, both of them are indeed informed by the same cosmological myth of the "fall" of the Ideal Man, his descent into the underworld (earth) and his "resurrection" into the heavens as the sun. The primacy of the mass as a Christian sacrament corresponds to that of the various solar sacrificial rituals of the brāhmanical religion. On the other hand, despite ancient coincidences with Jewish Kabbalistic lore, the dimly developed cosmological aspect of the sacred symbolism of the Kabbala and the relative insignificance of Kabbala itself in relation to Jahvist Judaism reveal the incompatibility of Christianity with any form of Judaism, which is rather considered by the former as a perverse rejection of the fulfilment of the Scriptures. Indeed, while Judaism and, to a certain extent, Islam may be considered Abrahamic religions "in Reinkultur". Christianity has more complex origins than facile references to "Judeo-Christianity" might suggest. And it is clear also that it was not just the spread of Christianity among the Greeks of southern Europe or the Germanic tribes of the Holy Roman Empire that endowed it with certain "pagan" characteristics but, rather, Christianity as a "mystery" religion possessed from its very inception an unmistakably Indo-European cosmological character.

---

[435] Cf. A. Jacob, *Brahman*, p.226.

VI. DIONYSUS AND MURUGA
Notes on the Dionysiac religion

WHILE MOST PEOPLE recognise Zeus and Dionysus as two of the most important deities of the ancient Greek pantheon, few are aware that the cult of Dionysus is closely related to that of Skanda/Muruga, the son of the preeminent Indian deity, Shiva. It would, therefore, be instructive to investigate the religious relations between the several Indo-European cultures that extended in antiquity from Crete in the west to the Indus Valley in the east.

***

I. The Origins of the Dionysiac Religion

If we attempt to identify the geographical location wherein the widespread Dionysiac mythology was first developed, we find that the name Zagreus used by the Cretans for Dionysus (the Zeus that finds himself in the Underworld) points to a Near Eastern origin of this god since it must have been derived from the Zagros mountain range –

which is a southern extension of the Caucasus beginning in southeastern Turkey and running southwards between Iraq and Iran. As this mountain range is also the region in which Mt. Ararat is situated and the latter is generally identified by the ancients as the resting place of the boat that saves the First Man ('Noah', in Genesis 6-9), we may assume that this is the cradle of the entire Indo-European cosmological theology from which arose the several variant mythologies that spread from there eastwards and westwards.

We may recall also that, in the Indian Purānas, the process of developing life on our earth is supervised by the First Man, or Manu, and that the latter is described in the *Bhāgavata Purāna* VIII,24, as being the King of 'Drāvida'. This Manu is responsible for the continuance of mankind on the earth as well as for its spiritual evolution. In this task, he is assisted by seven Sages, who represent the wisdom and culture of enlightened man and are considered to be the ancestors of the Brāhmans. We may, therefore, assume thus that the entire cosmological mythology behind the Dionysiac religion, as well as of the Brāhmanical religion of India, is the legacy of a proto-Dravidian race.

As regards the proto-Dravidian folk, we may remember Lahovary's pioneering research into the Mediterranean people, which he identified with the Dravidian, as being the original inhabitants of the ancient Near East 'in its largest meaning', that is, including

> Anatolia, Syria, Palestine, Caucasia, Persia, Mesopotamia with its extensions towards India, as well as Arabia and the African regions facing Arabia, i.e. from the Nile valley to the high tablelands of East Africa.[436]

---

[436] See N. Lahovary, tr. K.A. Nilakantan, *Dravidian Origins*, p.2.

Lahovary goes on to remark that

> It was from this world of Anterior Asia, where the foundations of civilization had been already laid, that the bearers of the neolithic and chalcolithic civilizations of the Near East spread, by successive migrations, in general of relatively small groups, over a period of more than three thousand years, first towards North-East Africa, and later, during the fourth, third and second millennium, towards Europe.[437]

It is possible that one of the earliest regions to be settled by the proto-Dravidians from neighbouring Armenia was Anatolia. This is suggested by the great antiquity of the Neolithic archaeological finds at Çatal Hüyük in (ca. 7th millennium B.C.). The civilisation of Syro-Palestine may be even as old as that of Anatolia since settlements in Jordan are traceable from the late 7th millennium B.C. and in Byblos from the 6th.[438]

The early neolithic/chalcolithic sites of Yarim Tepe II (7th millennium B.C.) in northern Iraq give some evidence of fire rituals in connection with funerary practices and fire-rituals signal an ethnic group associated with the Indian and Iranian Āryans.[439] The chalcolithic sites (ca. 5000 B.C.) of northern Mesopotamia also provide similar evidence and these may point to the presences of early Vedic peoples, whom we might call proto-Āryan.

---

[437] For the possible relation of the proto-Dravidians to the Druids, see A. Jacob, *Brahman*, Ch.VI.

[438] See G.W. Ahlstrom, *Ancient Palestine*; J. Cauvin, *Religions néolithiques*,1972; S.A. Cook, *op.cit*. For Jericho, see K.M. Kenyon, *Digging up Jericho*.

[439] See P. Charvat, *Mesopotamia Before History*, p.90.

Charvat has also recently revealed that the fundamental social and religious forms of later Mesopotamian culture, including that of Uruk, are evident already in embryonic form in the early chalcolithic sites of northern Mesopotamia.[440] Crematory practices associated with fire-rituals are noticed here[441] and Tell Arpachiyah (TT6) also gives the first evidence of the use of the white-red-black colour triad which persists from chalcolithic times to Uruk[442] and is representative of three of the four castes—the brāhman, kshatriya, and vaisya—amongst the Indo-Āryans.[443]

The proto-Dravidians are most probably identifiable with the proto-Hurrians. The Hurrians spoke a language that possessed Dravidian characteristics and F. Bork[444] and G.W. Brown[445] have revealed the intimate linguistic relationship between Hurrian (along with its Mitanni dialect),[446] Elamite, and Dravidian. The Hurrians, who are found widespread throughout the ancient Near East, are closely associated with the Indo-Āryans as well as with the Hittites in the seventeenth century B.C. So we may assume

---

[440] *Ibid.*, pp.92,96.

[441] *Ibid.*, pp.45,90.

[442] *Ibid.*, p.92. This triad corresponds to the three basic energies in Indian philosophy, Tamas, Rajas, Sattva.

[443] See, for instance, *BrdP* I,ii,15,18ff. The Vaisya caste is in India represented by the colour yellow since black denotes the shūdra caste. The absence of yellow in the pottery of this period suggests that the original "caste"-system of the Hurrians was a tripartite one comprised of priests, warriors and agriculturists (these are the same as the three "castes" mentioned in the Iranian Farvardin Yasht XIII,88).

[444] See F. Bork, "Die Mitanni Sprache", *MVAG,* I and II, 1909.

[445] See G.W. Brown, "The Possibility of a Connection between Mitanni and the Dravidian languages", *JAOS,* 50 (1930), pp.273-305.

[446] For the dialectal relationship between the language of Tushratta's letter to Amenophis III and Hurrian, see Knudtzon, *Die el-Amarna Tafeln*, no.24; cf. S. Smith, *op.cit.*, p.71; cf.

that the Hurrians formed an integral part of the original Āryans – Indians, Iranians and also Hittites.

In the eastern Mediterranean, the possibility that Anatolia was the source of the Cretan and Greek religious culture was suggested early by Arthur Evans, who considered Crete,[447] in its Neolithic period, to be merely "an insular offshoot of an extensive Anatolian province".[448] A Linear B tablet of the 14th century B.C. from Knossos also mentions the name 'Ionians' before the Dorians dominated Crete.[449] A.B. Cook too surmised that

> This name [Zagreus], we may suppose, travelled from Mesopotamia, *via* Phoinike, to Crete at about the same time and along much the same route as the Assyrian influences manifest in [a bronze shield found in the Idaean Cave in Crete dating from the eighth or ninth century B.C.]. From Crete it would readily pass to Argos, and so northwards to the rest of Greece.[450]

Further, the Cretan Zeus was originally called Kouros.[451] This would be related to the term 'kur' (mountain) applied to the Sumerian god of Wind, Enlil, as well as to his son, Ninurta.

When we explore the rise of the Indic civilisation around the Indus Valley, we note that the first settlements in Afghanistan resembling those of Elam (western Iran) and the Indus Valley are from ca.3000 B.C. in Mundigak,

---

[447] See A.B. Cook, *Zeus: A Study in Ancient Religion*, (1914-25), I:644ff.; cf. M.L. West, *The Orphic Poems*, Oxford: Clarendon Press, 1983, p.50.

[448] Quoted in G. Childe, *The Dawn of European Civilization*, p.17.

[449] M. Ventris and J. Chadwick, *Documents in Mycenaean Greek: Second Edition*. Cambridge University Press. 1973, p. 547.

[450] See A.B. Cook, *Zeus*, I:651.

[451] See M.L. West, *op.cit.*, p.131.

which is somewhat later than that of the Sumerian Uruk civilisation. From 2200-1700 B.C., there is clear evidence of typical Indo-Āryan settlement in the BMAC complex, which is not far north of Mundigak. It is difficult to determine whether these Āryans represent a continuation of the early Elamite Hurrians of Mundigak or are new immigrants from the Andronovo culture (1800-900 B.C.) north-east of the Aral Sea that is associated with the Indo-Āryans. The latter is indeed the more probable.[452]

Of the three Noachidian tribes mentioned in the 'Table of Nations' in Genesis 10, Japhetic, Semitic and Hamitic, the Japhetic or Āryan seem to have moved northwards to the Pontic-Caspian steppes to create the Yamnaya culture there (3300-2600 B.C.), which is considered the major source of the Āryan tribes.[453] The Andronovo culture of the Indo-Āryans is itself derived from the Hut Grave and Catacomb Grave culture of 2800-2000 B.C. and the Sintashta culture of the southeast Urals (2300-1900 B.C.),[454] which may have been proto-Āryan rather than proto-Indo-Āryan. The fact that there is clear evidence of fire-worship in the BMAC and little evidence of it in Mundigak suggests that the former is derived from the Andronovo rather than from the Elamite colonies. Elaborate fire altars are evident in the ruins of the BMAC complex which correspond to the Āryan fire-sacrifices. The temples also contain rooms with "all the necessary apparatus for the preparation of drinks extracted from poppy, hemp and ephedra" that may have been used for

---

[452] Andronovo type pottery has been found in the early layers of Margiana (see A. Parpola, "The problem of the Aryans and the soma", in G. Erdosy (ed.), *The Indo-Aryans of Ancient South Asia*, Berlin: Walter de Gruyter, 1995, p.363).

[453] See A. Parpola, *Ibid.*, p.356.

[454] See J.P. Mallory and V.H. Mair, *The Tarim Mummies*, p.260f.

the soma-rituals.[455] The BMAC may have thus been the centre of cultural contact between the proto-Dravidian/Hurrian peoples of Mundigak and the later Indo-Āryans.

The Indo-Āryan, both the Vedic Indians and the Avestan Iranians, seem originally to have been nomadic peoples, as is attested by the language of the Old Avesta, wherein the cosmos is viewed as an enormous tent.[456] We may remember also Megasthenes' report that

> The Indians were in old times nomadic, like those Scythians who did not till the soil, but roamed about in their wagons, as the seasons varied, from one part of Scythia to another, neither dwelling in towns nor worshipping in temples;[457] and that the Indians likewise had neither towns nor temples of the gods, but were so barbarous that they wore the skins of such wild animals as they could kill ... they subsisted also on such wild animals as they could catch, eating the flesh raw, - before, at least, the coming of Dionysus into India. Dionysus, however, when he came and had conquered the people, founded cities and gave laws to these cities, and introduced the use of wine among the Indians, as he had done among the Greeks, and taught them to sow the land, himself supplying seeds for the purpose ... It is also said that Dionysus first yoked oxen to the plough, and made many of the Indians husbandmen instead of nomads, and furnished them with the implements of agriculture; and that the Indians worship the other gods, and Dionysus himself in particular, with cymbals and drums, because he so

---

[455] *Ibid.*, p.262.

[456] See P.O. Skjaervo, "The Avesta as source for the early history of the Iranians", in G. Erdosy (ed.), *op.cit.*, p.168.

[457] The fact that the Scythians did not build temples or worship divine images is mentioned also by Herodotus, *Histories*, I,131.

taught them ... and that he instructed the Indians to let their hair grow long in honour of the god ....[458]

Since Dionysus belongs to the tradition of a reviving god prevalent in the Near East and Crete, we may assume that the cultural contact being referred to by Megasthenes is that between the early Scythian settlers of India and Elamite Dravidians/Hurrians from the Zagros region. Though the Orphic religion derived from the Dionysiac is itself not attested much earlier than the 6th B.C., the name of the god Dionysus, as we have noted above, is mentioned already in a Mycenean Linear B tablet from the Bronze Age.

Even the Indic Vedic culture itself seems to have been developed by the Indo-Āryans after an original sojourn in Iranian lands. This is suggested by the greater elaboration of the name of the god 'Tvoreshtar' amongst the Iranians —representing the older religion of the proto-Āryans— compared to the shorter Vedic 'Tvashtr'.[459]

The Mitanni, who were Indo-Āryans who called themselves 'kings of the Hurrians' in northern Syria and eastern Anatolia in the 16th century B.C. may also have been derived from an early westward migration of the BMAC folk in Afghanistan. The first coherent list of Indic gods indeed appears in the treaty of the Mitanni-Hurrian king Šattiwaza and the Hittite king Šuppililiumas I dating from the sixteenth century B.C., which includes the names Mitra-Varuna, Indra, and Nāsatyas.[460] It is important to

---

[458] See Arrian, *Indica*, VII (in R.C. Majumdar, *The Classical Accounts of India*, Calcutta: Firma K.L. Mukhopadhyay, p.220f.).

[459] Cf. A. Jacob, "Cosmology and Ethics in the Religions of the Peoples of the Ancient Near East", *Mankind Quarterly* 140, no.1 (Fall 1999), p.96.

[460] The text (CTH 51 and 52 (see D. Yoshida, *op.cit.*, p.12; cf. V. Haas, *Geschichte*, p.543) reads "$^{Dingir\ Meš}$Mitraššiel, $^{Dingir\ Meš}$Uruwanaššiel, ^{D}Indar, $^{Dingir\ Meš}$Našattiyana", where the uncertain suffix "šiel" may be a dual

note that the Hurro-Akkadian version of the Lord of the Waters among the Mitanni is 'Uruwana' or 'Aruna'. The similarity of 'Uruwana' to the Greek "Ouranos" is evident. And in the Vedic *Gopatha Brāhmana*, I,1,7, Varana[461] is the secret form of the name Varuna.[462] The form 'Aruna' is also related to the Hittite term for 'ocean' 'arunas'.[463]

Although the importance of fire-worship is typical of the Vedic Indo-Āryans and the Avestan Iranians, there is as yet not much evidence of fire-worship among the Mitanni Hurrians. It should also be remembered that the fire-worship of the Indo-Āryans is employed in the celebration of deities who are little different from those of the solar religions of the Sumerians or Egyptians. In the Sumerian religion too, the chief sky-god An is equated to Girra, the fire-god (in an Assyrian exegetical text)[464] and Re in Egypt is the same as the solar force, Agni. So that it is possible that the adoration of the solar force as divine fire may have been an integral part of the original proto-Dravidian religion that was shared by Semites, Hamites, and Japhetites. But the actual fire-rituals may have been preserved more carefully by the Japhetic Indo-Āryan stock that had migrated at a very early date northwards to the Yamnaya and Andronovo cultures whence they moved southwards again later, in the second millennium B.C., towards northern Mesopotamia, Iran, and India.

---

indicator.

[461] Following the example of the Latin pronunciation, we may assume that the original Sanskrit of this region also favoured the "u" sound for the phoneme later transcribed with a "v".

[462] "being Varana, he is mystically called Varuna, because the gods love mysticism" (see U. Chouduri, *op.cit.*, p.95).

[463] See G. Wilhelm, "Meer" in *RLA* VIII:3.

[464] RA 62-52,17-8 (see A. Livingstone, *Mystical and Mythological Explanatory Texts of Assyrian and Babylonian Scholars*, Oxford: Clarendon, 1986, p.74).

Pargiter suggested that the Brāhmanical institution was originally Dravidian and considerably transformed by the Āryans. While the original [proto-] Dravidian priesthood was characterised by the practice of yogic austerities (tapas) which gave them magical powers, the Āryan seem to have been preoccupied with the performance of sacrifices, especially revolving around the worship of fire.[465] The Indo-Āryan religion thus seems to have combined the ancient proto-Dravidian wisdom of the Elamite/Mesopotamian Hurrians with more northerly fire and soma-rituals and horse-sacrifices. Also, the original proto-Dravidian or Noachidian wisdom[466] is best preserved in the cultivated [sanskrit=refined] and inflected language of the upper castes of the Indo-Āryans.

As for the modern Dravidians (whom we may call Tamils, to distinguish them from the proto-Dravidians), the historical evidence of their entrance into South India is of relatively recent date, perhaps around the 13th century B.C. This means that there are only a few dim hints of the Near Eastern origins of the Dravidian peoples in the earliest archaeology and literature of South India. The earliest archaeological evidence (ca. 1200-80 B.C.) of the entrance of the Tamils into South India is from dolmen burial sites in Adichanallur (similar to those in Palestine and Cyprus), where some of the finds such as golden "mouth-pieces", bronze representations of cocks and spear-heads may be related to the worship of Muruga/Marduk/Ninurta.[467] The megalithic graves of the

---

[465] See F.E. Pargiter, *Ancient Indian Historical Tradition*, London: Milford, 1922, p.308f.

[466] That the biblical Noah, a descendant of Adam's son, Seth, represents the wisdom of Seth is evident from the Gnostic tradition (see G.G. Stroumsa, *Another Seed: Studies in Gnostic Mythology*, Leiden:E.J. Brill, 1984, p.107).

[467] See K. Zvelebil, *Tamil Traditions on Subrahmanya-Murugan*, Madras: Institute of Asian Studies, 1991, p.75f.

Madurai district dating from around 1000 B.C. also reveal resemblances to the early Iron Age graves of the Caucasus and the Central Iranian Sialk Necropolis B.[468]

II. *The Dionysiac Theogony*

In order to decipher the nature of the principal deities associated with the Dionysiac religion, we must study the original cosmological theogony of the Indo-Europeans. This is especially necessary in view of the fact that even a significant Indologist like Alain Daniélou has, in spite of his several fascinating studies of Shaivism,[469] expressed the rather misleading view that Shaivism—which he considers the Indic counterpart of the Dionysiac religion—'is essentially a nature religion.'[470] In fact, Shaivism and Yoga are the bases of all the major Dravidian and Āryan religio-philosophical systems of India and they are derived not from an adoration of natural phenomena but from a spiritual vision of the formation of the cosmos and of its reflection in the human microcosm.

The ancient Indo-European cosmogony—which I have reconstructed in my work *Ātman*[471]—begins

---

[468] See B. and R. Allchin, *The Birth of Indian Civilization*, Harmondsworth: Penguin Books, 1968, p.230.

[469] See (in translation) A. Daniélou, *Shiva and Dionysus: The Omnipresent Gods of Transcendence and Ecstasy*, London: East-West Publications, 1982; (revised edition) *Gods of Love and Ecstasy: The Traditions of Shiva and Dionysus*, N.Y.: Inner Traditions, 1992; *Shiva and the Primordial Tradition: From the Tantra to the Science of Dreams*, N.Y.: Inner Traditions, 2006.

[470] Alain Daniélou, *Gods*, p.15.

[471] For a full reconstruction of this cosmology see A. Jacob, *Ātman:*

after the cosmic deluge that ended the first cosmic age (kalpa), when the Divine Soul/Self (Ātman) present within the cosmic ocean gradually recreates the cosmos by first assuming the form of an Ideal Macroanthropos (Purusha). The breath or life-force (Vāyu/Wotan) of this macroanthropos first unites with the matter of the cosmic ocean to form a closely united complex of Heaven (the substance of the Purusha) and Earth. But the temporal aspect (Kāla, Chronos/Shiva) of the rapidly moving breath or wind also separates the two elements, an event represented as a castration of the Purusha. The semen that falls from the castrated phallus impregnates the Purusha himself with a cosmic Egg from which emerges the manifest cosmos comprised, again, of Earthly substance and Heavenly light (Brahman). This luminous Brahman is also represented anthropomorphically as a Cosmic Man.

However, this light that is represented in anthropomorphic form continues to possess a stormy quality that is a persistence of Chronos in the manifest cosmos. The violence of Chronos (Hurrian: Kumarbi), who caused the castration of the Ideal Man, persists particularly in the turbulent nature (Angra Manyu) of his offspring, Ganesha/Zeus/Teshup.[472] This force castrates the anthropomorphic Light and forces it to descend to the lower regions of Earth (the 'Underworld'), where it lies moribund as Osiris/Varuna.

A Reconstruction of the Solar Cosmology of the Indo-Europeans, Hildesheim: Georg Olms, 2005.

[472] This attack on the initial Light of the cosmos may be reflected in the speculation of modern astronomers too that the first gigantic fireball, as the source of all the suns of the incipient universe (or 'Mid-region', between 'Heaven' and 'Earth'), collapsed after about 3 million years and thus created the seeds for all the future stars and solar systems of the universe (see T. Folger, "The real Big Bang", *Discover*, Dec. 2002, p.45).

However, the same storm-force represented by Zeus has, in its assault on the manifest Light, swallowed the divine phallus and eventually revives the moribund Light in the Underworld and its sexual potency. Infused with the divine 'soma', Zeus/Indra emerges as a universal phallus (or Tree) of Life that separates the substance of Earth (the Underworld) into the nether and heavenly edges of our own universe and rises through the cleft between them into the 'mid-region' of the stars. The seed of this newly erect universal phallus is then emitted within our galaxy – first as the moon, and then, at the top of the Tree/Phallus. as the sun. It is this divine seed that is deified as Dionysus/Skanda/Muruga.

A: *Zeus in the Primal Cosmos*

When we turn to the individual gods of the ancient Indo-European pantheon, we find that the god Zeus is recognisable under different names among the Hurrians as well as the Mesopotamians, Egyptians, and Indians.[473] Since the proto-Hurrians are closely associable with the proto-Dravidians, we may consider the Hurrian mythology first in order to comprehend the nature of the gods Zeus/Ganesha and Dionysus/Skanda (Muruga).

In the Hurrian epic of the 'Kingship in Heaven', one of the offspring formed in Kumarbi's belly when Kumarbi

---

[473] The Hebrew god Yahweh is the same god as Zeus but robbed of his original cosmological significance by the Hebrews who made him the focus of a new, strictly tribal, monotheism. The Abrahamic aversion to cosmological religion is evident from the references in Josephus' *Jewish Antiquities*, I,157 and Philo the Jew's *De mutatione nominum*, 72-6. The identity of Yahweh to the storm-gods under consideration is confirmed by the "wrathful" nature frequently attributed to him in the OT (see. A.R.W. Green, *The Storm-God in the Ancient Near East*, Winona Lake, IN: Eisenbrauns, 2003, Ch.IV).

(Chronos)[474] bites off the genitals of the sky-god An is Teshup, the Weather-god,[475] along with the other gods of the Mid-region including Ta-shmishu (Suwalliyat, the sun-god), and Marduk. All of these three major Hurrian gods are intimately related to, and sometimes indistinguishable from, one another. Teshup is indeed regularly coupled with his "pure brother" Suwalliyat, just as the Akkadian Adad[476] is with Shamash.

Teshup is not merely a son of Kumarbi, but also of his 'grandfather' An (Heaven/Ouranos), since it is the latter's seed that is preserved in Kumarbi when Kumarbi bites off An's genitals. Teshup's mother is thus said to have been Earth,[477] who is the consort of Heaven.

Just as Seth in Egypt is represented as having 'felled the sky'[478] and dragged Osiris down into the Underworld of Earth, and just as Zeus, in the Orphic theogony,[479] swallows Phanes, the divine Light, or his genitals, their Hurrian counterpart Teshup uses a sickle (much like that used by Kumarbi to castrate An) to sever the phallus of Heaven, Ullikummi, from off the shoulders of the giant Uppelluri (Atlas) who bears Heaven and Earth. The figure of Uppelluri represents the Cosmic Egg constituted of Heaven and Earth and the severing of the "stone"

---

[474] Chronos is the same as the Canaanite god El who was originally worshipped by the Hebrews as well. This is clear from the Phoenician (=Canaanite) mythology reported by Sanchuniathon in the work of Philo of Byblos cited in Eusebius' *Praeparatio evangelica* (i.9; iv.16).

[475] Teshup is the Hurrian form of the earlier Hattian deity adored in the form of a bull, Taru, Taurit (see V. Haas, *Geschichte der hethitischen Religion*, Leiden: E.J. Brill, 1994, p.322).

[476] See below.

[477] Text Ib9 of the epic (see H.G. Güterbock, *Kumarbi, Istanbuler Schriften*, 16, 1946. p.87).

[478] Pap. Bremner-Rhind, 5,7,8 (see H. Te Velde, *Seth, God of Confusion*, p.85).

[479] See M.L. West, *The Orphic Poems*, p.85.

Ullikummi from it denotes Teshup's seizure of the phallus of An (Heaven/Ouranos) from it. From the Orphic evidence considered below, we may assume that Teshup finally swallows this phallus so that the universal life that it contains moves into his own body.

The storm-force represented by Teshup also encourages the resurgence of the solar energy in the form of the incipient sun of our system. In the cuneiform treaty of alliance between Hattusilis and Rameses II, Shamash (the Akkadian original of the Hurrian Tashmishu/ Suwalliyat) and Teshup are mentioned in the same way as Shamash and Adad in Assyria are.[480] The "vizier" [brother] of Teshup is said to be Ninurta [Marduk],[481] The solar gods (Ninurta/Marduk and Tashmishu) and the weather-god (Teshup) are thus two aspects of the same deity and co-operate in the formation of the sun of our system. That is why the two are often considered as dual deities (Tashmishu-Teshup/Shamash-Adad).

When we turn to the Greek Theogony of Hesiod, the castration of Ouranos is followed by the reign of his enemy Chronos (who, in the Orphic Theogony is responsible for the birth of the cosmic Light of Phanes from the Egg formed in the body of Ouranos as Ideal Man).[482] Unfortunately, Chronos has an alarming habit of swallowing his children and thereby preventing them from becoming manifest. So, in order to save the life of her baby Zeus, Chronos' consort Rhea, on the advice of her parents, Heaven and Earth, resorts to a special ruse.

---

[480] S. Langdon and A.H. Gardiner, "The treaty of alliance between Hattusili, king of the Hittites, and the pharaoh Rameses II of Egypt", *JEA* 6 (1920), p.187.

[481] See H.G. Güterbock, "The God Suwalliyat", p.4. Suwalliyat (Skt. Sūrya/Hurrian Tashmisu) is considered to be the "pure brother" of Teshup in Kbo V2 (*ibid.*).

[482] See M.L. West, *The Orphic Poems*, p.70.

This involves the substitution of a stone for the baby so that Chronos swallows the stone and thereby allows the baby to be born. This stone is an analogue of the phallus of Phanes, who is a product of Chronos and the Cosmic Egg, according to the Orphic theogony.

It is interesting to note also that, according to Pseudo-Apollodorus' *Bibliotheca* (I,1,5-7), Rhea travelled to Crete to give birth to Zeus, and that Zeus was guarded at his birth by Kouretes (Korybantes) who clashed their spears on their shields in order to prevent Chronos from hearing the baby cry.

In Homer, Zeus is recognizable as a storm-god, and, according to Diogenes of Apollonia, the Homeric Zeus is the "apotheosis of air [Vedic: Vāyu/Avestan: Wāta/Germanic: Wotan]".[483] From the Orphic theogony, we know that Zeus as a storm-force destroys his father Chronos and then swallows the phallus of Ouranos/Phanes which had been stuffed into Chronos. In this way, he forces the life and light of Ouranos down into Earth, from whence however he himself will help it rise into our universe as the sun.

The Indic counterpart of the Near Eastern storm-god is Ganesha, who is considered to be a 'son' of Shiva (who is the same as Kāla/Time/Chronos) and 'brother' of Skanda. In the *Shiva Purāna,* Ganesha, who is delineated with sinister traits, attacks Brahma (Phanes) after he attacks his father Shiva (Chronos). This is probably a reference to the attack on Kumarbi by Teshup after An had similarly been attacked by Kumarbi. Also, like Zeus, who, according to the Orphic Theogony, swallows the phallus of Ouranos/Chronos, Ganesha too is depicted with a "pot-belly" which contains the entire universe.[484]

---

[483] See A.B. Cook, *Zeus*, I:351.

[484] See S.L. Nagar, *The Cult of Vinayaka,* N.Delhi: Intellectual Publishing House, 1992, p.115.

Further, Ganesha obstructs the sacrificial devotions of the gods (*Brahma Purāna*) and hinders men from worshipping Soma (*Skanda Purāna*).[485] In the *Brahmavaivarta Purāna*, Ganesha is visited at birth by Sani (Saturn, who is the same as Shiva/Kāla/Chronos himself), whose maleficious gaze causes Pārvatī's son to lose his head, which is then replaced by Vishnu (a god representing the sun) with the head of an elephant.[486] The trunk of this elephantine head is a clearly phallic representation.[487] In the *Shiva Purāna* and the *Skanda Purāna* too, it is Shiva who beheads his son, though, on Pārvatī's pleading, he himself finds an elephantine replacement for it.[488]

Like the Egyptian Seth, Ganesha was apparently considered originally as a malevolent deity called Vināyaka who caused obstacles to men and inflicted barrenness and delirium on them.[489] The licentious aspect of the Sethian cults is reflected in some of the Tantric Ganesha cults in India, which are given to worshipping an obscene image of the god in the course of drunken and sexually promiscuous revels.[490] However, Ganesha is also identified in the *RV* and the *Aitareya Brāhmana* with Brahmanaspati, the power of light.[491]

---

[485] *Ibid.*, pp.16, 49, 52.

[486] *Ibid.*, p.12f.

[487] Indeed, in some Tantric statuary representations of Ganesha, the deity is depicted with a female counterpart, also with an elephantine head, representing his Shakti (energy) into whose 'yoni' (female organ) the tip of his trunk is inserted (see L. Cohen, 'The wives of Ganesha' in R.L. Brown (ed.), *Ganesh: Studies of an Asian God*, N.Y.: SUNY Press, 1991, p.121).

[488] S.L. Nagar, *op.cit.*, p.8f.

[489] See the *Mānavagrihyasutra* and the *Vājapayagrihyasutra* (in S.L. Nagar, op.cit., p.45).

[490] See 'Ganesa' in *Hindu World* 1:378.

[491] *RV* II,23,1; X,112,9; *AB* IV,4; I,21 (cf. S.L. Nagar, *op.cit.*, p.44).

Another, more famous, Indic god who bears a close resemblance to Ganesha is Indra. Indra is identifiable with Ganesha as the assailant of his Heavenly father Dyaus (Ouranos), who survives as Prajāpati (Brahman) at the stage of the formation of the Cosmic Egg. Indra's father is indeed said to be Dyaus in *RV* IV,17,5, and in *RV* IV,18,12 Indra is said to have "slain" his father: "What God, when by the foot thy Sire thou tookest and slewest, was at hand to give thee comfort?" However, in *KYV* V,7,1, Indra is directly identified with Prajāpati (the creator of the manifest cosmos), suggesting that he is not merely a son of Prajāpati but indeed an aspect of him and the sacrifice of Prajāpati is indeed a self-sacrifice.

The birth of Indra, the chief of the gods, resembles that of Seth, who is said to have emerged "sideways from his mother".[492] At *RV* IV,18,1-2 Indra is said to have issued sideways from his mother Aditi and, on his birth, his mother hid him (IV,18,5). This awkward manner of his birth associates Indra with Seth, as well as with Zeus.

Indra's vital and heroic quality—that of Zeus/Teshup—is emphasised by his frequent epithet of divine 'Bull'. The Bull is also a typical epithet of Teshup of the Hittites, who is a counterpart of Zeus Adados.[493] Similarly, in Sumer, the term "Bull of Heaven" is used of Girra (Agni), and it also serves as an appellation of the god of Wind, Enlil, (CT 24,5,41 and CT 24,41), as well as of Adad (CT XV, 3f.), that is, of the stormy wind-like stages of solar evolution which, finally, are of greater importance in the formation of the sun than the purely luminous element represented by the pure brother of Adad/Teshup/Ganesha.

---

[492] See Plutarch, *De Iside et Osiride*, Ch.12 (cf. H. te Velde, *Seth*, p.27).

[493] See G. Wilhelm, *Grundzüge der Geschichte und Kultur der Hurriter*, Darmstadt: Wissenschaftliche Buchgesellschaft, 1982, p.70.

B: Zeus in the Underworld

The Tree of Life

Once the Light of Heaven has sunk into the 'Underworld', or the Earthly part of the Cosmic Egg, it is the task of Zeus—the force that attacked Chronos, the violator of Heaven, and swallowed the divine phallus—to revive it in our universe. We may remember that in the Egyptian *Book of Caverns*, when Re passes over Osiris, the latter becomes ithyphallic.[494] This betokens the rise of the universal life contained in the phallus of Heaven (Horus the Elder-Osiris) into the Mid-Region between the heaven and earth of our universe. The rising phallus is also often represented as a "tree" of life which is indeed symbolic of the entire universe.

In the Vedas, this tree is identified with Indra who serves as the axis that holds the heaven and earth of our universe together. In *RV* III,31, Indra develops into a universal tree as a result of his consumption of 'soma', the spiritual stimulant that causes that causes the phallus to become erect. Under its inspiration Indra separates earth and heaven and holds them together:

> 12. ... With firm support [Indra] parted and stayed the Parents [Heaven and Earth], and sitting, fixed him there erected, mighty.

> 13. What time the ample chalice [of soma] had impelled him, swift waxing, vast, to pierce the earth and heaven.

and *RV* II,15:

---

[494] See E. Hornung, *Ancient Egyptian Book of the Afterlife*, tr. D. Lorton, Ithaca: Cornell University Press, 1999.

> High heaven unsupported in space he established: he filled the two worlds [earth and heaven] and the air's Mid-region.
>
> Earth he upheld, and gave it wide expansion. These things did Indra in the Soma's rapture.

Indra's intoxication with soma is related to the wine-rituals of his 'brother' Muruga/Dionysus.

It may also be noted that a majority of the Vedic hymns are devoted to the god Indra in relation to the Tree of Life and to his battle with the demon Vrtra. So it is possible that the Indo-Āryans were mostly interested in the phallic and heroic significance of this god, especially in the Underworld.

That the tree of life is a symbol also of the Sumerian Enlil's warrior son, Ninurta, is made clear in the epic *Lugal e* (l.189), where Ninurta is called "the cedar which grows in the Abzu" (l.189)[495] as well as "the great Meš tree" (l.310).[496] Ninurta is also called the "date-palm", ^{d}Lugal.giš.gišimmar (ŠA$_6$), in the An=Anum god-list, Tablet I.[497]

The Divine Semen

The deity in the Underworld representing the divine seed that will be ejected through the phallus is in India called Skanda (Tamil: Muruga), whose name means 'jet of semen'. In the *Mahābhārata*, Āranyakaparva (IX,43,14ff), we find an account of the birth of Shiva/Chronos' son,

---

[495] See J. Van Dijk, *Lugal ud me-lam-bi Nir-gal*, Leiden: E.J. Brill, 1983, p.75.

[496] *Ibid.*, p.90.

[497] See R. Litke, *A Reconstruction of the Assyro-Babylonian God-list An:^{d}A-nu-um and An: anu šá amēli*, New Haven, CT: Yale Babylonian Collection, 1998, p.46.

Skanda. It states that the daughter of Daksha (Aditi/Pārvathī) made love to Agni/Shiva six times (in spite of Shiva's famed asceticism), taking the guise of the wives (who are identifiable with the Pleiades) of six of the Seven Sages (who, as we have seen, represent the wisdom of the previous cosmic ages), and then, taking his seed in her hand, flew in the form of a Gārudī bird[498] to a golden lake[499] on the peak of the "white mountain"[500] guarded by Shiva-Rudra's armies. The seed of Shiva turns into an embryo [or egg] and the mountain itself turns into gold, while Earth is infused with metals of diverse colours.[501] From this embryo is born Skanda, who, representing the jet of divine semen, emerges from atop a mountain (Shiva being typically called Parvatha/Kur/Mountain).[502]

In the *MBh* account, the birth of Skanda is described as being accompanied by terrific storms and blizzards.[503] The gods are at first disturbed by the violence of his birth and suspect the infant of being a potential usurper of their role.[504] The reason for the unusual violence accompanying the birth of Skanda is that his father Shiva is a powerful

---

[498] The Gārudī bird is the female of the Garuda, which, iconographically represented in fierce form, is an early manifestation of the sun.

[499] In the *Haracharitachintāmani* of Jayaratha, the lake itself is formed when Agni vomits after swallowing the powerful seed of Shiva (see W. O'Flaherty, *Asceticism and Eroticism in the Mythology of Śiva*, London: Oxford University Press, 1973, p.274). The swallowing of Shiva's seed by Agni is represented in the Brāhmanical rituals by the insertion of oblations into the sacred fire (*ibid.*, p.278).

[500] In Kālidāsa's *Kumārasambhava*, V, the mountain itself as well as the lake of the forest of reeds, Saravana, were formed of Agni's entrance into the semen of Shiva when it was dropped onto Earth.

[501] cf. Kālidāsa, *Kumārasambhava* V.

[502] Vāyu, the god of Wind, is also called "Parvatha" (mountain), in *RV* I,132, 6.

[503] *MBh* IX, 44.

[504] *Ibid.*

ascetic and his child is imbued with an extraordinary amount of "tejasic" or solar virtue.[505] So Indra as the stormy aspect of Shiva/Ganesha attempts to kill Skanda with the aid of the 'Mothers', the seven cosmic streams, who act as Skanda's nurses. However, the latter refuses to follow Indra's instructions and instead protect the infant against Indra's attacks. Finally, Indra concedes his impotence against the invincibility of Skanda and appoints him as his general. We may detect here a resemblance of Skanda's birth to that of Dionysus (see below).

In the *MBh* account of the birth of Skanda we also note that Indra first acts as the adversary of the solar force, Skanda. But Skanda and Indra/Ganesha are two aspects of the same deity (and considered as the 'sons' of Shiva in India), just as Shamash (Suwalliyat) and Adad (Hanish), are. As Skanda represents the solar virtue of the seed of Brahman, so Indra and Ganesha bear the violent nature of Shiva/Chronos. Indeed, in spite of Indra's malevolence against Skanda, Indra himself, like Zeus, helps in the formation of the sun in the underworld, since, as we shall see below, it is Indra who possesses the solar energy, "kshatram", especially in his phallic 'vajra'.[506]

Among the Dravidians, Skanda is called Muruga, a name that is possibly related to the nominal variant 'Marukka' for the Babylonian Marduk in the An=Anum god-list, Tablet II.[507] Just as Marduk is four-headed,[508] and Ninurta is called Sagash (six-headed),[509] Muruka too is six-headed and therefore called Shanmukha ('the Six-

---

[505] *MBh* XIII,83,45;47-8 (cf. W. O'Flaherty, *op.cit.*, p.268).

[506] See p.234.

[507] The name is spelled "Ma-ru-uk-ka" (see R. Litke, *op.cit.*, p.91).

[508] See *Enuma Elish* I:95.

[509] See K. Tallquist, *Akkadische Götterepitheta* (Studia Orientalia 7), Helsinki, 1938, p.422.

faced'),[510] since he is born of Pārvatī in the six-fold form of the wives of six of the seven sages.

That this divine seed is the source of the sun is clear in the earliest Tamil literature, such as the *Tolkapiyam* and the Sangam texts, from the 4th c. B.C., where there are numerous references to Muruga as 'ceyon', the 'red' god, representing the rising sun.

In Sumer, Ninurta himself represents the seed of Enlil, particularly as Ningirsu Lord of the Flood). In the Sumerian myth "Lugal-e", Ningirsu is represented as the reddish floodwaters of the mountains and equated to the mountain's "semen".[511] It is interesting that the flood of which Ningirsu is lord is both the semen of his father, Enlil (who is often adored as Kur/Mountain) and the cosmic flood from which the sun will arise.

In Babylon, Marduk is equated with Nergal (the incipient sun of the Underworld) in KAR 142 rec.iii 28.[512] In fact, the original form of Marduk's name was Amarutuk, sun-calf.[513] And in VAT 8917 rev.5, where Nabû represents the seed of the moon or "the one inside Sin [the Moon]", Marduk is called the "one inside Šamaš [the Sun]".[514]

In Greece, the deity most closely associated with the Tree of Life as its sap or seed must have been Dionysus, since his name itself may be construed as 'Zeus of the Tree'. The word 'dios' is the genitive of Zeus and, according to

---

[510] *Shiva Purāna* V.1.34; I.1.27, etc.

[511] See T. Jacobsen, *Treasures of Darkness: A History of Mesopotamian Religion*, New Haven: Yale University Press, 1976, p.131. We see that the attribute "mountain" regularly applied to Enlil is a phallic one and that Ninurta represents Enlil's seed.

[512] See A. Livingstone, *op. cit.*, p.235.

[513] See W. Lambert, "Studies in Marduk", *BSOAS*, 47, p.8.

[514] See A. Livingstone, *op. cit.*, p.83.

Pherecydes of Syros, 'nūsa' was an archaic word for 'tree'.[515] This is also confirmed by another name that Dionysus bears, as "Dionysus in the tree".[516]

Dionysus is considered to be the Cretan Zeus, Zagreus. In one version of the Dionysus story reported by Diodorus Siculus, Dionysus is the son of Zeus and Persephone.[517] Zeus' other wife Hera, filled with jealousy, sends the Titans to destroy the child. These details of the birth of Dionysus clearly resemble those of the birth of Skanda and the attack on the latter by Indra. Unlike Skanda, however, Dionysus is not quite protected and is finally torn apart by the Titans. He is then revived by Zeus himself, who takes Dionysus' still-beating heart and inserts it into his thigh. The references to Dionysus' 'heart' and Zeus' 'thigh' are to be understood in the context of the seminal and phallic roles of these gods. We remember the phallus of Phanes that Zeus had swallowed and the representation of Ganesha with an elephantine head and a phallic trunk.

The Birth of the Sun

In the Vedas, the tremendous power of the heroic god Indra which allows the solar energy to emerge as the light of the universe is contained in his phallic weapon, 'vajra'.

---

[515] K. Müller (ed.), *Fragmenta Graecorum Historicorum* 3, p. 178.

[516] Plutarch, *Quaestiones Convivales*, V,3.

[517] Diodorus, *Bibliotheca Historica* III;63ff. However, Diodorus also refers to two other accounts of Dionysus, the first claiming that he was of Indian origin, and a third that posits Semele as Dionysus' mother. This last version of Dionyus' origin is presented in the *Theogony*, l.940, as well as in Nonnus (*Dionysiaca* VII.136ff), where Zeus is said to have consorted with Semele, daughter of Cadmus, King of Thebes, to produce Dionysus. This must be a later variant of Dionysus' parentage.

The dragon of material resistance that Indra battles with his weapon is called Vrtra.[518]

In *RV* IX,42,1, Indra/Soma is said to engender the sun in "floods" along with the other stars.[519] The flood is the result of the separation of earth and heaven in the Underworld as well as the condition of the creation of the light of the mid-region of our universe. That this process is similar to the ejaculation of seminal fluid is not surprising considering the significance of the phallus in the macrocosmic creation.

Indra is the counterpart of the Mesopotamian Marduk and also of Enlil's son, Ninurta, since they bear the same phallic weapon.[520] But since Marduk and Ninurta are more properly identified with Skanda/Muruga, we see that Marduk and Ninurta assume the roles of both the sons of Shiva. In the Babylonian *Enuma Elish*, IV, Marduk splits Tiamat, the consort of the Abyss from which Anu (Heaven) emerged, into two halves and thus forms the heaven and earth of our universe. The Assyrian ritual text K 3476 rev. l.9 reveals the phallic role of Marduk in this aggression: "Marduk, who with his penis ... Tiamat".[521] The separation of heaven and earth resultant on the destruction of the dragon facilitates the rise of the sun to its position within the 'mid-region' of our universe between them.

---

[518] It is interesting that the epithet Verethraghna (destroyer of Vrtra) is applied in the Iranian Avesta to Mithra rather than to Indra (who is generally considered a demonic 'deva' in the Avesta). We may note here a deficiency of cosmogonical understanding in the Zoroastrian reform.

[519] 'Engendering the Sun in floods, engendering heaven's lights, green-hued,

Robed in the waters and the milk'

[520] It is clear that the Germanic Thor who wields a 'hammer' is also a counterpart of Indra (see Ch.VII).

[521] See A. Livingstone, *op.cit.*, p.123.

The storm-force of the Sumerian Ninurta in his battle against monstrous creations such as Asakku is called Ramman (Adad). Adad is called the stormy aspect of Marduk also in CT 24,50,10b,[522] Marduk being identical to Ninurta. That the exact storm that Adad represents is identical to the flood which forms the sun is made clear in several sacred Sumerian texts, including the epic *Lugal e*.

When Ninurta undertakes a mighty battle against certain mountainous "regions of resistance",[523] Enki calls to Nin-ildu, "the great carpenter [or demiurgus] of Anu", to fashion the mighty mace of Ninurta. Ninurta's "arm", or weapon, is itself represented as a separate deity called Sarur. The stormy nature of this mace is revealed in Gudea's Cylinder B, where the mace of Ningirsu [Ninurta as lord of the flood] is described as being the "fiery stormwind". This fiery stormwind is deified as the storm god Ri-ha-mun or Adad.

That the stormwind is related to a cosmic flood is suggested by the Sumerian term 'amaru' for a weapon, which may be interpreted also as "flood", as a hymn to Nergal makes clear:

> So strong was his Weapon, its upward rising was unopposable,
>
> In its aspect as a storm, it was the great Flood which none could oppose;[524]

---

[522] "ⁱˡAdad=ⁱˡMarduk ša zu-un-nu".

[523] Ninurta/Marduk is also described as fighting a 'dragon' and facilitating the development of the sun.

[524] See J.V. Kinnier Wilson, *The Rebel Lands: An Investigation into the Origins of Early Mesopotamian Mythology*, Cambridge: Cambridge University Press, 1979, p.53.

From the reference to the floods which Soma engenders in *RV* IX,42,1 when liberating the sun, also, we may identify this flood as being the universal storm in which the incipient sun is formed and borne aloft. Ramman is, again, called "bel abubi", lord of the deluge.[525]

In Greece, Zeus, rather than Dionysus, is properly identified with Teshup's Syrian counterpart, Adad, as Zeus Adados.[526] Zeus Dolichaios is also represented bearing the same axe and lightning in his hands as Ramman does.[527]

The Mastery of the Manifest Universe

Although the erection of the Tree of Life as the divine phallic support of our universe represents the rejuvenation of the fallen Heaven (Osiris/Varuna) and is the instrument of the birth of the sun, it too has to be overcome spiritually.

The baneful aspect of the material manifestation of the universe (which is the central focus of the Zoroastrian reform of the Vedic religion) is to be found in the Dravidian version of the *Skanda Purāna*, *Kantapurānam*. Here, the mango tree situated in the midst of the ocean is the second form taken by the demonic Asura, Sūrapadman, who is concealed in a mountain (exactly as Asakku is in *Lugal-e* or Vrtra in the Vedas).[528] The first form assumed by Sūrapadman is a monstrous multiform

---

[525] H. Zimmern, 'Religion und Sprache' in E. Schrader, *Die Keilinschriften und das Alte Testament*, Berlin: Reuther und Reichard, 1903, p.448; p.555.

[526] By the end of the second century B.C., Zeus comes to be identified quite commonly with Adad as Zeus Adados (see A.B. Cook, *op.cit.*, I:549).

[527] See A.B. Cook, *op.cit.*, I:604ff.; cf. H. Zimmern, *op.cit.*, p.448.

[528] See D. Handelman, "Myths of Murugan: Asymmetry and Hierarchy in a South Indian Puranic Cosmology", *History of Religions*, 27, no.2, p.143.

mockery of the Purusha characterised by a thousand arms and legs.

The son of Shiva born especially for the martial purpose of defeating the Asura Sūrapadman is Muruga (Skanda). Like Ninurta and Marduk in Mesopotamia, and Indra in the Vedas, Muruga is the god in the Underworld who has to combat the asura that represents the forces blocking the emergence of the sun into our universe. Muruga destroys Sūrapadman's first form by revealing his own true, and eternal, form as the Purusha. Sūrapadman's second form, that of the "mango" tree, is also cloven into two by Muruga when he casts his Maya-destroying lance ("vel") against it.[529] The tree is then transformed into a cock and peacock, which are symbols of death and the Underworld.

In Babylon, just as Muruga in the Dravidian version of the myth is said to have cloven the "mango" tree,[530] Marduk is also said, in the *Poem of Erra*, I,148, to have 'altered' the position of the tree.[531] We note that Muruga and Marduk are finally involved in an effort to master the universal Tree/Phallus represented by Indra.

The cult of Dionysus too was, like the Indian Murugan,[532] a deeply philosophical one since it aimed ultimately at guarding men from the cycle of reincarnation. This is evident in the Orphic account of Dionysus' effort, after his

---

[529] Muruga is always iconographically represented with this characteristic weapon, his 'Vel'. This, unlike the 'Vajra' of Indra, is not particularly a phallic symbol, unless perhaps it represents a 'spiritual lingam' such as described in the *Linga Purāna* (see below).

[530] See D. Shulman, "Murukan, the Mango and Ekambaresvara-Siva Fragments of a Tamil Creation Myth", *Indo-Iranian Journal* 21 (1979), p.32.

[531] See L. Cagni, *The Poem of Erra*, Malibu, CA: Undena Publications, 1977, p.32.

[532] See p.245.

resurrection, to save men from rebirth with the aid of his mother Kore/Persephone.[533]

III. *The Dionysiac Religion*

If we now consider the spiritual importance of the deities within the cosmological structure studied above, we note that the principal god of the Yogic religion of the proto-Dravidians is Shiva since he is the same as the Divine Self or Soul, Ātman. In his wind-like form of Vāyu/Enlil/Wotan Shiva seems to have been the major deity even in the ancient Near East. For there are references in the Sumerian epic of *Enmerkar and the Lord of Aratta*, 141-6, to a time when all the peoples of the region "in unison/ To Enlil in one tongue [gave praise]."[534] Charvat has also recently noted the emergence of the first "universal religion of Mesopotamia" already in the Chalcolithic cultures of Tel el Halaf and Ubaid.[535]

As for the original Āryan religion of which the Mitanni and the Indo-Āryans represent the western and eastern branches we note that the Mitanni reference to Mitra-Varuna, Indra and the Nāsatyas suggests worship of the forces that created the sun. For, Mitra is the Heaven/Ouranos that was felled by Chronos/Kāla/Shiva and lies sunk in the Underworld as Varuna/Osiris, Indra is the revived phallus of Ouranos, and the Nāsatyas are twin deities associated with the sun.

---

[533] See M.L. West, *Orphic Poems*, p.74; cf. p.95. Kore is the mistress of Zeus.

[534] See S. N. Kramer, *Enmerkar and the Lord of Aratta*, Philadelphia: University Museum, 1952, p.15.

[535] See P. Charvat, *Mesopotamia Before History*, p.236.

The Near Eastern and Greek religious cults of Dionysus are similarly focused on the reviving solar force in the Underworld. In the archaic Greek cultures stemming from Anatolia in the seventh and sixth centuries B.C., we find cults related both to Zeus—the chief of the children of Chronos, and leader of the Olympian gods—and to the children of Zeus. Of the latter, Dionysus seems to have been one of the most important since his religion is the most widely spread. The religion of Dionysus may have developed in Lydia or Phrygia in Anatolia, as Euripides' tragedy *The Bacchae* makes clear:

> I have left the wealthy lands of the Lydians and Phrygians, the sun-parched plains of the Persians, and the Bactrian walls, and have passed over the wintry land of the Medes, and blessed Arabia and all of Asia which lies along the coast of the salt sea with its beautifully-towered cities full of Hellenes and barbarians mingled together; and I have come to this Hellene city first, having already set those other lands to dance and established my mysteries there, so that I might be a deity manifest among men.[536]

Although the details of the Dionysiac religion as a 'mystery' religion involving initiation are mostly lost, we may infer from literary evidence that the devotees indulged in orgies of wine-drinking[537] in order to achieve an elevation of the mind to a state in which it could be filled by the god, or 'enthused'. The participants of the Dionysiac rituals, which included ecstatic dancing, included female votives called 'maenads' and men representing satyrs that bore the phallus and thyrsus symbolic of the deity.

---

[536] Translated by T.A. Buckley.

[537] For Dionysus' discovery of the vine see Apollodorus, *Bibliotheca* III.4.5; cf. Diodorus Siculus, *Bibliotheca Historica* III,62ff, IV.1.6, IV.2.5.

Omophagia, or the eating of raw meat, along with the consumption of wine, seems to have been an important part of the Dionysiac celebrations since it recalled the devouring of Dionysus by the Titans. A.B. Cook has pointed to the significance of these Dionysiac sacrifices:

> In Crete, the ritual of Dionysos, the re-born Zeus, included a yearly drama, at which the worshippers performed all that the boy had done or suffered at his death. The Titans' cannibal feast was represented by a bovine omophagy, and those who took part in this sacrament thereby renewed their own vitality. For *ipso facto,* they became one with their god and he with them. The true mystic was 'éntheos' in a twofold sense: he was in the god, and the god was in him ... Dionysos was at once the god of the Mysteries and the mystic ... the bull eaten and the bull-eater.[538]

Nevertheless, in Euripides' *The Bacchae* we find that purity of life is a condition of a Bacchant:

> Blessed is he who, being fortunate and knowing the rites of the gods, keeps his life pure and has his soul initiated into the Bacchic revels, dancing in inspired frenzy over the mountains with holy purifications, and who, revering the mysteries of great mother Kybele, brandishing the thyrsus, garlanded with ivy, serves Dionysus.[539]

Also, from Porphyry's reference in *De Abstinentia* to Euripides' now fragmentary play *The Cretans*, we may infer that the ultimate aim of the Dionysiac religion was asceticism:

---

[538] A.B. Cook, *Zeus* p.673; see also p.673ff.
[539] Translated by T.A. Buckley.

> In the mystic rites
> Initiated, life's best delights
> I place in chastity alone,
> Midst Night's dread orgies wont to rove,
> The priest of Zagreus and of Jove;
> Feasts of crude flesh I now decline[540]

Plutarch too points, albeit disdainfully, to the philosophical significance of the Dionysiac cult in his essay 'On the E at Delphi':

> And as for his turning into winds and water, earth and stars, and into the generations of plants and animals, and his adoption of such guises, they speak in a deceptive way of what he undergoes in his transformation as a tearing apart, as it were, and a dismemberment. They give him the names of Dionysus, Zagreus, Nyctelius, and Isodaetes; they construct destructions and disappearances, followed by returns to life and regenerations—riddles and fabulous tales quite in keeping with the aforesaid transformations.[541]

We may assume also that the Dionysiac rituals were informed by the same concentration on the spiritual significance of the divine phallus and its solar seed that we will find in the Purānic literature related to Shiva and Skanda in India.[542] The mystery aspect and orgiastic/ascetic tendencies of the Dionysiac cult may thus have involved a quasi-Tantric understanding of the need to control the magical power of sexuality in the microcosm as well as macrocosm.

---

[540] Porphyry, *On Abstinence from Animal Food*, tr. Thomas Taylor, IV:19.

[541] Translated by F.C. Babbit.

[542] See p.246.

The Dionysus cult is continued by the traditions of Orphism that appear around the 6th century B.C. The survival of crucial details of the Zeus story in the Orphic papyrus discovered recently in Derveni[543] points to Orphism as a major resource of the Dionysiac mythology and mysteries. Orphism was principally located in Thrace (Macedonia and the Balkans).[544] And A.B. Cook stated that he inferred, 'that the Orphic poem took shape somewhere in Asia Minor as the result of early Ionian speculation brought to bear on primitive Thracian-Phrygian beliefs.'[545]

The Orphic mysteries also had a definite relation to Greek philosophical inquiries of the 6th c. B.C. on the nature of the soul, and especially to Pythagoreanism, which influenced the Idealistic philosophy of Plato in the 5th c. B.C. as well.[546] The revivification of Dionysus may have been considered in Orphism as representative of a rebirth of the soul and even of metempsychosis, as Plato's reference to 'an ancient theory' in *Phaedo* 70c suggests.

The Cretan Dionysiac rituals, which were based on a mystic communion of the celebrants with the god, may also have been the origin of the Attic drama of the 6th century B.C. Attic tragedy may have evolved from the

---

[543] Derveni, near Thessaloniki, was part of the Macedonian kingdom of Philip II (382-336 B.C.), from which period the Derveni papyrus dates.

[544] Thrace is where, according to the *Prose Edda* of Snorri Sturluson, Wotan first travelled to in his migration from Anatolia to central and northern Europe (cf. A. Jacob, 'On the Germanic Gods Wotan and Thor' in this journal).

[545] A.B. Cook, *Zeus*, II, ii, p.1021.

[546] Platonism in turn was crystallised in the 3rd century A.D. by Plotinus in a way that returned to Greek thought its original mystical insights. Among the Ideal or 'intelligible' hypostases of Neoplatonism we find that the 'One' is the counterpart of the original Self/Soul of the Upanishadic philosophy, the 'Mind' is that of the Divine Light and Consciousness of Brahman, and the 'Soul' that of the Prakriti (Māyā) of the macrocosmic Purusha.

ritual recreations of the passion of Dionysus. And, as G. Murray suggested, the comedy too may have developed from the satyr-play which 'coming at the end of the [tragic] tetralogy represented the joyous arrival of the Reliving Dionysus and his rout of attendant *daimones* at the end of the *sacer ludus* [sacred play].[547]

The Dionysiac religion that is centred on the concept of the revival of the battered Light of Heaven in the Underworld also bears a close resemblance to the Christ story, and the spread of the latter in the first centuries A.D. through the Christian religion must have derived sustenance from the Dionysiac traditions of the peoples of the Mediterranean.

Murugan Worship

As we have noted above in Megasthenes' account of the ancient Indians, the Dionysiac cult may have been influential in the formation of the religious traditions of the Indic peoples as well. In India, there are not many references to the counterpart of Dionysus, Skanda/Muruga, in the Vedas. Only a few passages such as *RV* V,2,1 refer to 'Kumāra', a name of Skanda/Muruga. The *Chandogya Upanishad,* however, refers to Sanāta Kumāra (the Eternal Son) as being identical to Skanda, who is represented as imparting the doctrine of the soul to the sage Nārada. And in the *Shiva Purāna* it is again Skanda who imparts the Shaivite cosmology and rituals to the sage Sūta. Muruga is also said to be the one who revealed the doctrines of the Shaiva Siddhānta school of philosophy, which, though it may have originally been widespread throughout India, is now best preserved, after the Muslim invasions, in South India.[548] This major branch of Indian

---

[547] Quoted in A.B. Cook, *Zeus*, I, p.695f.

[548] See G, Flood, *The Tantric Body: The Secret Tradition of Hindu*

philosophy has as its goal the liberation of the individual soul, through initiation, into a state approximating that of the god Shiva.

The Kushan Empire of the 1st to the 4th c. A.D. shows some evidence of the worship of Kārtikeya (son of the Krittikas/Pleaiades). In the following period, the worship of this deity becomes common both in the Gupta Empire and in the South Indian Pallava kingdom. The earliest textual references to Muruga from the Dravidian literature of the first three or four centuries A.D. bear witness to a Dionysiac god who is capable of infusing women with love-sickness and possessing his devotees in a frenzy.[549] In this context, we may also note that Muruga's mother is Shiva's consort Parvathi in her form as "Korravai". The adjective 'kuravanji' (nowadays translated as "gypsy") is cognate with the Greek 'korybantes' (associated with the birth of Zeus) and refers originally to the deities of the mountain (which in Sumerian is called "kur").

Muruga is worshipped by the Tamils especially during the festival called 'Thāipūsam', which commemorates the granting of the spear (vel) to Muruga by his mother Pārvathi. During this festival, the devotees of Muruga are committed to abstinence, self-flagellation and the bearing of a burden in the form of (phallic) mountains symbolising the transcendence of the physical universe.[550] Some of the participants also dance a typical Murugan dance (kāvadi) with representations of these mountains on their shoulders.[551]

Religion, London: I.B. Tauris, 2005, p.34.

[549] See K. Zvelebil, *Tamil Traditions on Subrahmanya-Murugan*, Madras: Institute of Asian Studies, 1991, p.78.

[550] Self-flagellation, especially during Lent, is also an ancient tradition in the Christian religion related to the passion of the Christ on the Cross.

[551] The Murugan rituals, like the Indian Tantric rites, were open to people of all classes of society. Indeed, even the classical choreographic

We note that the rituals associated with Murugan worship as preserved today in South India are ultimately as ascetic as the Dionysiac rituals since Muruga's father Shiva is indeed the source of Yogic wisdom. The *Linga Purāna* also makes clear that there are two types of phalluses, an external material one and a subtle internal one. According to the *Linga Purāna*, I:75,19-22, 'simple people worship the external Linga and carry out rites and sacrifices' because 'The purpose of the phallic image is to stir the faithful to knowledge.' However, 'The subtle and eternal Linga is only perceptible to those who have attained knowledge."[552] The same Purāna states that Skanda is imbued with secret knowledge: 'Skanda knows the meaning hidden in the teachings of the Vedas and other sacred texts. He knows the meaning of all ritual acts.' (*Linga Purāna*, I:82, 92-95).[553] In the *MBh*, Āranyakaparva (IX,45, 87ff.), the title "Yogeshvara" (Lord of Yoga) is applied particularly to Muruga/Skanda Thus, along with the continued worship of Muruga in South India as a Dionysiac deity, his importance in Indian philosophical history is mainly as a disseminator of the philosophy associated with his father Shiva, who is traditionally considered to be the original Yogi.[554]

***

and theatrical art expounded in Bharata's *Nātya Shāstra* (ca.6th c. B.C.) was originally devised by Brahman (and edited by Bharata) as a 'fifth Veda' meant for the diversion and edification of those outside the high-born, or 'twice-born', castes (see *Nātya Shāstra: A Treatise on Dramaturgy and Histrionics Attributed to Bharata*, tr. Manmohan Ghosh, Ch.I, pp.7-12).

[552] Cited in A. Daniélou, *op.cit.*, p.58.

[553] *Ibid.*, p.97.

[554] The *Hathayoga Pradīpika*, for instance mentions Shiva as the author of the various Yogic āsanas, or postures.

It is difficult to determine the location in which the Yogic insights into the cosmological myths that underlay the early IE religions were first fully enunciated – apart from the general identification of Manu as a 'King of Drāvida', or proto-Dravidian, that we have noted above. If the Sāmkhya-Yoga system may be located in the Bactro-Margiana Archaeological Complex—as the identification of the founder of the Sāmkhya system, the sage Kapila, with the Bactrian region suggests[555]—the earliest Brāhmanical religion in India nevertheless seems to have been more centred on fire- and soma-sacrifices than on ascetic Yogic precepts. It is possible that Brāhmanism may have received an orgiastic stimulus from West Asia, as Megasthenes' comments on the civilising force of Dionysus among the ancient Indians indicate. And this stimulus may have contributed to the rich development of Yogic doctrines within the subcontinent itself not only in the Sāmkhya-Yoga school of philosophy (beginning around the 1st c. B.C.) but also, more significantly, in the numerous Upanishadic and Tantric systems dating from the last centuries B.C.

---

[555] See Ch.III above.

VII. ON THE GERMANIC GODS WOTAN AND THOR

> Apparently everyone had forgotten that Wotan is a Germanic datum of first importance, the truest expression and unsurpassed personification of a fundamental quality that is particularly characteristic of the Germans.
>
> C.G. Jung, 'Wotan', 1936[556]

MANY WILL BE familiar with the citation above from a perceptive article by Jung that attempted to show that Nietzsche's rhapsodic appeals to Dionysus should really have been addressed to the old Germanic god, Wotan, and was indeed an unconscious revival of an ancient Odinist religion among the Germans. It is, however, doubtful that all Germans were, or are, 'ergriffen' (possessed) by Wotan, as Jung claimed, and it might even be proven that Odinism was not really native to Germany but was, like Christianity after it, imported into it from Asia Minor. Furthermore, Jung focuses on only the stormy, orgiastic aspects of Odinic religion and

---

[556] C.G. Jung, 'Wotan', *Neue Schweizer Rundschau* III (March, 1936), pp.657-69 (tr. Barbara Hannah in *Essays on Contemporary Events*, London, 1947, pp.1-16).

does not attempt to understand the full significance of the god Wotan within the original solar mythology of the Indo-Europeans.

According to Snorri Sturluson,[557] the author of the thirteenth century *Prose Edda,* the Germans and Scandinavians, in fact, derived their religion from Anatolians who moved into Europe.[558] The leader of the Anatolians (the "Aesir") was called Odin (the Scandinavian form of the German 'Wotan'), In the *Prose Edda,* 'Gylfaginning', ch.6, the Primordial Man, equivalent of the Indic Purusha, is called Ymir and he has a son called Búri whose grandsons were Odin, Vili, and Ve. Odin originally lived with Ymir in the Elder Asgard.

The originators of the Odin/Wotan mythology may have actually been located first east of the Don, as Sturluson's narrative in the *Heimskringla* suggests. According to the 'Ynglingasaga', ch.1, Odin's original homeland was east of the Don river, the river in Russia that flows into the Sea of Azov, the north-eastern extension of the Black Sea. The Don itself

> was formerly called Tanakvísl (fork of the Don) or Vanakvísl (fork of the Vanir). It reaches the sea in Svartahaf.[559]

---

[557] See *The Prose Edda*, Prologue, tr. A.G. Brodeur, London: OUP, 1916.

[558] This is confirmed by the earliest archaeology of Europe, where the first formation of the earliest Germanic cultures is to be located in the south, in modern day Czechoslovakia, which it may have reached from "the Mediterranean or Anatolia" (G. Childe, *The Dawn of European Civilization*, p.101). Geoffrey of Monmouth (*History of the Kings of Britain*, Chs.3-16) points to the Trojan origin of even the earliest Britons, since Britain was, according to him, first settled by a great grandson of Aeneas called Brute.

[559] Snorri Sturluson, *Heimkringsla*, Vol.I, tr. A. Finlay and A. Faulkes, London: Viking Society for Northern Research, 2011.

The land around the Don delta was the land of the rivals of the Aesir, the Vanir:

The land within Vanakvíslir (delta of the Don) was then called Vanaland (Land of Vanir) or Vanaheimr (World of Vanir). This river separates the thirds of the world. The region to the east is called Asia, that to the west, Europe.

East of Vanaland was Ásaland (Land of the Æsir) or Ásaheimr (World of the Æsir). The capital city of Asaheimr was called Ásgarðr (ch.2):

> To the east of Tanakvísl in Asia it was called Ásaland (Land of the Æsir) or Ásaheimr (World of the Æsir), and the capital city that was in the land they called Ásgarðr. And in that town was the ruler who was called Óðinn. There was a great place of worship there. It was the custom there that twelve temple priests were of highest rank. They were in charge of the worship and judgements among people. They are known as díar or lords. They were to receive service and veneration from all people.

Now, the earliest cultures north of the Black Sea, those of the Pontic-Caspian Steppe, are the Sintashta (2100-1800 B.C.) and the Andronovo (2000-900 B.C.), both associated with the Indo-Iranian, or Āryan, culture. So we may assume that both the Aesir and the Vanir belonged to this predominant group. The battle between the Aesir and the Vanir may reflect the beginning of the split between the Indian and Iranian branches of the Āryan tribes since the Iranians, especially by the time of the Zoroastrian reform, worshipped only the Asuras and considered the Daevas as demons. However, the language spoken by the Aesir and Vanir may have been the original Indo-Iranian since even the Āryan Mitanni who appeared in south-eastern Anatolia and northern Syria in the 16th century B.C. exhibit elements of both branches of the Indo-Iranian language.[560]

In the *Prose Edda*, 'Gylfaginning',9, Asgard is said to have been constructed after the killing and dismembering of Ymir. Odin and his brothers then fashion the human race out of two trees, a male child called Ask and the other a female called Embla. The gods and their semi-divine human offspring then dwell in Asgard, which is located south of the Black Sea, in Anatolia:

> Next, they made for themselves in the middle of the world a city which is called Ásgard; men call it Troy. There dwelt the gods and their kindred;[561]

Asgard is firmly identified with Troy and glorified in its opulence:

> Near the earth's centre was made that goodliest of homes and haunts that ever have been, which is called Troy, even that which we call Turkland. This abode was much more gloriously made than others, and fashioned with more skill of craftsmanship in manifold wise, both in luxury and in the wealth which was there in abundance. There were twelve kingdoms and one High King, and many sovereignties belonged to each kingdom; in the stronghold were twelve chieftains.

---

[560] Several Median words are traceable in Old Persian (see P.O. Skjaervo, in G.Erdosy, (ed.) *The Indo-Aryans of Ancient South Asia*, Berlin: Walter de Gruyter, 1995, p.159). That the term 'Mede' might be related to the term 'Mitanni' was suggested early by J. Charpentier, "The Date of Zoroaster", *BSOS* 3 (1923-25), 747-55, among others.

[561] Snorri Sturluson, *The Prose Edda*, tr. A.G. Brodeur, London: OUP, 1916.

***

The chief of the Aesir, Wotan, and his people eventually migrated to the German lands:

> And wherever they went over the lands of the earth, many glorious things were spoken of
>
> them, so that they were held more like gods than men. They made no end to their
>
> journeying till they were come north into the land that is now called Saxland; there Odin
>
> tarried for a long space, and took the land into his own hand, far and wide.

Odin's three sons, Vegdeg, Beldeg (Baldur) and Sigi ruled over East Germany, Westphalia, and France, respectively. Further expeditions took Odin to Denmark, Sweden and Norway, In the process of these migrations the Aesirs mingled with the local peoples and thereby succeeded in spreading the "language of Asia" all over Europe.

> The Aesir took wives of the land for themselves, and some also for their sons ; and these
>
> kindreds became many in number, so that throughout Saxland, and thence all over the
>
> region of the north, they spread out until their tongue, even the speech of the men of Asia, was the native tongue over all these lands.

The date of the Odinic migration may have been around that of the Trojan War (ca.12th century B.C.).

Odin is endowed with quasi-magical powers, as Sturluson recounts in the 'Ynglingasaga', ch.6:

> But there is this to be said about why he was so very exalted – there were these reasons for it: he was so fair and noble in countenance when he was sitting among his friends that it rejoiced the hearts of all. But when he went to battle he appeared ferocious to his enemies. And the reason was that he had the faculty of changing complexion and form in whatever manner he chose. Another was that he spoke so eloquently and smoothly that everyone who heard thought that only what he said was true. Everything he said was in rhyme, like the way what is now called poetry is composed. He and his temple priests were called craftsmen of poems, for that art originated with them in the Northern lands.

Not only did he introduce the poetic art into the lands that the Aesir settled but he also established the laws of Anatolia in the north:

> he chose for himself the site of a city which is now called Sigtun. There he established chieftains in the fashion which had prevailed in Troy; he set up also twelve head-men to be doomsmen over the people and to judge the laws of the land; and he ordained also all laws as there had been before in Troy, and according to the customs of the Turks.

Odin is said to have two ravens that

> sit on his shoulders and say into his ear all the tidings which they see or hear; they are called thus: Huginn and Muninn. He sends them at day-break to fly about

all the world, and they come back at undern-meal;
thus he is acquainted with many tidings. Therefore
men call him Raven-God. ('Gylfaginning', ch.38)

Huginn in Old Norse mean 'thought' and Muninn
'memory'. The more accurate understanding of the latter
term is perhaps as the desire ('munr') which impels
thought.[562] We shall encounter these assistants of Wotan
again when we consider the Indian Purānic evidence.

Odin's fellow-Aesir include Baldr, ('Gylfaginning'
ch.22), Tyr, Bragi, Heimdallr, Hodr, Vidarr and Loki
(chs.25ff.). Thor is another Aesir (ch.21) and he is
loosely identified with Hector, the Trojan prince just
as Loki is identified with Ulysses, the Greek (ch.54). In
the Prologue to the *Prose Edda*, "Tror", or "Thor", is the
son of a Trojan king called Mennon or Munon who had
married a daughter of King Priam. He is said to have been
brought up in Thrace In the 'Ynglingasaga', ch.5, Thor is
represented as one of the Aesir appointed as priests in the
northern lands after their colonisation by Odin. It may be
noted that in the 'Prologue' to the *Prose Edda*—unlike in
'Gylfaginning'—Voden (Wotan) or Odin is said to be a
distant descendant of Thor. But this may be explained by
the fact that, although the Wotan of Asgard appears in the
universal Tree of Life later than Thor whose battling of the
serpent precedes the full rise of the Tree, Wotan is already
a major god in the Elder Asgard.

***

If we attempt to ascertain the linguistic affinities of the
culture imported into Europe by the Aesir of Anatolia,
we have to choose between the shatem Mitanni and the

---

[562] This has been suggested online by the Norwegian novelist, Bjørn
Andreas Bull-Hansen.

centum Hittite languages as the two likely ancestors of the Germanic languages (which are centum languages). While the Hittites were Indo-Europeans who ruled in central Anatolia in the 17th century B.C., their religious culture is heavily dependent on that of the earlier non-Indo-European Hattic culture of Anatolia. The Mitanni who ruled in eastern Anatolia and northern Syria in the 16th century B.C. exhibit a more Sanskritic culture since the first coherent mention of Indic gods appears in the treaty between the Mitanni-Hurrian king Šattiwaza and the Hittite king Šuppililiumas I dating from the sixteenth century B.C. and including the names Mitra-Varuna, Indra, and Nāsatyas.[563]

The collective name 'Edda' for the sacred poems of the Germanic peoples is clearly related to the Indo-Āryan 'Veda', as well as to the Zoroastrian Iranian 'Avesta'. In the Eddic poem 'Rigsthula', Edda is given as the name of the ancestress of the human race who bears three children Thrall, Karl and Jarl, representing serfs, freemen engaged in farming and crafts, and warrior nobles. The protagonist of the poem himself is called Rig and identified with the god Heimdall. The juxtaposition of Rig (a word signifying radiation or glory) with Edda seems to point to Indic origins, where Rig is the first of the Vedas. Further, in the 'Purusha Sukta' (*Rig Veda* X,90,9ff), the Rig Veda, as well as the Sāma and Yajur Vedas, is said to have been formed out of the cosmic sacrifice of the First Man, Purusha, who contains within his personal form also the four castes of men, his mouth representing the Brāhmanical caste, arms the Kshatriya, thighs the Vaisya and feet the Shūdra. It

---

[563] The text (CTH 51 and 52 (see D. Yoshida, *Untersuchungen zu den Sonnengottheiten bei den Hethitern*, Heidelberg: Universitätsverlag C. Winter, 1996, p.12) reads "[Dingir Meš]Mitraššiel, [Dingir Meš]Uruwanaššiel, [D]indar, [Dingir Meš]Našattiyana", where the uncertain suffix "šiel" may be a dual or plural indicator since the Sumerian prefix 'Meš' along with 'Dingir' (god) is a plural indicator.

may be noted that the castes in the Germanic literature are depicted as racial distinctions since the thralls are black, the karls red-haired and the jarls blond, whereas the Āryan castes are spiritually based professional divisions of the Āryan peoples themselves into philosophical brāhmans, warrior kshatriyas and labouring vaisyas (=the common people). The three colours ('varnas') associated with the three principal Hindu castes,[564] white, red and black (the last turned into yellow with the addition of the shūdras, who were then associated with black), are based on the colours traditionally used to represent the three 'gunas' or primal energies, sattva, rajas and tamas, attributed to the brāhmans, kshatriyas and vaisyas/shūdras respectively.

In the *Prose Edda*, "Gylfaginning, or The Deluding of Gylfi", the end of the universe, Ragnarök, is heralded by a long winter exactly as in the Yima story of the Vendidad.[565] Also, the German form of the god of Wind, Wotan, is recognisably related to the Āryan Wāta, a god of Wind who is more prominently mentioned in the Iranian sacred literature than in the Indic.[566] This may suggest that the Aesir that emigrated from the Anatolian region belonged to the Indo-Iranian tribes before the separation of the Indic from the Iranian Āryans. Furthermore, a trace of the transmission of the early religion to the European north through the Sumerians and their Anatolian neighbours

---

[564] The fourth caste of shūdras was probably added to accommodate the indigenous non-Āryan inhabitants of India.

[565] See H. Usener, *Die Sintfluthsagen*, Bonn: Friedrich Cohen, 1899, p.208ff.

[566] The Avesta (Yasht 14, Yasht 8) uses the form Wata to denote the more corporeal form of the god of wind Vāyu (cf. *RV* X, 136,4 which refers to "the steed of Vāta, the friend of Vāyu"). The name Wata is also reflected in the Hittite divine name, Huwattassis, god of Wind (see E. Laroche, *Recherches sur les noms divins hittites*, *RHA* VII, 45 (1946-7), p.69). The Germanic Wotan/Odin is etymologically related to Otem/Atem (breath) and mythologically to Vāta/Vāyu.

may be found in the name of the Eddic Ocean-god, Aegir, which resembles that of his Sumerian counterpart, Enki (=Lord of Earth).[567]

***

To understand the identities of the two major Germanic deities, Wotan and Thor, we may briefly consider the cosmological basis of the mythology of both the Germanic and the Indic peoples – which I have reconstructed in my study *Ātman*.[568] At the end of the first cosmic age, the supreme Soul (Ātman/Shiva), desirous of creation, assumes an ideal, and androgynous, form as a macroanthropos (Purusha). From the nostrils of this macroanthropos emerges the wind-form of the deity, Vāyu (in the form of a Boar) which recovers the Earth sunk at the bottom of the cosmic ocean during the flood that brought the first cosmic age to a close. The boar/Vāyu then impregnates and spreads Earth, producing as a result extended Earth (Prithvi) and its "cover" primal Heaven (Dyaus) in a closely united complex.

However, the temporal concomitant of the rapidly moving Wind-form of the supreme deity, Shiva/Kāla/Chronos, divides the united Heaven and Earth by castrating the Purusha. The semen that falls from the castrated phallus of Heaven impregnates the Purusha itself with the Cosmic Egg, from which then emerges the manifest cosmos constituted of Earth, in the form of a lotus, crowned with a Heaven of divine Light and Consciousness (Brahman/Helios).

---

[567] Earth is the infernal region of the cosmos and is surrounded by an Ocean (Okeanos). Hence the Lord of Earth is also the Ocean-god.

[568] See A. Jacob, *Ātman: A Reconstruction of the Solar Cosmology of the Indo-Europeans,* Hildesheim: Georg Olms, 2005.

This ideal Light (Ouranos/Horus the Elder) is, however, shattered by the stormy aspect (Zeus/Ganesha) of the Light itself and forced to descend into the nether regions of the "lotus" Earth. Zeus/Ganesha, nevertheless, preserves the castrated phallus of the ideal Man (containing the life of our yet unmanifested universe) by swallowing it.

In the underworld, where the solar force lies moribund as the Lord of Earth (Enki/Aegir/Varuna), the stormy and vital aspect of the same force (Indra/Thor) destroys the serpent of material resistance and divides its body into the heaven and earth of our own universe so that the divine phallus may emerge between these regions in the Mid-region of our universe.

The entire universe—which is informed by the vital force of Soma—is now shaped in the form of a "tree" [an analogue of the divine phallus itself] whose roots are in the underworld, branches in the mid-region and peak in heaven. When the passionate force of the storm-god is also controlled and the Tree of Life has been purified of all its chthonic elements, the life and light of the original Ideal Man are finally free to emerge in our universe as the sun.

In the Vedic literature, the fiery force of the divine Soul, Agni, is said to have been born three times, first from Heaven, then from Earth (*Shatapatha Brāhmana*,[569] VII,iv,1,9)—or in the navel of the Earth (*SB* VI,vi,3,9)—and finally from the Waters (his third birth, as Mitra/Āditya). The second birth of Agni in our universe is as Vāyu, the Wind-god. In *KYV* IV,2,2, the second birth of Agni from Earth is described thus:

From us secondly [was born] he who knoweth all

---

[569] Henceforth abbreviated as *SB*.

The first person refers to the Vedic brāhman priests who represent Agni, while the reference to the god "who knoweth all" is clarified by the Eddic reference to Wotan's acquisition of higher knowledge on the Yggdrasil.[570]

In the *Brahmānda Purāna* I,ii,10, the different forms of Agni are presented. The first form of Agni is Rudra, and is said to be embodied in the sun, the second, called Bhāva, in the waters, the third, called Sarva, in the earth, the fourth, called Īshana (Desire) in the wind (Vāyu), the fifth, called Pashupati (Lord of Creatures), in the fire, the sixth, called Bhīma in the ether, the seventh, called Ugra, in the initiated brāhman priest and the last, called Mahādeva (the Great God), in the moon. The order of manifestations in the *BrdP* is as a series of concentric circles, for we note that the first and last forms, in the *BrdP* account, are constituted by the sun and moon respectively, the second and seventh by the waters and the Mind, the third and sixth by Earth and Heaven, the fourth and fifth by the Wind (Vāyu) and plantal life (Pashupati).

In *BrdP* I,ii,10,76ff, the corporeal manifestations of these fiery forms are presented. The corporeal form of Rudra is called Raudri and his son is the planet Saturn. Similarly, the body of Bhāva is Apāh (the waters), and his son is Venus, the body of Sarva is Earth and his son is Mars, the body of Īshana is Wāta and his sons are Avignātagati ("of inscrutable movement") and Manojava ("rapid as the mind"), the body of Pashupati is Agni (fire) and his son is Skanda (Muruga), the body of Bhima is the Ether and his son is Heaven, the body of Ugra is the Brāhman priest and his son is Santāna, the body of the Moon is Mahat and his son is Budha. In the Wāta form of Agni and his 'sons', we clearly recognise the original of Wotan and his 'ravens' Huginn and Muginn.

---

[570] See p.274

***

The Germanic Wotan must be the same cosmic force as the Indo-Iranian Wāta, who is coupled with Vāyu, the god of 'Wind' (the source of Prāna/life-breath). We have seen that Vāyu is closely associated with Time (Kāla) in the original separation of Heaven from Earth, or the 'castration' of the former. While Wāta is not a clearly defined deity in the Vedas, he is, in the Middle Persian version of Zoroastrianism called Zurvanism (from 'Zurvan', Time/Chronos/Shiva), represented as a companion of Vāyu and denoting the spatial aspect of the original Wind.

As regards the cosmological background of the Germanic literature, we find that, in the *Prose Edda* ("Gylfaginning"), the Mid-region (Ginnungagap) of our universe between Muspell (Heaven) and Niflheim (the underworld) is said to be vitalised by the sacrifice of the First Man, or "giant", called Ymir. Ymir, who is the Germanic counterpart of the Indic Purusha/Prajāpati/Brahman and the Avestan Ymir, is sacrificed by Wotan and his brothers, Wili and We. From the corpse of Ymir are fashioned the firmament (his skull) and earth (his flesh) and the surrounding ocean (his blood). The ocean represents the waters whence the sun of our system emerges, and corresponds to the Greek Okeanos surrounding Earth. The substance of the sacrificed Ymir thus constitutes the material universe of the Mid-region between primal Heaven (Muspell) and Earth (Niflheim).

In the Indic literature, the attack on Brahman or the Divine Light (as the Cosmic Man Prajāpati) is attributed to the son of Shiva, Ganesha, who is akin to Indra.[571] In the *Shiva Purāna*, Ganesha, who is delineated with sinister traits, attacks Brahma (Phanes) after he attacks his father

---

[571] See p.228.

Shiva (Chronos). Also, like Zeus, who, according to the Orphic Theogony, swallows the phallus of Ouranos/Chronos, Ganesha too is depicted with a "pot-belly" which contains the entire universe.[572]

Ganesha's alter ego, Indra, is characterised by the violent rage called Manyu (*SB* IX,i,1,6). Indra is particularly identified with Angra Manyu in *RV* X,83, as well as in *AV* IV,31,5. Indra is said to have "slain" his father: "What God, when by the foot thy Sire thou tookest and slewest, was at hand to give thee comfort?" (*RV* IV,18,12). Indra's father is said to be Dyaus in *RV* IV,17,5, but in *KYV* V,7,1, Indra is directly identified with Prajāpati, suggesting that he is not merely a son of Prajāpati but indeed an aspect of him (just as Odin must be an aspect of Ymir). The sacrifice of the Purusha/Prajāpati is thus a self-sacrifice. This is confirmed by *KYV* IV,6,2, which declares: "Do thou thyself [Vishvakarman=Prajāpati] sacrifice thyself to thyself, rejoicing".

Further, in the *Skanda Purāna* and *Shiva Purāna*,[573] Shiva himself is represented as once losing his phallus, when he is cursed by some sages for his lasciviousness. The phallus, however, becomes an immense fiery pillar which pierces the three worlds until it is fixed in the vulva of Shiva's consort and worshipped as the "source of the universe".[574] In the *BrdP* I,ii,27,23, it is Indra who loses his phallus when he is cursed by the sage Gautama for violating his wife Ahalyā. This incident reinforces the association of Indra with his father Shiva/Chronos.

In *RV* X,90 ('Purushasūkta'), Purusha is offered as a sacrifice by the gods and out of him are formed the

---

[572] See S.L. Nagar, *The Cult of Vinayaka*, N.Delhi: Intellectual Publishing House, 1992, p.115.

[573] Henceforth abbreviated as *ShP*.

[574] *ShP* XII:17ff. (see A. Daniélou, *Shiva and Dionysus*, tr. K.F. Hurry, London: East-West Publications, 1979, p.62f).

universe and its creatures. The sacrifice of Prajāpati/Purusha has the result that "three-fourths" of him remains in heaven as life eternal, whereas one-fourth of him descends to the manifest universe as the creation (v.3). The creation itself involves the emergence of animal life, the Vedic hymns, and the castes of men. The moon arises from Purusha's Mind (v.13) and the sun from his eye, Indra and Agni from his mouth and Vāyu from his breath. From his head is formed the sky and from his feet, earth, while from his navel arises the mid-region (v.14). We see that the emergence of the entire universe is due to this original sacrifice.

The Zoroastrians who abhor Indra seem not to appreciate the Promethean significance of this cosmic phenomenon. Indeed, the Zoroastrian reform, like the Hebrew religion dependent on it, seems not to be based on comprehensive cosmological insight so much as on a moralistic obsession with the perfection of the ideal Heaven and the relative corruption of the material universe which will emerge from Earth after the violent separation of Heaven and Earth by Chronos.[575]

In the *Bundahishn*, Ch.IV, Angra Mainyu attacks and draws part of the ethereal expanse of Heaven into the Mid-region, the Void, where the solar system ruled by the sun will be finally located. The text reports that Angra Mainyu attacked the sky in its ideal form [i.e. as Heaven] and "dragged it down into the Void", so that only "one-third of the sky was above the station of the stars on the inner side". The Void thus becomes the region of the material universe.

---

[575] The rather negative view of the creation of our universe as a sinful one in the Avestan literature is perhaps the source of the story of the Fall of Man in the Hebrew Bible. However, the Hebrew literature does not possess the cosmological understanding that impels the higher idealistic and ascetic impulses that have become so highly developed in Indian and, to a certain extent, Christian thought.

In the Avesta, too, Angra Mainyu destroys all the pure creations of Ahura Mazda and is considered to be a completely evil force that counteracts the splendid goodness of Ahura Mazda and his creative aspect, Spenta Mainyu. That is why the Daivas (Indic 'Devas') and their leader, Indra, are considered demons by the dualistic Zoroastrians. It is interesting to note that Indra is considered by the Zoroastrians not as identical to Angra Mainyu but as an evil *assistant* of this arch-fiend.

The Germanic Wotan too is akin to Angra Mainyu in that he possesses a praeternatural and passionate energy that he imparts to his warriors, the Berserkers, in war. This is confirmed in the 'Ynglingasaga', ch.6:

> Óðinn could bring it about that in battle his opponents were struck with blindness or deafness or panic, and their weapons would cut no better than sticks, while his men went without mail and were as wild as dogs or wolves, biting their shields, being as strong as bears or bulls. They killed the people, but neither fire nor iron took effect on them. That is called berserk fury.

Wotan is thus closely identifiable with the Vedic Indra, and through him to Ganesha, the son of Shiva, and Zeus.

***

In the Sumerian and Indic mythologies the solar force that is sunk in the underworld, or Earth, after it has been castrated by the storm-force, is represented by the gods Enki (Lord of Earth)/Varuna (Ouranos). It is these gods who are revived by the storm-god and who sustain the phallic Tree of Life that rises from them.

Like the Sumerian Enki, the Vedic Varuna is the Lord of Earth, or the Underworld, from whence arises the Tree of Life. *RV* I,24,7 states that Varuna "sustaineth erect the Tree's stem in the baseless region [the Abyss/(Sumerian 'Apsu')]". The roots of the tree arise from deep within the Abyss, while the trunk proper represents the Earth. The branches of the Tree of Life represent the Mid-Region of our universe. The summit of the tree, that is, the highest point of its branches, represents Heaven, the domain of the sun. There are three heavens and the highest of the three serves as the seat of the gods (*AV* V,4,3,4). There the Ādityas enjoy their nectar of immortality, just as the Asuras/Aesir are located in Muspell.

The Norse god, Aegir, represents Enki/Varuna, the castrated primal Heaven that is sunk in the underworld (Earth) waiting to be revived by the storm-god. The name Aegir is itself possibly related phonetically and semantically to the Sumerian Enki (Lord of Earth), who is the counterpart of the Indic Varuna. He is represented as a sea-god in 'Skaldasparmal' (*Prose Edda*) and in the 'Hymiskvida' (*Poetic Edda*) as a god who brews ale (the equivalent of the Indic 'soma') for the Aesir. However, in the 'Hymiskvida' he complains that he does not possess a cauldron (a phallic symbol) to brew ale for his guests in. Thor ventures to obtain such a cauldron from Hymir, a 'giant' who clearly represents the phallic aspect of Ymir in the underworld just as Zeus and Ganesha do. Wotan, however, is not directly identified with Hymir. However, in the *Hymiskvida* Tyr is said to be the son of Hymir whereas Snorri Sturluson declares, in the *Skaldskaparmal* of the *Prose Edda*, that Tyr was the son of Odin. So the two figures are probably identical. Only, the fact of the divine phallus being swallowed by Wotan is not apparent in the extant Norse literature.

***

Just as Wotan may be identified with Indra in the earlier phase of the cosmic evolution which witnessed the separation of the substance of Heaven from that of Earth, the second appearance of Indra (now representing Ganesha, the 'son' of Shiva, as the deity that contains the divine phallus, or the life of the universe, in his stomach[576]) in the Underworld may also be associated with Wotan through the Tree of Life called Yggdrasil.[577]

In the Vedic literature, Indra is said to have imbibed the soma in the dwelling of Tvashtr, who is the formative aspect of Dyaus. Soma is described in *RV* III,48,2-3 as that milk which Indra's mother, Aditi, "poured for thee [Indra] in thy mighty Father's dwelling / Desiring food he came unto his Mother, and on her breast beheld the pungent Soma." At *RV* III,48,4, Indra is said to have conquered his father and borne off the soma in beakers thereafter. Indra is the deity that resuscitates the divine Light sunk in the Underworld with the potency of the 'soma' that he has drunk.

RV II,15 gives an account of Indra's development into a universal Tree of Life as a result of his consumption of soma and this soma-inspired growth holds Earth and Heaven together:

> High heaven unsupported in space he stablished: he filled the two worlds [earth and heaven] and the air's Mid-region.
>
> Earth he upheld, and gave it wide expansion. These things did Indra in the Soma's rapture.

---

[576] See p.226.

[577] We may remember also the swallowing of Ouranos' phallus by Chronos/Shiva's son, Zeus (see M.L. West, *The Orphic Poems*, Oxford: Clarendon Press, 1983.p.85).

Indra is indeed represented as the vital force of Agni/Shiva in all its three forms, in the underworld, the mid-region, and the heavens, thus as Agni, Vāyu and Āditya (*RV* X,31):

> 8. ... With power divine he makes his skin a filter, when the Bay Coursers bear him on as Surya [=Āditya]
>
> He passes o'er the broad Earth like a Stega:[578] he penetrates the world as Wind [=Vāyu] the mist-cloud.
>
> He balmed with oil, near Varuṇa and Mitra, like Agni in the wood, hath shot forth splendour.

Indra's association with soma causes him to be called the "lord of the seed".[579]

The Tree of Life through which the solar energy rises is, in the Indic literature, said to span the entire universe comprising the three regions of earth, the mid-region, and the heavens, which are dominated respectively by the three forms that the solar energy assumes in its development in our universe – Agni, Vāyu, Āditya. Agni is, in *KYV* V,5,1, called "the lowest of deities", while Vishnu (i.e. as Āditya) is the highest.

The Germanic name of the Tree of Life, Yggdrasil, is commonly understood by scholars to be derived from Old Norse 'drasil' meaning horse and 'Ygg', an epithet of Wotan's. This is possible since the name of the sacred tree in Sanskrit, 'ashvatta', is derived from 'ashva' (horse) and denotes the rampant energy of the god of Wind, Wāta/Wotan. The tree is associated with the horse also in Shamanistic rituals which depict the "ride" or "ascent" of the shaman to heaven.[580]

---

[578] The meaning of this word is uncertain, though it may refer to the penetrating power of Agni.

[579] *Mahābhārata*, I, 57, 1-27.

[580] See Mircea Eliade, *Shamanism: Archaic Techniques of Ecstasy*, N.Y.:

In the poem 'Voluspa' the tree is said to contain nine worlds, those of the gods (Asgard), the Vanir (Vanaheim), the elves (Alfheim), men (Midgard), giants (Jotunheim), fire (Muspellsheim), the dark elves (Svartalfheim), the dead (Niflheim), and another world that is unidentified. These nine worlds correspond to the three Heavens, three Mid-Regions and three Earths of the Vedas.[581]

The Germanic Yggdrasil grows sidewards, and one of its roots is said to be based in Heaven, Muspell, where the gods (Aesir/Asuras) hold court. Under this root is the well of Urd.[582] In one region of heaven called Valaskjalf (the hall of the slain) is to be found the seat of Odin, called Hlidskjalf, whence he surveys the nine worlds covered by the tree.

The second root reaches the Ginnungagap where the "frost ogres" dwell. This region represents the waters from which the sun is finally born (just as it is born earlier also from Heaven and from Earth). Here is to be found an oracular spring guarded by the sage Mimir.

The third root ends in Hel, or Niflheim, which is Earth as well as the land of the dead, the underworld. At the base of this region dwells the serpent Nidhogg in the well called Hvergelmir.

The tree represents the entire universe that comes to be in Midgard, which is the Mid-Region between Heaven and Earth that includes all the stars. That the Nordic tree also represents the axis from which the sun is born is made clear in the verses that refer to "Arvak and Alsvid", two horses which "must pull wearily the sun from

---

Pantheon Books, 1964, p.270.

[581] According to *AV* XIX,27,4f., there are, along with "three heavenly vaults", also "three oceans ¨[Earths]… three atmospheric regions" (see W. Kirfel, *Die Kosmographie der Inder*, Hildesheim: G. Olms, 1967, p.14f).

[582] *Prose Edda*,"Gylfaginning", p.15.

here".[583] These horses are related to the horse-twins that are common in Indo-European mythology such as the Ashvins, Nāsatya, and Dasra, in the Vedas, the Ašvieniai in Baltic mythology that pull the carriage of the sun, and the Graeco-Roman Dioscuri.

The Norns inscribe on the tree the fates of all human beings:

> Laws they made there, and life allotted
> To the sons of men, and set their fates. ('Voluspa', 20)

As in India, the destruction of the Yggdrasil, which represents the universe, heralds the end of a cosmic age, Ragnarok, which however will be followed by a renewed creation of the universe from the life-bearing trunk (earth) of the tree.[584]

***

In the Germanic myths ale is the equivalent of the soma with which Indra is infused while he rises as the Tree of Life manifest as our universe. Thor, who is the deity who finds the cauldron (phallus) in which Aegir might brew his ale, represents the seed of the rising sun that will course through the Tree of Life, or the revived phallus of the debilitated solar Light. It is possible that the name Thor is derived from the same root thor- denoting the ejaculation of semen which is noted in the epithet 'thoreni' applied to Aphrodite as sprung of Zeus' seed in the Derveni Orphic writings.[585] If so, this would approximate Thor to

---

[583] *Poetic Edda*, 'Grimnismal', 37.

[584] Snorri Sturluson, *The Poetic Edda*, 'Völuspá', 59ff., tr. H.A. Bellows, Princeton: Princeton University Press, 1936; cf. *The Prose Edda*, 'Gylfaginning'.

[585] *Ibid.*, p.91.

the Sumerian Ninurta/ (Babylonian Marduk), son of Enlil (Lord of the Wind), and Skanda/Muruga, son of Shiva. Indeed, just as Ninurta is considered the semen of the "great mountain" Enlil, Skanda, the son of Shiva in Indic mythology, has a name signifying "jet of semen". We may thus consider Thor to be the counterpart of the Indic Skanda, the son of Shiva, who represents the solar force growing within the Tree of Life and emitted through it into our system as the sun.

The birth of Skanda is recounted in the *Aitareya Brāhmana*. Prajāpati's seed falls when Rudra (Shiva)'s arrow pierces him and from this seed arises a lake surrounded by fire which is then agitated by the winds and the force of Agni. The kindled seed that ultimately turns into the sun is the same as Skanda.

Just as Skanda is the seed of the sun, his Dravidian form, Muruga, is associated with the rising sun in the *Paripātal* (ca. 300-400 A.D.) where he is described thus: "his body was of the colour of fire, his garment and garland red, the colour of the shaft of his 'vel' like coral, and his face like the rising sun". Hence he is called 'Ceyon', the red god.[586]

***

The name Thor may also be related to Taurit, the Anatolian bull-god who is later identified with Teshup, the son of Kumarbi (Chronos/Shiva), whom we have recognized as a counterpart of Zeus/Indra. As in the case of Ninurta/Marduk, we note that Thor appropriates some of the heroic qualities of Wotan as a storm-god.[587] Like Teshup, who is the slayer of Hedammu (CTH 348), Thor

---

[586] Thor is also traditionally represented as a god with a red beard (see the 13th century *Saga of Erik the Red*, ch.8).

[587] See p.235.

battles the Midgard serpent ('Gylfaginning', ch.48). In the *Prose Edda* ('Gylfaginning'), the slaying of the serpent is represented in the battle of Thor against the Midgard serpent, which is, in the end, consigned to the Ocean around Earth, which it then encircles.[588] The root of the Yggdrasil tree that reaches to Niflheim also harbours the serpent Nidhögg, which must be related to the Midgard serpent.

In the 'Hymiskvida' from the *Poetic Edda*, Thor kills the serpent Jörmungandr while on a boat with Hymir, who owns the cauldron that Aegir needs to brew ale in. Thor has to battle the serpent of 'tāmasic' power (or 'inertia') at the base of the Tree in the underworld (Earth) before he can rise through the Tree as the sun. That is why he is typically represented as wielding a hammer, Mjölnir.

***

In the Indic mythology, Indra, rather than Skanda, fights the dragon Vrtra and is represented with a weapon, the Vajra, rather like Thor and his hammer. In the Vedas, Vrtra is a serpentine cosmic phenomenon represented as a demon of resistance which prevents the "mountain" from ejecting its life-giving seed.[589] In *TS* II,iv,12,2, Vrtra is said to have grown and enveloped the three worlds. Again it is not Skanda/Muruga who destroys the dragon but Indra himself, when all of the Adityas, Vasus, Rudras, and gods were paralysed by the monster (*RV* 10,48,11). Indeed, Indra's freeing of the waters from the restriction imposed on them by the dragon Vrtra is associated with the creation of our heaven and earth, which are formed out of Vrtra's body (*RV* I,36,8).

---

[588] *The Prose Edda*, Ch.47; cf. "The Deluding of Gylfi".

[589] The etymology of the word is more accurately preserved in the Avestan "Vrθra" meaning "resistance" (see A.K. Lahiri, *Vedic Vrtra*, Delhi: Motilal Banarsidass, 1984, p.73).

In *BP* VI,9,18, Vrtra is said to cover the universe in darkness, which is not surprising considering that his father Tvashtr is the same as Tartarus, who, according to the Greek tradition, is the parent of Typhon.[590] Indra is associated with the discovery of the "lights" for the benefit of living creatures and men in particular (*RV* VIII,15,5). The association of Indra with the birth of the sun is evident also in *RV* II,19,3: "Indra, this mighty one, the dragon's slayer, sent forth the flood of waters to the ocean/ He gave the sun his life, he found the cattle [the solar rays]."

***

Another figure that appears in the Germanic mythology that warrants examination in conjunction with the rising solar force Thor, is Mimir, for he is instrumental in the process of the strengthening of the nascent sun. In the 'Gylfaginning' we have seen that Mimir's spring lies at the base of the Mid-Region. Mimir may be the Germanic counterpart of the Babylonian Mummu, who in the poem Babylonian *Enuma Elish*, I,98, is called a "vizier" (or son) of the personified Apsu/Abyss and is the formative force of the Abyss. The Abyss and Mummu are later conquered by Enki (Babylonian Ea) so that the latter rules as the Lord of Earth/the Underworld.

The history of Mimir is recounted in Chapter 4 of "Ynglingasaga", where it is stated that, in the war between the Aesir and the Vanir,[591] a truce was agreed upon whereby the Vanir sent their gods Njörðr and Freyr to the Aesir and the latter sent to the Vanir Hoenir and the 'wise' Mimir to the Vanir. Delighted, the Vanir send their own wise man, Kvasir, to the Aesir. However Hoenir, who

---

[590] Hesiod, *Theogony*, 820-22.

[591] Since the Aesir are Asuras, we may reasonably surmise that the Vanir are Devas, their name perhaps being a contraction of Devānir.

was made a chieftain of the Vanir, proved to be lacking in independent judgement and reliant on Mimir, so the Vanir seized Mimir, cut off his head and sent it back to the Aesir. Odin preserved the head of Mimir magically so that it would reveal secret knowledge to him.

In the "Völuspá" (29) of the *Poetic Edda*, Odin pledges his eye (that is, the sun)[592] to Mimir in exchange for the latter's wisdom, while Mimir himself drinks mead from this eye, which lies within his spring. The secret knowledge of the universe is thus juxtaposed with the growing force of the sun. In "Gylfaginning" (15), Mimir is said to imbibe mead from this eye using the horn Gjallarhorn which the god Heimdallr will use to announce the Ragnarök, the end of the gods. Heimdallr's "horn" is represented in the 'Völuspá', 27, as being

> ... hidden
> Under the high-reaching holy tree;
>
> On it there pours from Valfather's pledge [eye]
> A mighty stream.[593]

Mimir's imbibing of mead from the sun bears some similarity to the consumption of solar energy by the infant sun in *RV* III,I,7, where 'Agni' (the solar force that assumes three forms as Agni-Vāyu-Āditya)[594] is said to be nourished by the "milch-kine" (solar rays) which are present in the seven cosmic rivers that issue out of the mountain when Indra destroys the serpent Vrtra.[595]

---

[592] In the royal horse-sacrifice of the Indo-Āryans, the horse is said to be produced from the "left eye" (the sun) of Prajāpati (*SB* XIII,iii,1,1) and the sacrifice of the horse is meant to restore this eye to its proper place.

[593] *The Poetic Edda*, tr. H.A. Bellows, Princeton: Princeton University Press, 1936.

[594] See p.259.

[595] We may remember that the seven cosmic streams are associated

***

Although the erection of the Tree of Life as the divine phallic support of our universe represents the rejuvenation of the fallen Heaven (Osiris/Varuna) and is the instrument of the birth of the sun, it too has to be overcome spiritually.

The final sacrifice that purifies the Tree of Life itself is that undertaken by Wotan himself. In the poem 'Havamal' Wotan is said to have undergone an ordeal on the Yggdrasil tree that resulted in his acquisition of the knowledge of the magical runes that bear the fates of all men. This ordeal is a self-sacrifice of Odin to himself that repeats in the Mid-Region the original killing of Ymir, the First Man, by Odin:[596]

> 139. I ween that I hung on the windy tree, [597]
> Hung there for nights full nine;
> With the spear I was wounded, and offered I was
> To Othin, myself to myself,
> On the tree that none may ever know
> What root beneath it runs.
>
> 140. ... I took up the runes, shrieking I took them,
> And forthwith back I fell.
>
> 142. Then began I to thrive, and wisdom to get,
> I grew and well I was;
> Each word led me on to another word,
> Each deed to another deed.[598]

---

with the birth of the solar Skanda/Muruga as well (see p.103).

[596] See p.261.

[597] The reference to the "windy" tree reminds us of Wotan's own nature as Wind-god.

[598] *The Poetic Edda*, tr. H.A. Bellows.

The baneful aspect of the material manifestation of the universe (which is the central focus of the Zoroastrian reform of the Vedic religion) is to be found in the Dravidian version of the *Skanda Purāna*, *Kantapurānam*. Here, the mango tree situated in the midst of the ocean is the second form taken by the demonic Asura, Sūrapadman, who is concealed in a mountain (exactly as Asakku is in *Lugal-e*, or Vrtra in the Vedas).[599] The first form assumed by Sūrapadman is a monstrous multiform mockery of the Purusha characterised by a thousand arms and legs.

The son of Shiva born especially for the martial purpose of defeating the Asura Sūrapadman is Ganesha/Indra's 'brother', Muruga (Skanda). Like Ninurta and Marduk in Mesopotamia, and Indra in the Vedas, Muruga is the god in the Underworld who has to combat the asura that represents the forces blocking the emergence of the sun into our universe. Muruga destroys Sūrapadman's first form by revealing his own true, and eternal, form as the Purusha.

Sūrapadman's second form, however, is that of a mango 'tree', which is also cloven into two by Muruga when he casts his Māya-destroying lance ("vel") against it. The tree is then transformed into a cock and peacock, which are symbols of death and the Underworld. This episode is also similar to Shiva's burning of his erotic aspect Kāma in the form of a tree in the *Skanda Purāna*, I,1,21,82-99 and maybe a representation of Yogic discipline.

It is true that the Germanic mythology does not exhibit any clear understanding of the Yogic bases of the cosmic events it describes and represents these events rather in a fabulous, 'fairy tale' form. However, we may

---

[599] See D. Handelman, "Myths of Murugan: Asymmetry and Hierarchy in a South Indian Puranic Cosmology", *History of Religions*, 27, no.2, p.143.

assume that, as a result of his penance on the Tree in our nascent universe, Odin also recovers the full divine force that he originally bore in the Elder Asgard and that is reflected in the twelve names he possessed there:

> He is called in our speech Allfather, but in the Elder Ásgard he had twelve names: one is Allfather; the second is Lord, or Lord of Hosts; the third is Nikarr, or Spear-Lord; the fourth is Nikudr, or Striker; the fifth is Knower of Many Things; the sixth, Fulfiller of Wishes; the seventh, Far-Speaking One; the eighth, The Shaker, or He that Putteth the Armies to Flight; the ninth, The Burner; the tenth, The Destroyer; the eleventh, The Protector; the twelfth, Gelding"[600] ('Gylfaginning', ch.3).

In conclusion, we may return to Jung's descriptions of Wotan in his article as a 'god of storm and frenzy, the unleasher of passions and the lust of battle … a superlative magician and artist in illusion'.[601] We see from our study that Jung did not consider that the storms and battles and illusions recounted in the Eddas were enacted on a cosmic level and that Wotan is indeed a far more complex mythological phenomenon than merely a 'storm-god'. Furthermore, rather than representing 'a wind that blows into Europe from Asia's vastness, sweeping in on a wide front from Thrace to the Baltic, scattering the nations before it like dry leaves,'[602] the original followers of Wotan seem, from Sturluson's account, to have been forces of civilisation that introduced architecture and poetry, as well as laws, into the northern lands.

---

[600] A gelding is a castrated horse, which should be understood within the context of the solar cosmology outlined above.

[601] C.G. Jung, *ibid.*

[602] *Ibid.*